Voting for Policy, Not Parties

How Voters Compensate for Power Sharing

Voting for Policy, Not Parties proposes an institutionally embedded framework for analyzing voter choice. Orit Kedar argues that voters are concerned with policy, and therefore their votes reflect the path set by political institutions leading from votes to policy. Under this framework, the more institutional mechanisms facilitating post-electoral compromise are built into the political process (e.g., multi-party government), the more voters compensate for the dilution of their vote. This simple but overlooked principle allows Kedar to explain a broad array of seemingly unrelated electoral regularities and offer a unified framework of analysis, which she terms compensatory vote.

Kedar develops her compensatory logic in three electoral arenas: parliamentary, presidential, and federal. Drawing on institutional variations in the degree of power sharing, she analyzes voter choice, conducting an empirical analysis that brings together institutional and behavioral data from a broad cross section of elections in democracies.

Orit Kedar is an Associate Professor in the Department of Political Science at MIT. Her dissertation, on which this book is based, was the winner of the Noxon Toppan Award for Best Dissertation in Political Science at Harvard University. Her work has appeared in the *American Journal of Political Science, American Political Science Review, Electoral Studies,* and *Political Analysis.* She also serves on the editorial boards of *Electoral Studies* and *Political Analysis.*

Cambridge Studies in Comparative Politics

General Editor
Margaret Levi *University of Washington, Seattle*

Assistant General Editors
Kathleen Thelen *Northwestern University*
Erik Wibbels *Duke University*

Associate Editors
Robert H. Bates *Harvard University*
Stephen Hanson *University of Washington, Seattle*
Torben Iversen *Harvard University*
Stathis Kalyvas *Yale University*
Peter Lange *Duke University*
Helen Milner *Princeton University*
Frances Rosenbluth *Yale University*
Susan Stokes *Yale University*

Continued after the Index

To my parents

Voting for Policy, Not Parties

How Voters Compensate for Power Sharing

ORIT KEDAR

Massachusetts Institute of Technology

CAMBRIDGE
UNIVERSITY PRESS

CAMBRIDGE UNIVERSITY PRESS
Cambridge, New York, Melbourne, Madrid, Cape Town, Singapore,
São Paulo, Delhi, Dubai, Tokyo

Cambridge University Press
32 Avenue of the Americas, New York, NY 10013-2473, USA
www.cambridge.org
Information on this title: www.cambridge.org/9780521764575

First published 2009

Printed in the United States of America

A catalog record for this publication is available from the British Library.

Library of Congress Cataloging in Publication data
Kedar, Orit.
  Voting for policy, not parties : how voters compensate for power sharing /
Orit Kedar.
    p.   cm – (Cambridge studies in comparative politics)
  Includes bibliographical references and index.
  ISBN 978-0-521-76457-5 (hardback)
    1. Voting.   2. Political parties.   3. Political planning.   4. Representative
  government and representation.   5. Public opinion.   6. Comparative government.
  I. Title.   II. Series.
  JF1001.K43 2009
  324.9–dc22   2009009401

ISBN 978-0-521-76457-5 Hardback

Contents

List of Tables and Figures

TABLES

Acknowledgments

It is a pleasure to thank teachers, colleagues, friends, and institutions who have been so generous with me over the years. This study builds on my dissertation work. Gary King, my dissertation committee chairman, was a source of inspiration not only for creativity, well-argued logic, and presentational clarity but also for true mentorship. Gary's ability to see right to the heart of an argument served as a compass that kept me focused during the ups and downs of dissertation writing. Conversations with Torben Iversen were always constructive. His insights and gentle guidance immensely improved this study. Torben's skill in making analytic connections across realms of research usually seen as unrelated is a model to which any political scientist strives. Ken Shepsle's door was always open. I am grateful for his generosity and willingness to offer advice. His challenging questions made this project stronger and made me grow as an academic. And Rise's cooking was an extra treat!

My friends and colleagues at the University of Michigan deserve special thanks. Although January in Ann Arbor turned out to be a challenge for a Middle Easterner like me, I am extremely fortunate to have spent intellectually formative years in the Institute for Social Research and in the Department of Political Science. I am grateful to Anna Grzymala-Busse for her encouragement and sound advice. Anna, Nancy Burns, Bill Clark, Rob Franzese, and Mark Tessler, joined by Jim Reische, took the time to meticulously read an early draft of the manuscript and provide immensely helpful comments. My deep appreciation to Bill Clark, Liz Gerber, Allen Hicken, and Ken Kollman for their guidance and support. I also thank Allen for his permission to use data on constitutional authorities of presidents, which we collected in collaboration in Chapter 4 of this book. Skip Lupia has my deep gratitude. His wisdom, sound advice, generosity, support, and friendship are invaluable.

I am thankful to numerous individuals who gave me much good advice, asked probing questions, and supported my endeavor. My teacher, mentor, and now colleague and friend Michal Shamir originally sparked my interest in electoral politics, encouraged me to follow my curiosity, and supported me in my journey. Alan Zuckerman welcomed me at Brown University, generously helped me get accustomed to the U.S. graduate school system, and taught me a great deal about comparative political behavior. A few weeks before this book was due to come out, Alan passed away. I will miss his wisdom, kindness, and generosity.

The first incarnation of this project was heavily influenced by Mike Alvarez and Jonathan Nagler's joint work. Their encouragement set me on track. Numerous instructive conversations with Jonathan prevented me from falling off track. Jim Alt has provided ongoing support and advice since I entered the graduate program at Harvard. Chris Achen, Jim Adams, and Jamie Druckman each encouraged me to pursue my research and gave me sound advice at critical junctions. I was fortunate to receive the attention of a terrific team at Cambridge University Press. I am greatly indebted to Margaret Levi for her ongoing guidance and encouragement. Her support and advice were immensely helpful. Lew Bateman believed in me and kept us on track from the very beginning. Emily Spangler got us through logistical hurdles effectively and kindly. Ronald Cohen, the editor of the manuscript, handled it with exceptional care, wisdom, and sensitivity.

Brainstorming with Alan Jacobs, Eric Dickson, and Macartan Humphreys in Cambridge and with Rob Mickey in Ann Arbor was as rewarding as can be – their friendship even more so. Leeat Yariv repeatedly offered both a heart-to-heart conversation over gin and tonic and game-theoretic advice. I am most grateful for her friendship. Dear friends and family members in Israel and the United States, Amit, Daniela, Evelyn, Irit, June, Kira, Leora, Pazit, Ran, and Yael, were patient with me and supportive of my physical, personal, and intellectual journeys. This work would not have been completed without Elizabeth's wisdom, insights, and patience.

I have greatly benefited from comments and suggestions from numerous colleagues and friends. The list is too long to include here in its entirety, and I have undoubtedly omitted many, but it includes the following: John Aldrich, Alberto Alesina, Jim Alt, Steve Ansolabehere, Enriqueta Aragones, David Austen-Smith, Andy Baker, Laia Balcells, Larry Bartels, Bob Bates, Kathy Bawn, Neal Beck, Ken Benoit, Pablo Beramendi, Suzanne Berger, Ray Duch, Bob Erikson, Jeff Frieden, Ken Greene, Bernie Grofman, Thomas Gschwend, Bob Jackman, John Jackson, Karen Jusko, Paul Kellstedt, Herbert Kitschelt, Bob Luskin, Bonnie Meguid, Sam Merrill, Thomas Plümper, Markus Prior, Rob Salmond, Ethan Scheiner, Ken Scheve, Wendy Schiller, Jas Sekhon, Phil Shively, Lenka Siroky, Jim Snyder, George Tsebelis, Jonathan Wand, Greg Wawro, and Chris Way. Their advice greatly improved the final product.

Some of the ideas and data included in this book were published earlier in journal articles. I thank the following publishers and publications for kindly granting me permission to include excerpts from these articles in this book: "When Moderate Voters Prefer Extreme Parties: Policy Balancing in Parliamentary Elections," Orit Kedar, *American Political Science Review*, Vol. 99 (2), May 2005, pp. 185–199. Copyright © 2005 by the American Political Science Association. Reprinted with the permission of Cambridge University Press; Orit Kedar, "How Diffusion of Power in Parliaments Affects Voter Choice," *Political Analysis*, Vol. 13 (4), 2005, pp. 410–429. Copyright © 2005 Oxford University Press. Reprinted with permission; Orit Kedar, "How Voters Work around Institutions: Policy Balancing in Staggered Elections," *Electoral Studies*, Vol. 25 (3), 2006, pp. 509–527. Copyright © 2006 Elsevier Limited. Reprinted with permission.

Part of the project was written when I was a visiting scholar in the Department of Politics at New York University. Another part was written when I was a Fellow in the Department of Political Science at Tel Aviv University. I greatly appreciate the warm and lively hospitality of both institutions and the financial support of VATAT, which allowed me to visit Tel Aviv University. In fall 2004, Phil Shively and I co-convened a workshop at the Center for the Study of Democratic Politics at Princeton University on methodological and substantive questions commonly asked in the analysis of multi-level data such as those used in this project.

I thank Phil, workshop participants, and especially Larry Bartels and the staff of CSDP for hosting us.

I received helpful feedback from audiences in various venues, including seminar participants at Ben Gurion University, Duke University, IDC-Israel, MIT, New York University, Northwestern University, Ohio State University, Princeton University, Tel Aviv University, UCLA, UC Davis, University of Haifa, University of Mannheim, University of Michigan, and Yale University. I also greatly benefited from feedback from participants of the Comparative Study of Electoral Systems Plenary Meeting (2005), EITM summer school (2006), and Context and the Vote Decision Conference at Nuffield College, Oxford (2007).

I was fortunate to have had the support of an outstanding team of research assistants at the University of Michigan. Carolina Greer de Miguel Moyer gathered the bulk of the parliamentary and electoral macro-level data used in Chapter 3. Jae-Jae Spoon added additional parliamentary cases and gathered data on the United States used in Chapter 4. Dan Magleby analyzed and coded constitutional authorities of presidents used in Chapter 4. Daniela Stockmann assembled the data on regional and federal elections used in Chapter 5. I am grateful to them for their tireless, meticulous, and thoughtful efforts. I thank DeAundria Bryant, Kim Dorazio, and Stephanie Wang for their excellent research assistance at various points along the way. At MIT, Greg Distelhorst rolled up his sleeves and provided superb research assistance at the last stages of the project. Mike Sances throughly and thoughtfully assisted at the final stages.

Last, I wish to express my deep gratitude to my family. My parents planted in me a sense of curiosity about the world, engagement with the public sphere, and determination. Since my childhood, they have been patient with me and encouraging of my endless list of questions and my (usually unsatisfied) insistence on finding a satisfactory answer. Heated political discussions with my brother, a man of science and humor, taught me to be a sharper thinker. His affection and teasing energized me to continue. I am forever grateful for all that they have given me.

PART I

VOTING FOR POLICY

I

Introduction

Institutional Sources of Voter Choice

I.I INTRODUCTION

This book is about electoral politics in democracies. It examines the way ordinary citizens make their choices at the voting booth under various, complex, political environments. At the heart of the study is an old question, fundamental to electoral politics: how do voter views translate into electoral choice? I propose a new approach with which to investigate, and a new answer to, this old question.

The main principle from which I derive insights is straightforward, and can be summarized in a few sentences. Voters are concerned with policy. In order to achieve policies most beneficial to them, they work around complicated institutional and political structures that set the rules of the game. Their calculus is more far-reaching than we might expect, and their time horizon extends beyond the night on which election results are announced, deep into subsequent post-electoral stages of policy formation. In making their choices, voters take into consideration the path parties or democratic institutions more broadly are likely to encounter the day after votes are counted, and compensate for post-electoral negotiations that will dilute their votes. Simply put, in polities and under circumstances in which policy formation is diffused among multiple players, and negotiations and compromise are likely to water down their votes, voters respond by preemptively overshooting, supporting parties that will be effective in guarding their interests under the particular institutional circumstances. Being policy minded, voters compensate for the dilution of their vote by institutional mechanisms. In other words, voter choice varies predictably with institutional mechanisms that convert votes to policy; in fact, it reflects these mechanisms. To achieve the policy most beneficial to them, voters use parties as instruments at the voting booth. *Parties, then, are not the real object of voter choice; they are the means.*

This simple, key principle allows me to derive a set of predictions that shed light on a variety of electoral regularities. I develop this principle in three electoral arenas: parliamentary, presidential, and federal democracies. In each of these arenas, I analyze a variety of elections over time and geography using both individual-level and institutional data. I show that my argument unifies a variety of regularities, furthering our understanding of voter choice in multiple contexts.

1.2 THREE REGULARITIES

In September 1998 Sweden held its elections for the Riksdag, its 349-member national parliament. Over 5 million voters participated in the elections, delivering seats in the parliament to seven parties. The results were a mixture of consistency with, and break from, past elections. On the one hand, the Social Democrats experienced their worst performance since 1921, while the Left Party enjoyed a dramatic increase in support, as did the Christian Democratic Party. On the other hand, in line with recent trends that they had been experiencing, the Center Party and the Liberal Party both experienced a decline in voter support. Finally, the Moderate Party on the right and the Green Party on the left both preserved their base of support (Möller 1999).

While I do not presume to explain the results of these particular elections here, an interesting picture arises from an examination of the views held by supporters of the Moderate Party and the Left Party, the two parties at the ends of the spectrum. Its name notwithstanding, the Moderate Party, supporting privatization, free markets, and personal liberties, is an extreme rightist party in the Swedish landscape. When asked to place the party on an ideological scale, Swedes assigned it an average placement of 9.1 on a 0–10 scale.[1] However, when those

---

[1] Supporters of the Moderate Party alone assigned it an average position of 9.0.

who supported the Moderate Party were asked about their own position, they reported a more moderate position (an average position of 7.7). In fact, only 21 percent of supporters of the Moderate Party reported holding the same views as the party, while 74 percent of its supporters reported holding more moderate positions.[2]

A similar pattern emerges on the Left. When asked to place the Left Party on an ideological continuum, voters assigned it an average placement of 1.2.[3] When asked about their own views, however, supporters of the Left Party reported a more moderate position (2.1) on average. Only 39 percent of supporters of the Left Party reported holding the same positions as the party, while 53 percent of its supporters reported positions more moderate than those of the party.

Figure 1.1 presents the positions of voters and parties on unidimensional ideological spectra in a sample of seven parliamentary polities: The Netherlands (1998), Sweden (1998), Norway (1989), Denmark (1998), Japan (1996), Switzerland (1999), and New Zealand (1996).[4] The top scale in each panel presents the average placement of each party as perceived by those voters who supported it. Corresponding with each party, the bottom scale presents the average self-reported placements of those who supported each party. As an example, the leftmost point on the top panel marks the position of the Green Left in the 1998 Dutch elections as perceived by its own supporters. The point linked to it on the bottom scale is the average reported ideological self-placement of voters of the Green Left. Although these are aggregate measures, individual-level data reveal a similar pattern. Parties often place themselves in a position more extreme than, rather than next to, their constituencies, and voters, for their part, often support parties whose positions are more extreme than their own. In fact, I depict here a conservative picture of the discrepancy. Since party positions are measured as perceived by their own voters, the fact that voters may project their own views onto the parties they support (Krosnick 2002) suggests that the discrepancy between ideological positions of voters and those of their supported parties might be even greater than captured in Figure 1.1.

---

[2] Analysis based on figures extracted from the CSES (2001).
[3] Supporters of the Left Party alone assigned it an average position of 1.2.
[4] The figure utilizes data from the Comparative Study of Electoral Systems for all cases but Norway, for which it utilizes data from the Norwegian Elections Study.

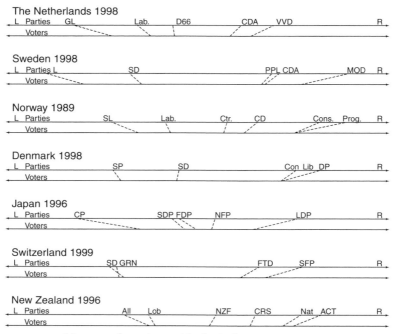

FIGURE 1.1. Voters and parties on ideological spectra

Notice that some voters, in spite of the presence of a party in their ideological proximity, support one more distant from them (examples on the left are the Japanese Communist Party and the Socialist Left in Norway, and on the right, the Progress Party in Norway and the People's Party in Switzerland). And although the scales of voters and parties within each system are comparable (voters were asked about both their own ideological placement and those of parties in their country), the observed regularity does not rely on the assumption that the scales are comparable across systems.

I am not the first to document this regularity. Students of electoral politics have long observed an ideological discrepancy between voters and elected elites in different polities, various types of elections, and using alternative measures. Iversen (1994a) observes it with respect to thirty-seven parties in seven West European polities. Utilizing mass surveys along with surveys administered to party delegations at national party conventions, Iversen identifies two dimensions – traditional left-right and a New Politics dimension. With party placements measured as reported by the party elites, he finds that only three parties unanimously adopt positions similar to those of their supporters on both dimensions. Most others deviate from their supporters toward the extremes. Dalton (1985) observes a similar pattern in his study of elections for the European Parliament. Drawing on a survey of candidates for the 1979 European Parliament, along with a survey of the public in the same member states, Dalton finds that on nine out of thirteen issues, elite positions are more extreme than those of the public. This discrepancy is particularly pronounced on the liberal side of the spectrum. Adams and Merrill (1999a) find a similar pattern in the 1989 elections for the Norwegian Parliament. The authors show that average party positions as perceived by all voters are more extreme than the positions of their voters, and that the discrepancy is greater for extreme parties compared to moderate ones. Holmberg (1989) finds this in Sweden. Utilizing interview data with both voters and members of the Swedish parliament from 1968 to 1969, and then 1985, Holmberg shows that averaging twenty issues, members of the parliament of all five main parties held more extreme views than their supporters in 1985, although there was a systematic left bias of representatives compared with their voters in 1968–69. Finally, drawing on both cross-national and individual-level comparisons and various types of analyses, the research team of Rabinowitz, Macdonald, and Listhaug (in various orders) finds evidence for party systems being more ideologically dispersed than their respective electorate in a variety of contexts (1978, 1989, 1990, 1991, 1993, 1998, 2001).

Focusing on the voters' side of the picture, I seek to understand the voter choices that lead to this puzzling regularity in parliamentary democracies. In particular, I analyze why, and under what circumstances, voters support parties whose positions differ from, and are often more extreme than, their own views.

Consider a different regularity from a different political arena: presidential democracies. In November 2006, under the presidency of George W. Bush, the United States held its elections for the 110th Congress. More than three years after the United States invaded Iraq, an end to the war was not in sight, the number of U.S. casualties was increasing, opposition to the United States in the international

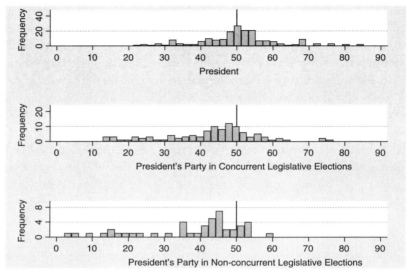

FIGURE 1.2. Presidential and legislative elections: vote share of the president and her party

arena was gaining momentum, and the Republican administration, initially pledging fiscal responsibility, ran a growing budgetary deficit. The Democrats, previously a minority in both houses, gained seats in both the House of Representatives and the Senate, and became the majority party. But was it really the war, the economy, and the international resentment that led to the defeat of the Republican Party?

Figure 1.2 presents electoral returns from 189 presidential and 151 legislative elections in thirty-four democracies between 1945 and 2000. The sample includes presidential systems such as South Korea, the United States, Chile, and Bolivia. The top panel presents presidential vote share, averaging 50.8 percentage points. The second panel presents vote share of the president's party in concurrent legislative elections, with an average of 43 percentage points, and the bottom panel presents vote share of the presidential party in non-concurrent legislative elections, such as the United States' 2006 elections, with an average of 37.5 percentage points. As the figure shows, the president almost always wins more votes than her party when presidential and legislative elections are concurrent. Moreover, the president's party loses support in non-concurrent legislative elections compared with concurrent ones. Although, as the figure suggests, there is substantial variation within each of the three quantities, the three distributions are statistically different. The party of the president loses on average over 13 percentage points in non-concurrent legislative elections compared with the electoral fortunes of the president, and about 6 percentage points compared with the party of the president in concurrent elections.

Time and again, in both stable and fragile democracies, in developed and developing economies, in two-party and multi-party systems, in thriving and stagnating markets, the party of the incumbent president loses support in legislative elections. What can explain this pattern? Why do voters withdraw their support from the party of the president, and what explains the variation in the magnitude of withdrawal?

Finally, consider an entirely different (although, I will argue, related) regularity. In September 1998, after sixteen years of federal rule by a coalition of the Christian Democrats and Liberals over West Germany and then reunified Germany, the Social Democrats led by Gerhard Schroeder won the federal elections and formed a coalition with the Greens. Between the 1998 and the 2002 federal elections, fifteen of the sixteen länder (states) held regional elections. Since each land is on its own electoral schedule, over four years of a federal cycle, different land elections take place in different times, such that the fifteen were spread over the four-year cycle from Fall 1998 to Spring 2002, only five months prior to the 2002 federal elections. Figure 1.3 presents the fifteen elections. The vertical axis represents the change in the combined vote share of the parties in control of the Bundestag – the SDP and the Greens – between the federal elections and each of the subsequent land elections. As an example, the third bar shows a 10 percent combined drop in support for the two parties from their performance in Bremen in the 1998 federal elections to their performance in Bremen's land election nine months later. As the figure shows, the Social Democrats and the Greens lost support in all but one of the regional elections following the federal ones. Importantly, in the following federal elections in September 2002, the Red–Green coalition reestablished its power in the Bundestag. And although Gerhard Schroeder and the SDP won these elections with a thin majority, the fifteen elections documented

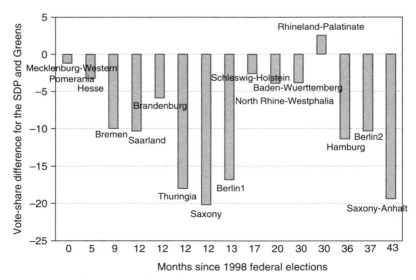

FIGURE 1.3. Germany: 1998–2002 federal cycle

in the figure were not part of a trend culminating in the 2002 federal elections.

Over the past fifty years, land elections in Germany have systematically resulted in loss of support for the parties in power in the Bundestag. Time and again, the parties in power did poorly in regional elections, and the national opposition fared well. This was the case both for the left and the right, both before and after reunification. The figure, along with the more general pattern, raises the question as to why the parties in power lose support in regional elections. And while a few regional elections are concurrent with federal elections, it is important to note that most land elections are staggered, taking place from as early as a month after the federal election to a few months prior to the next ones.

These regularities bring up numerous questions pertaining to principles of voter behavior in democratic polities. The general underlying question is: how do voter positions on issues translate into vote choice? Another way of asking the same question is: what is the object of voter choice? And how do voters vote to achieve this object? In answering these questions, I search for a unifying principle behind the regularities I present here, a principle that will account for variation in voter decision rules observed in different polities. I analyze the way different institutional environments lead voters to employ different decision rules and support different parties.

1.3 WHAT IS NEW

The literature on electoral politics in general and voter choice in particular is vast. Numerous studies – theoretical and empirical, case-oriented and comparative, cross-sectional and longitudinal, utilizing individual-level and aggregate data, grounded in psychological, behavioral, and rational research traditions – have taught us a great deal about voters, electoral institutions, and their interaction. This project draws on insights from previous studies to yield new ones. Doing so, it speaks to several intellectual debates in the study of electoral politics. First is what voters are concerned with. Numerous fields of inquiry in political science focus on policy (e.g., gender politics, conflict studies, macro political economy). Several areas of research within the study of electoral politics as well have incorporated the importance of outcomes into the study of voter behavior, and in doing so have analyzed the effect of institutions as a mediating factor. A few notable examples are the study of economic voting following the path-breaking work of Powell and Whitten (1993), the study of turnout (Powell, 1986), party attachment (Huber et al., 2005), and referenda (Hug and Sciarini, 2000). In contrast, the study of issue voting has focused almost entirely on voter evaluation of party positions with respect to their own views, leaving post-electoral activity such as bargaining and compromise, coalition formation, portfolio allocation, and policy formation, themes often considered as residing at the heart of politics, out of the picture. This project conceptualizes voters as having longer time horizons and being concerned with policy as the ultimate object of their choice rather than merely with parties or candidates.

Second, and related to the first, is the ubiquitous division of labor between students of behavior and students of institutions in the study of electoral politics. Unlike many studies of voter behavior, this study, while focusing on individuals, examines the logic voters employ as one that is embedded in, affected by, and reflecting particular political contexts. Doing so, it integrates institutional context into the analysis of voter choice. Different institutional environments, I argue, lead voters to make different decisions. Hence, to capture voter decision making, a micro-foundational study ought to incorporate the macro-level, and in particular, institutional conditions under which voters make their choice into its analysis.

Third is the standing debate between supporters of the proximity and the directional models. As I have mentioned, numerous studies have observed an ideological discrepancy between voters and parties whereby parties are ideologically more extreme than their supporters. The literature, however, is not in agreement about a micro-foundational explanation consistent with this regularity; although the empirical study of issue voting has focused on voter evaluation of party positions with respect to their own views, evidence as to the particular micro-foundational model is mixed. On the one hand, the intuitive benchmark model, proximity, is unable to explain the systematic discrepancy between voters and parties. On the other hand, the directional model, although addressing the discrepancy, is contested extensively on both theoretical and empirical grounds (for a summary, see Westholm, 1997, 2001). The logic put forth in this study reinterprets the debate between these two standard accounts of voter choice, providing an alternative rationale for voting of directional nature, as well as identifying conditions under which it is likely to emerge.

Lastly, and related to the last two contributions, is the generalized approach to the study of voter choice across institutional regime types. Many of the studies that inform my analysis conceptualize voter behavior in particular polities. My framework allows me to unify some of the insights from these studies into an encompassing logic of compensatory vote across institutional regimes, focusing on the degree of power fragmentation. This is particularly relevant in my analysis of presidential systems. I demonstrate how results of previous analyses of Congressional elections in the United States imply a broader logic on the part of voters.

In general, under my framework, voter choice reflects the path of policy formation leading from votes to policy. In parliamentary elections, under a concentration of power (e.g., single-party majority government) and hence a straight, short path from election results to policy, voters may support the party whose position is most similar to their own views, expecting that the party in power will pursue their preferred policies. If, on the other hand, they predict a fragmented decision-making process involving multiple actors, and hence a long and winding path of bargaining and compromise leading to policy (e.g., a coalition government), they may support a party whose positions differ from their own views, taking into consideration the likely dilution of their vote by post-electoral negotiations.

A similar logic holds when policy formation involves multiple institutions. Policy produced in presidential regimes is often a product of compromise between the executive and the legislature. In federations, policy reflects a combination of policy inputs (or simply a compromise) between regional and federal agents. When voters are called to the voting booth under either of these regimes, their choice may reflect such cross-institutional bargaining. Incorporating post-electoral bargaining between the executive and legislature or regional and federal agents into their calculus, voters may use their votes at one level to compensate for post-electoral compromise with the other. Thus, the more weighty one governmental arm is, the greater the pull voters will attempt to achieve in the opposite direction. Voters might not compensate as much against a weak president as they do against a strong one, and similarly, voters in a highly centralized federation might compensate more in regional elections than voters in decentralized federations. Overall, the strategy that policy-oriented voters employ will vary predictably depending on the degree to which their votes will be watered-down along the policy-formation path.

1.4 DATA AND METHOD

In my endeavor to understand the decisions voters in various democracies make at the ballot booth, I seek to both generalize and dwell on the differences. On the one hand, I am in search of a unifying principle to explain voter choice that goes beyond a context of a particular set of parties on the ballot, a particular electoral system, and a particular institutional regime. I attempt to develop a general principle that travels across parliamentary polities from Icelandic to New Zealand voters, across federations from German to Canadian voters, and across presidential systems from American to Bolivian voters. At the same time, to carry explanatory power, a cross-polity study of individual-level behavior ought to incorporate specific contexts, political and social cleavages, and characteristics of the party system that frame voter decisions in particular polities.

This careful balance is reflected in my theorizing and my empirical analysis. On the theory side, I construct a simple abstract model of voter choice from which I derive predictions. I start with a general version of the model – one that only captures the intuition of the key principle of policy-oriented voting but does not tell us much about the specifics. I then introduce institutional context into the general version and show its implications under parliamentary, presidential, and federal regimes.

Empirically, the study spans across democracies in several continents, including Western Europe, North America, Latin America, and Africa. I conduct parts of the analysis from a bird's eye view, comparing large pieces of political reality and analyzing polity-level similarities and differences in patterns of voter choice with a broad brush. I complement these analyses with targeted, more nuanced data analysis, generally employing individual-level data, focusing on a particular election in a particular polity. Overall, the data I use include a combination of behavioral and attitudinal data and institutional data, election returns, constitution articles, parliament and government compositions, portfolio allocations, parliamentary norms and procedures, details of the electoral system, and electoral calendars.

My analysis is of several kinds. In parliamentary environments, I construct an empirical model parallel to the theoretical one. I test the argument using micro-level data of voter behavior in a variety of polities, drawing on cross-sectional institutional variation. To test the argument in presidential systems, I employ aggregate data of election returns along with institutional data. The data span across polities and over time, allowing me to make inferences about the institutional effect across presidential systems versus contextual effects that vary within polities over time. Having established the effect of institutional variation in these two electoral arenas, in the third electoral arena I focus on a single polity (Germany) as a case study of federations. This precludes me from investigating the effect of the degree of power diffusion – I only have one federation with relatively similar degree of autonomy across its regions – but it allows me to complement the two chapters that do examine the effect of such variation that rely on cross-sectional comparison within their respective arenas with a focused analysis of voter behavior in a single polity over time.

1.5 PLAN OF THE BOOK

To my knowledge, this study is the first systematic comparative study of voter choice as policy motivated. In my journey to integrate institutional environment into the analysis of voter behavior, I move back and forth between the micro and the macro. I spend time on understanding micro-foundational principles that guide voters, and how institutions (specifically, aspects of institutions relevant for voter decision) affect voter choice.

The book consists of three parts. Part I presents the main principle driving the argument and derives implications for three electoral arenas. After this introduction (Chapter 1), Chapter 2 presents an intuitive as well as a formal version of the argument, and derives a model of compensatory vote in parliamentary, presidential, and federal regimes. I model voter decision as motivated by two considerations: supporting the party that best represents her views, and supporting the party that pulls policy in her direction. I show that these two motivations converge in systems in which power is concentrated and diverge in ones in which policy is formed by compromise and bargaining. In the latter, expecting post-electoral bargaining, voters have an incentive to compensate for the watering-down of their votes. They do so by incorporating into their decision rule the manner and degree in which political institutions facilitating compromise diffuse their votes.

Part II tests empirically the argument in three electoral arenas. Chapter 3 focuses on parliamentary systems. I derive an empirical model parallel to the theoretical model and estimate it on a sample of fourteen parliamentary democracies that vary in their institutional design. I conduct the analysis in two steps. First, I estimate a model of voter choice in each polity, analyzing the degree to which voters compensate for the watering-down of their vote. Second, utilizing measures of diffusion of power in parliaments, I account for variation in compensatory vote across parliamentary systems. I demonstrate that the more fragmented is the policy-formation process in the parliament, the more voters compensate for the dilution of their vote by supporting parties whose positions differ from their own views, parties that will be more effective in pulling policy in their direction.

Chapters 4 and 5 analyze the way voters utilize multiple ballots they have at their disposal to compensate for cross-institutional bargaining.

Chapter 4 focuses on horizontal balancing in presidential polities. I analyze legislative and presidential elections taking place concurrently and non-concurrently in most presidential democracies during the post-war era. I demonstrate that in almost all non-concurrent legislative elections, the party of the incumbent president loses support. Moreover, I show that the power the constitution grants to the president is directly related to the magnitude of the loss of the president's party in non-concurrent legislative elections: the more powerful the president is, the greater the loss.

Chapter 5 analyzes vertical compensation in federations. I focus on a single polity over time – the Federal Republic of Germany – and its sixteen länder (twelve before reunification). I employ individual-level and aggregate data of election returns from land and federal elections between 1961 and 2002, demonstrating how voter choice reflects the vertical diffusion of power between regional and the federal governments.

While this project examines voter choice under the new proposed framework, it leaves party strategy untouched. Part III (Chapter 6) builds on insights from the previous five chapters and opens a door to revisiting our understanding of party strategy, incorporating processes of policy formation and voter motivations. The study ends with theoretical questions about the meaning and quality of representation in light of the insights developed.

2

A Theory of Compensatory Vote

2.1 VOTER CHOICE: THEORIES AND REGULARITIES

What is the object of voter choice? And what logic do voters employ in pursuit of this object? To answer these questions, we need to identify an underlying principle that can explain cross-national and cross-institutional similarities and differences in the logic voters employ. In this chapter, I propose a theory of issue voting – compensatory vote – that rests on such a unifying principle. Different contexts call for different strategies, however. Once such an objective has been identified, the next step is to understand how voters living in different countries and under different institutional regimes vote to maximize it. This will allow me to account for regularities (and variations in them) along the lines of those I presented in Chapter 1, such as differences in behavior between British and Dutch voters, each participating in their respective parliamentary elections but under radically different electoral systems; between American and Brazilian voters, each participating in presidential and legislative elections but under different constitutional frameworks; and among German voters, participating in regional (federal) elections but under different federal (regional) governments.

Studies of elections in various polities suggest that issue voting has become increasingly important in explaining voter choice (Barnes, 1997). Nonetheless, political scientists to date have not reached a consensus over a theory of voting that accounts for cross-national regularities; disagreements about an underlying theoretical model, a desired methodological approach, and measurement are common-place. While I do not attempt to provide a comprehensive review of the voluminous literature on voter choice, I review some of the key issues at the heart of current debates as they pertain to my interest.

The familiar spatial model (Hotelling, 1929; Downs, 1957) char-acterizes party competition in a two-party system in which a short path leads from elections to policy: the winner can implement its policy plat-form. Under this model, each voter chooses a party such that the resulting policy will be as similar as possible to her own bliss point. This repre-sentation of the model appears in most theoretical accounts (e.g., Davis and Hinich, 1966; Davis, Hinich, and Ordeshook, 1970). The result of this model is well known: parties will adopt the policy position of the median voter, and the competition will result in policy convergence. According to the standard characterization of majoritarian polities, the winning party is almost always able to govern alone, and can therefore implement its preferred policy. In particular, in the Downsian two-party system, once election results are known, the winner is immediately announced. Generally speaking, assuming a binding platform, policy in a unitary two-party system is identical to the winner's position.

What does the short path from election results to policy in unitary two-party systems tell us about voter motivation? As I mentioned earlier, the Downsian model conceptualizes voters as supporting a party such that the resulting policy will be as ideologically similar (spatially close) to their own views as possible. If they are concerned with policy outcomes, voters in such systems will maximize their interests by supporting the party ideologically most similar to them. In a two-party system, there is no apparent reason to support the party ideologically remote from one's position – considerations of party viability aside, the party more similar to the voter will always yield greater utility for her. In a two-party environment, voting for policy and voting for party platform (positions) are observationally equiva-lent. That voters support the party ideologically similar to them is not necessarily an indication that they are concerned with *policy*. They might simply prefer parties whose positions are most similar to their own, and therefore best represent their views – parties with which they can comfortably declare their affiliation.

By voting for the party ideologically most similar to her, the voter declares who she is. This interpretation is consistent with Schuessler's

(2000) theory of expressive choice. Schuessler suggests that mass elections are an instance individuals use "to establish, reaffirm, demonstrate, and express" their partisanship to the world, as well as to themselves (2000, 15). Voting for a party ideologically close to one's own positions entails expressive attachment; it allows an individual to attach herself to a collective similar to her.

The observational equivalence of the two theoretically different accounts of voter motivation marks the beginning of my theoretical journey. While formal theoretical accounts of voting (following the Downsian model) adopt the interpretation of outcome-motivated choice, empirical research adopts the latter interpretation of voter motivation – voting over party positions. Enelow and Hinich (1984) define the utility of voter i ($i = 1,. . .,$n) for party j ($j = 1,. . .,$J) as negatively related to the distance between the voter's position and that of the party:

$$U_{ij} = \beta \left(v_i - p_j \right)^2 \qquad (2.1)$$

where v_i is the position of voter i, p_j is the position of party j, and β is a salience parameter. In multiple dimensions:

$$U_{ij} = \sum_d \beta^d \left(v_i^d - p_j^d \right)^2 \qquad (2.2)$$

where v_i^d is the position of voter i on policy dimension d, p_j^d is the position of party j on policy dimension d, and β^d is a salience weight of policy issue d.[1]

The proximity model has become the benchmark in studies of issue voting; following Enelow and Hinich (1984), the vast majority of empirical studies of voter choice include a vector of distances between the voter's ideal points and the party's platform positions on the relevant policy issues. In the past two and a half decades, however, an alternative model has persistently challenged proximity voting. Although accepting the general framework of voter evaluation of party positions, Rabinowitz (1978) and Rabinowitz and Macdonald (1989) propose an alternative theory of issue voting – directional voting. For issues to have impact, the authors claim, they have to convey a symbol

---

[1] For simplicity, I assume separability across dimensions.

and consequently evoke sentiments. Symbols have two qualities that trigger voter sentiments: direction and intensity. First, voters feel favorable or unfavorable toward a symbol. Second, the symbol conjures feelings with varying degrees of emotional content. Rather than responding to different levels of extremity of issue positions, voters respond to issues with different levels of intensity. Building on ideas of symbolic politics (Edelman, 1964), the directional model predicts that a voter will prefer a party placed farther away from her as long as she is on the same "side" of the issue as the party more similar to her ideologically but placed on a different side.

Contrary to the Downsian model, the prediction of the directional model is divergence of parties to highly intense positions. Parties are vote maximizers and will thus be more intense than voters. But how far can they go? The authors write: "Of course, it is possible for a candidate to be so intense as to become an unacceptable 'extremist'" (Rabinowitz and Macdonald, 1989, 97). While a party seeks to make the most effective use of a symbol, there are limits on how aggressive it may be; these are the bounds of reasonableness that a party should not cross, lest it lose voter support. The authors refer to these bounds as the region of acceptability. The prediction of the model, in turn, is that parties will place themselves right at the internal edge of the region of acceptability. The two components, direction and intensity, are integrated into a simple equation:

$$U_{ij} = v_i p_j \tag{2.3}$$

Assuming a policy scale with a neutral point at zero, when the party is on the same side of the issue as the voter, the product in Equation (2.3) is positive, and when they are on opposite sides, it is negative. Therefore, if a voter and a party are on the same side of an issue, the more intense is the party, the higher is voter utility for it. In multiple dimensions:

$$U_{ij} = \sum_d v_i^d p_j^d \tag{2.4}$$

While each of the two models carries its own logic about voter choice, empirical evidence has been mixed. Numerous studies examining the two models applied to different elections using different methodologies have reached inconclusive results (see, e.g., Adams and Merrill

1999b; Cho and Endersby 2003; Krämer and Rattinger 1997; Onizuka 2005). Others concluded that given current data, conclusive findings cannot be reached (Lewis and King, 2000).

A handful of explanations that depart from the notion of directional voting and account for the regularity of voters' support for parties that ideologically differ from their own views are found in the literature. Iversen (1994b) suggests that consistent with the directional model, voters look at politicians in search of direction, but also that party elites, on their side, pull electorates toward sharper positions. This model differs from other models of issue voting in that it perceives voter positions as endogenous to the political process.

Two studies of voter choice in separation-of-power systems put forth a discounting hypothesis. Lacy and Paolino (1998) argue that voters in a separation-of-power system differentiate between candidate positions and policy. Testing their hypothesis on data from a 1996 survey conducted in Texas, they show that ideological distance between voters' positions and policy predicts vote choice better than the distance between voter positions and party platforms. Bailey (2001) proposes a sketch of a formal model that acknowledges voter motivation to achieve desired policy in addition to being represented by a platform. The institutional distinction Bailey makes is between parliamentary and separation-of-powers systems. Under Bailey's conceptualization, in presidential systems, multiple institutions and veto players form policy, while in parliamentary systems a single institution is responsible for policy formation.

In addition, two formal works propose a framework for analyzing voter choice as incorporating post-electoral parliamentary activity. Grofman (1985) proposes a formal model in which voters evaluate the potential success of each party in implementing changes from the status quo in their preferred direction. He highlights the importance of the status quo relative to the party's platform in determining the voter's vote choice (i.e., the shift the voter hopes to achieve), as well as the party's impact ("performance weight"), which is a function of past performance and circumstantial constraints on its ability to implement its policy. Grofman's model provides a framework for thinking about voter choice in a new light. With its generality, however, comes the pitfall that it does not discriminate among institutional environments. Predictions of the model depend on the party's past performance and the spatial location of the status quo relative to the voter's bliss point, but not necessarily on institutional features of the political system. Austen-Smith and Banks (1988) develop a game-theoretic model of parliamentary elections under proportional representation in a three-party system. Inspired by the German party system prior to reunification, the model conceptualizes voters as strategic actors who support the leftmost and rightmost parties. The small center party ends up with slightly more votes than necessary for passing the parliamentary threshold. After the elections, one of the two big parties and the small party form a coalition government.[2]

While the debate between the directional and the proximity frameworks has conquered the center stage in the empirical literature on voter behavior in the past two and a half decades, this same literature has set aside the Downsian principle of voters voting to achieve beneficial policies. In this chapter, I offer an account for voter choice, acknowledging that voters might be policy oriented rather than party-platform oriented only. I first introduce a general logic and then apply it in specific forms to parliamentary, presidential, and federal institutional environments.

The rest of the chapter is organized as follows. The next section presents the intuition of the compensatory vote model, first in general terms, and then in each of three electoral arenas. The following section discusses voter sophistication. The next section presents a formal version of the model. The following section discusses the differences among compensatory vote, strategic vote, and protest vote. The final section offers a conclusion.

2.2 COMPENSATORY VOTE: THE ARGUMENT

In his famous book, Downs (1957) conceptualizes voter choice as a choice for the party that will provide him with the highest utility. To determine which party it is, a voter "compares the utility income he believes he would receive were each party in office" (39). Downs refers to this difference as the *expected party differential*:

... [I]f he is rational, he knows that no party will be able to do everything that it says it will do. Hence he cannot simply compare platforms; instead, he must estimate in his own mind what the parties would actually do were they in

---

[2] For a similar framework, see Baron and Diermeier (2001).

power. . . Therefore the voter must weigh the performance that the opposition party would have produced in period *t* if it had been in power. . . As a result, the most important part of the voter's decision is the size of her *current party differential*, i.e., the difference between the utility income he actually received in period *t* and the one he would have received if the opposition had been in power. (39–40)

The model I develop here is in line with the Downsian logic. After all, as Bailey (2001, 6–7) reminds us, to the extent that a voter wakes up in a sweat in the middle of the night thinking about politics, it is probably actual policy and its direct effect on her ("what will happen to my welfare benefits?") that concern her.

Picture a left-leaning moderate voter in the imaginary Western democracy Westland watching a story about her country's pension system on the evening news. The story describes the thin cushion of the pension system, the growing cohort of the elderly, and the shrinking working-age population. The story then turns to discussing policy suggestions including privatization, retrenchment of benefits, and an increase in taxes for the middle class. She might ask herself: Who is most similar to me ideologically? Who best represents my *views*? Or, alternatively, she might ask: Who will be most effective in pulling policy in my direction? Who will best represent my *interests*?

What would each question imply for her choice in the ballot booth? Let us imagine three different institutional environments, and predict voter choice under each environment in light of the two questions. The first is parliamentary democracy, in which policy is formed solely or mostly in the chamber whose representatives are up for election (e.g., the UK or the Netherlands). The second and third involve multi-institutional policy formation: presidential systems in which policy is determined by both the legislature and the executive (e.g., Brazil or the United States), and federations in which policy is determined by a combination of preferences of the central and regional governments (e.g., Germany). What decision rule might she employ if voting in each of these environments?

The proximity model assumes that a voter is concerned with the first consideration, representation of her views. This consideration leads to similar decisions under each of the three environments. If concerned with representation of her views, she will simply support the party with positions most similar ideologically to hers. By supporting the left-leaning Social Democrats in our example, she declares who she is. This consideration is consistent with Schuessler's (2000) notion of expressive voting and is constant across institutional environments; whether the path leading from votes to policy is straight or long and winding, a direct platform implementation or involving compromise, the party ideologically most similar to the voter is the same party. Under proximity voting, then, voters employ the same decision rule, regardless of the environment in which they vote.

The second consideration, however, might lead to different choices under different environments. According to this consideration, the voter evaluates how to use her ballot in a way that will most effectively guard her interests. This logic suggests that her vote will reflect her assessment of the manner in which her vote is converted to policy. The conversion from votes to seats to policy formation is set by institutions, and different institutional mechanisms will convert identical vote-share profiles to different policy outcomes. If voters are concerned with policy, institutional mechanisms converting their votes to policy will find their way into voter decision rules and consequently into voter choices. In systems in which power is straight platform implementation, voting for policy may lead voters to endorse the party ideologically most similar to their own views. In systems in which power is shared among multiple bodies, and policies are determined by compromise, voters may have an incentive to endorse a party whose positions differ from (and are often more extreme than) their own views in order to compensate for the dilution of their votes.

I turn now to an examination of this principle under each of the three institutional environments, beginning with parliamentary democracy.

2.2.1 Parliamentary Elections

If voting in a parliamentary democracy, our voter might ask herself what is the relative impact of the Social Democrats compared with that of other parties in the parliament. What would it look like in the absence of, for example, the radical Left Party? Will the Social Democrats coalesce with the Center Party in the absence of the left, and privatize public services? And what would it look like in the absence of the moderate Social Democrats? Will the Left Party, if in power, nationalize private property? Or will the right then acquire power?

Considering ideal types of parliamentary democracy or their close relatives can shed light on the entire possible range of outcomes. Suppose that Westland is characterized by a plethora of parties often governed by a minority government that relies on different compositions of ad-hoc majorities supported by the opposition, as is common in Norway. The path leading from votes to seats to government formation to policy formation is typically long and winding, with bargaining and compromise awaiting at each turn. Votes cast in this electoral environment will likely be routinely watered-down by bargaining in the Storting.

This rationale is not specific to the Norwegian case. Systems in which the opposition has major agenda-setting power via plenary meetings or the parliamentary committee system, as is the case in the Netherlands; systems in which power is horizontally fragmented by design, as in Belgium; or, similarly, systems in which short-lived multiparty coalitions are commonly formed, as is the case in Israel, will encourage similar motivation on voters' part. Voters may compensate for post-electoral compromise by overshooting, supporting an extreme party in order to effectively pull the center of gravity in their direction. In fact, almost any system characterized by diffusion of power in the parliament will encourage some version of such motivation.

Conversely, suppose that the voter casts her ballot in a single-member district, as in Australia, or a first-past-the-post electoral system, as in Canada, or a system characterized by a single-party majority government and a parliament in which the government has a strong agenda-setting power in comparison to the chamber, as in the UK. The Canadian party system notwithstanding, typically in such systems the parliament hosts only a few parties. The path leading from votes to policy is short and straight: policy formation is concentrated, and there is little watering-down by institutionalized bargaining. Considerations of winnability aside, she has no reason to overshoot since policy formation involves little compromise; the party in power is the party in power.

Voter choice, I argue, is directed by a combination of the two motivations: who guards her interests, and who represents her views. Depending on the path from votes to policy the two motivations converge or diverge. When policy formation is a straight path of platform implementation by the winner, power is concentrated and thus policy-minded choice and expressive choice lead voters to endorse the same party, the one ideologically similar to them. When the institutional environment is such that policy formation is a process incorporating input from multiple political actors, power is diffused, and policy-oriented choice will lead voters to endorse a party ideologically different from them, and hence the two motivations will diverge.

In polities characterized by concentration of power (e.g., the government secures a majority in the parliament, the government consists of a single party, the government is relatively strong vis-à-vis the legislature, or the opposition has little impact over policy formation via the committee system), policy is unlikely to be watered-down much by post-electoral negotiations. Take Canada in the late 1990s or Britain in the late 1990s as examples. Holding more than 50 percent of the seats in the parliament, the Liberals in Canada, like Labour in Britain, exercised near complete control over policy. Under such circumstances, supporting the party whose positions on pension policy are most similar to the voter's position is a de facto *vote* over *policy*; votes are unlikely to be watered-down along the path leading from elections to policy. Therefore, both representational and compensatory vote will lead the voter to endorse the party whose positions are most similar to her own views.

In polities in which power in the parliament is fragmented (the government often leans on no more than plurality, the government consists of a coalition of parties, or where the opposition has control over policy formation via the committee system), bargaining is a daily matter. Under such circumstances, representational considerations and compensatory considerations present a tradeoff, and will lead the voter to support different parties. Expecting that her vote will be watered-down by compromise, a voter in a highly fragmented system might "overshoot" in a way her counterpart in a majoritarian system might not.

One might wonder why voters would compensate at all in majoritarian systems. Indeed, in majoritarian systems there is little incentive for voters to compensate, since little bargaining and compromise take place. In some such systems, a single party is in power and the government has almost complete agenda-setting power. However, in others, the opposition has its say in formation of policy via various mechanisms. Avakumovic (1978) discusses how through placing issues on the agenda, the CCF-NDP has affected policy in Canada for years.

Similarly, Meguid (2005) shows how emerging niche parties take part in shaping the agenda by raising issues for public discussion, and, over time, forcing established parties to incorporate them into the discourse.

This argument directly leads to an empirical prediction: the more power-sharing facilitated by the institutional environment, the more voters will compensate for the watering-down of their votes. Therefore, *the more the political system is characterized by fragmentation of power, the more likely are voters to support parties whose positions differ from their own views. Thus, compensatory vote will increase with institutional power-sharing.*

I proposed here that, in general, an extreme party may have more momentum in pulling policy in a desired direction than a party closer to the voter's bliss point. Two factors should be taken into consideration, however. First is the direction in which voters will attempt to pull policy. Recall our left-leaning voter. Would the Left Party be able to more effectively guard her interests if the Social Democrats pursue a centrist policy resulting from parliamentary bargaining, or will the Center party guard her interests in case of a Social Democrat–Left Party alliance? In what direction will the voter turn when policy formation involves multiple actors? My argument is theoretically silent on the direction in which the voter will compensate. I am agnostic as to the a priori direction of overshooting; it depends on the political map. When expecting a weighty political force to her right, the voter will compensate to the left, and when expecting a weighty force to her left, she will compensate to the right. Empirically, however, we can often narrow down our prediction. Under proportional representation, policy is often in congruence with the position of the median voter (Powell 2000). This implies that when compensating, voters will more often than not compensate toward the poles of the ideological scale rather than toward its center. I will return to this point in the empirical analysis.

A related issue is the predictability of post-electoral bargaining. In some cases, parties announce their preferred coalition partner before election day, and even campaign with the declared partner (Golder 2006). The purple coalition in the Netherlands in 1998 is one such example, where the Dutch Labour Party (PvdA), the Conservative Liberals (VVD), and the Progressive Liberals (D66) coalesced for the second time. A similar example is the 2002 German elections, in which Gerhard Schroeder and Joschka Fischer campaigned together, the former announcing that he would like the latter to serve as his minister of foreign affairs (*International Herald Tribune*, September 13, 2002) and the latter that he had no desire to be a chancellor but would rather "bear responsibility for this country as a foreign minister ... under Gerhard Schroeder" (*Financial Times Information*, September 15, 2002). Other elections in the same two polities, however, had much more vague party groupings; the purple coalition was a surprising outcome of the 1994 Dutch elections. Similarly, the 2005 German elections brought much more uncertainty, with the grand coalition following the elections formed from one of at least four speculated party groupings (Proksch and Slapin 2006). When post-electoral grouping is clearly predicted or pre-electorally announced (Golder 2006), voters can more easily target their vote toward a desired policy outcome. When the configuration of parties yields multiple plausible scenarios, policy-oriented voting is harder to carry out.

Compromise in the parliament is only one form of power sharing. I turn now to a different one, compromise in multi-office elections.

2.2.2 Multi-Office Elections

Unlike in parliamentary systems, where policy inputs are from parties in parliament, power in both presidential and federal systems is diffused across institutions, each one on its own a host for parties (or their leaders). I now turn to a discussion of compensatory voting under both these environments.

2.2.2.a Presidential Elections

Imagine our left-leaning moderate voter, this time in a presidential democracy, watching the news about the crisis of the pension system. As in the example given earlier, she might ask herself who best represents her views or who best guards her interests under the given political circumstances. At the time of the elections, as before, if she is concerned with representation of her views, she will likely support the party most similar to her ideologically. If, however, she is concerned with the way policy serves her interests, she may incorporate policy formation into her choice. Voters in parliamentary elections may adapt their votes depending on the post-electoral compromise among parties in parliament. Their counterparts in presidential systems may take into consideration inter-institutional compromise in policy formation: how the president and the legislature form policy together.

What form does compensatory vote take under presidentialism? In parliamentary systems, the bodies the voter balances – parties themselves – are all within the legislative branch. In contrast, in presidential systems, the voter compensates for bargaining across government branches. The different parties balanced in a parliamentary system are of the same institutional species. One might argue that balancing the legislature against the executive is analogous to using apples to balance oranges. This type of compensatory vote works via at least two routes. First, given the involvement of the executive branch in policy formation through presidential signing of bills, presidential veto power, presidential budgetary powers, and the like, a vote cast in presidential elections affects those aspects of executive activity involving policy formation in the legislature. Second, since approval of the legislature is often required for appointments proposed by the president, a vote in legislative elections balances policy execution and implementation.

Before proceeding, it is important to note that students of American politics have examined a specific presidential form of policy balancing in an attempt to explain electoral patterns in Congressional elections in the United States (see, e.g., Alesina and Rosenthal 1995; Fiorina 1996; Mebane 2000). These and other studies find support for the balancing hypothesis, although others, in an attempt to explain the very same regularities, find no evidence of it (see Burden and Kimball 1998). I review the extensive U.S.-specific literature and the implications it carries in detail and discuss the advantages of a cross-sectional analysis in Chapter 4. Theorizing about and empirically analyzing compensatory vote in a comparative fashion allows me not only to demonstrate that the midterm slump in the United States is part of a broader, cross-sectional regularity in presidential systems but, more importantly, to draw on cross-country variation, and in particular on institutional variation, to understand what the off-year slump is about.

Still, it is worth mentioning a few of these works here. Fiorina (1996) argues that divided government in the United States is a product of voters' balancing the president and Congress against one another. Ticket splitting by middle-of-the-road voters, he argues, results in divided government and moderate policy. Alesina and Rosenthal (1995) develop a model of general and midterm elections in the United States, incorporating economic policy. They contend that the party of the president loses support at midterm because of a moderating strategy by voters. Mebane (2000) develops and tests a model of moderation of the executive and legislature as well as coordination among voters, showing that a small group of voters moderate and coordinate in general elections.

Next, I list the key principles of compensatory vote in presidential systems. I adopt a logic similar to the one employed by the U.S.-specific literature, and embed it in the broader concept of compensatory vote across institutional regimes. Thus, some of the principles or their implications I lay out have been examined by the U.S.-specific literature, while others have not been tested at all. None of them, to the best of my knowledge, has been tested comparatively. I specify them all here, although I explore empirically only a subset of them.

If voters are concerned with policy, and policy is a combination of policy inputs of the executive and those of the legislature, then they might incorporate into their choice of one their expectation of whether *and to what degree* their votes will be watered-down by the other. Thus, a vote of a compensatory voter might reflect three questions. First, who is (or who will likely be) in control of the executive and the legislative branches? Second, what is the decision-making process involving the executive and the legislature? And third, what are her positions relative to those of the ones in control of the two branches? The combination of these questions carries multiple implications. Let me take these three questions one by one, along with the implications that each question carries. First, voters might ask who is (or will likely be) in control of either branch. Voters will be better able to use their ballots in a targeted way when elections are non-concurrent than when elections for both institutions take place simultaneously. Using a seesaw analogy, when one arm of the government is fixed, voters can use their ballots for the other arm to balance the seesaw with respect to their views and pull policy in their direction with greater precision. In theory, elections for either the presidency or the legislature can serve as an opportunity to balance the other institution. In practice, given the centrality of the executive in presidential regimes, I take presidential elections to be the pivotal event, and legislative elections to be the reacting event. The first implication, then, is that the party of the president will do poorly in off-year legislative elections compared with concurrent elections.

Second, and central to my argument here, voters might consider the policy-formation process, and in particular the weight of either the executive or the legislature. The degree to which voters balance the executive depends on the power of the executive vis-à-vis the legislature. A strong executive will water down the policy input of the legislature more than a weak executive will. In those polities in which the executive is relatively powerful vis-à-vis the legislature, balancing of greater magnitude is required in order to achieve desirable policy. Conversely, when the executive has limited power, the position of the legislature will be diluted by post-electoral negotiations to a lesser extent, and hence voters will have less of a motivation to compensate. Therefore, the more power the constitution grants to the president, the greater the expected off-year electoral loss in legislative elections. The same macro-level relationship will not necessarily be observed in concurrent elections. Even if in those polities in which the executive has greater authority, and as a consequence voters are more likely to split their tickets in concurrent elections, it does not necessarily imply that the party winning the presidency is more likely to do poorly in the legislative elections. This is because ticket splitting in various directions does not necessarily aggregate to divided government.[3]

Third, a voter might consider the positions of those in power, and her positions in comparison to them. This carries several implications. Voters will engage in more or less compensatory vote depending on the ideological position of the party in control of the presidency. In particular, the fourth implication suggests that all else being equal, when the party in control of the presidency is relatively extreme, more voters will have an incentive to turn in the other direction in legislative elections in order to effectively shift the center of gravity of the political system.

Middle-of-the-road voters, and in particular ones whose positions are in between the positions of the large parties, are the ones most likely to switch in search of moderation (see Scheve and Tomz 1999). Therefore, the fifth implication suggests that the more moderate a voter

---

[3] I elaborate on this point in Chapter 4. As an example, a voter might vote for party A for president and B for the legislature, and her partner might do the reverse. The aggregate result will be identical to a situation in which they both voted the straight ticket – one for A, the other for B.

is, the more likely she is to switch her ballot in off-year legislative elections. However, not all moderate voters are as likely to switch their
ballot in non-concurrent legislative elections. Voters' likelihood of
switching in search of moderation depends on their poorly predicting the
outcome of the presidential elections preceding the legislative elections.
After all, if the results of the presidential elections are perfectly predicted,
the following legislative elections serve no corrective role. Therefore, the
sixth implication is that among moderate voters, the more surprised
voters are with the outcome of the last presidential elections, the more
likely they are to switch their vote in non-concurrent elections.

There is more than one potential reason for voters to switch their
ballots in non-concurrent elections. Perhaps the most obvious alternative candidate explanation is presidential coattails. When legislative
elections are held concurrently with presidential elections, a charis-
matic presidential candidate might help her party gain support in the
legislative elections. However, when the two are staggered, the party
of the president does not enjoy the electoral energy produced by the
presidential candidate – that party is already in power. Compensatory
vote implies that voters understand (or behave as if they understand)
key principles of how their votes are converted to policy. And while
my model does not assume that voters are aware of and understand the
specifics of policy formation and presidential-legislative relations, it
assumes that they understand that the executive and the legislature
jointly determine policy. Being policy-oriented rather than party-
oriented, compensatory voting is, therefore, more demanding than
proximity voting. Thus, the seventh implication is that (if voters switch
their ballot in non-concurrent legislative elections with policy-formation
in mind) voter sophistication should be correlated with switching among
moderate voters more than among others.

Lastly, other things being equal, some voters are more likely than
others to stick with a party. Those strongly attached to a party are less
likely to compensate for compromise by switching to another between
presidential and legislative elections. For voters with a weak party
attachment, on the other hand, vote switching away from their party (in
either presidential or legislative lections) is not as costly. Thus, I expect
party attachment to be negatively correlated with switching at midterm.

In this book, I examine a small subset of these implications. I focus
only on how institutional design affects and is reflected in voter choice.

My empirical analysis to follow will analyze the first and second implications: withdrawal of support for the party of the president in non-concurrent legislative elections, and the relationship between the power of the presidency and the loss of support.

2.2.2.b. Federal Elections

While power in presidential systems is horizontally distributed between the executive and the legislature, voters in federations face vertical inter-institutional policy formation by both central and regional governments. From the voter's point of view, there are some similarities between inter-institutional compromise in federal and presidential environments. However, particular features of electoral politics in federations make the federal arena a somewhat more complicated environment than the presidential arena. I begin by discussing some of these features, and then, reflecting on them, I discuss vertical compensatory voting in federations.

Presidential systems often consist of two-party systems, one in the legislature and one, often of fewer parties, competing for the presidency. The executive itself, however, is embodied in a single party, and sometimes in a single person. Federal environments, by contrast, not only often consist of both multiple regional party systems *and* a national one, but also often involve coalition governments at either level, such that a plethora of parties is directly involved in policy formation. The multiplicity of party systems creates challenges for us in attempting to understand voter choice across sub-national units. When party systems are integrated across levels, voters are able to identify parties at one level with those carrying similar labels at another level. When regional party systems are not integrated with the national one, such that similar parties do not necessarily compete at both levels and party labels do not necessarily encapsulate similar information either across regions or between regions and the national system, compensatory voting across government levels might not result in a familiar electoral cycle.[4]

Policy formation in federations, and hence compensatory voting, is largely a vertical process. The nature of federations implies that both the regions and the center provide policy inputs, and policy is a

---

[4] I thank Craig Volden for pointing out this distinction.

product of both government arms. Regional and federal inputs can be combined into policy in more than one way. A distinction between two federal models is relevant here. The first is cooperative federalism, in which policy responsibilities are divided along functional lines and the two levels share responsibility for most policy areas. This can manifest itself in the central government's responsibility for general policy framework, and the regions' for details, or the center's responsiblity for legislation and the regions' for implementation. Office holders at the regional level are involved in policy formation at the central level via the second chamber. Under cooperative federalism, therefore, "the two levels of political institutions are 'interlocking'" (Hix 1998). The second is one of dual federalism in which the center and the regions split policy competences between them along jurisdictional lines, such that each level is responsible for devising and implementing policy for a particular policy area and "the two levels of political institutions are said to be 'independent'" (ibid).

Compensatory voting is possible in both environments, although it is more straightforward in the former, in which inputs of the two levels of government are combined into a single policy. Under cooperative federalism, voters use their ballots for one office to balance the other in a given policy area (or each of multiple areas.) Somewhere along the path from votes to policy – between policy framework and detailed legislation or between legislation and implementation – there is room for watering down of the mandate voters give their government. And while they are probably uninformed about the details of the distribution of power between regional and national governments, they intuit that if one is governed by the left and the other by the right, jointly shaped policy will likely be somewhere in between. Thus, they use their ballots to pull a given policy (or policies) in a desired direction. Under dual federalism, in which policy formation is distributed along jurisdictional lines, compensation is not in any given policy area but across areas. Since the federal government is responsible for some policy areas and the regions for others, there is some averaging of "conservative policy on issue X with liberal policy on issue Y."

The implications of the vertical-compensation argument in federations are largely analogous to those of horizontal compensation in presidential systems. Here, too, while federal and regional elections in theory might be each reacting to one another, in practice, given the importance of the central government in federations, I assume that federal elections serve as a pivot to which regional elections react.

Returning to the seesaw analogy, voters in federal systems are able to use their ballots with relatively high precision when elections are staggered; when the federal government is intact, voters can use regional elections to compensate for expected post-electoral compromise. However, when both central and regional governments are up for election, both arms of the seesaw are unknown. Thus, if voters are concerned with policy, they might use staggered regional elections to pull the federal government in the direction they desire. The first implication, then, is that parties in power federally will do poorly in regional elections following the federal elections compared with regional elections held concurrently with federal elections.

Second, the degree of compensatory vote in federations may depend on the ideological makeup of the central government. In particular, the more ideologically defined and extreme the parties in control of the federal government are, the more likely are voters to shun them in regional elections.

Third, the degree of compensatory vote may depend on the distribution of power among the bodies participating in policy formation. In the federal arena, this has two implications. First, since policy is a combination of inputs from both central and regional governments, voters, when facing a strong central government, will pull away more strongly in regional elections. Thus, in general, the more centralized a polity is, the more voters will shun the central government in regional elections non-concurrent with federal elections.

Some federations (or multi-level governance systems more broadly), however, vary in the degree of autonomy they grant to different regions. Regions with a high degree of dependence on the central government will, I contend, be characterized by a high degree of compensation compared with regions enjoying more autonomy. This is for two reasons. First, politics of highly dependent regions are likely to be highly integrated with national politics, and thus national considerations might be especially potent in voters' minds. Such conditions allow the compensatory logic to be easily picked up by voters. Regions enjoying a high degree of autonomy, on the other hand, are likely to have their regional politics less integrated with national politics, and thus voters are less likely to focus on national issues when casting their ballots. Second, the logic applied to cross-polity comparison earlier applies here as well; the weight of the policy input of the central government is high in regions that are highly dependent on the central government, and this, in turn, increases the degree of compensation on the part of voters.

In my discussion of presidential systems, I mentioned Alesina and Rosenthal's (1996) argument about the effect of (un)predictability of the presidential election's outcome. The authors argue that the more surprising the results of the presidential race are, the greater the loss in subsequent legislative elections. Similar logic holds here. When the results of the federal race are surprising, voters are more likely to shun the parties represented in the federal government in subsequent regional elections.

The implications I have discussed so far are at the macro level. What about individual voters? Some voters are more likely to repeat their vote choices from national to regional elections, while others are more prone to switching. Voting to compensate for the power of the federal government is about the policy the federal government engages in. To compensate for the federal government, therefore, a voter first needs to be concerned with national-level politics; the more a voter is concerned with the national political agenda, the more likely she is to react to recent national developments in regional elections. Similarly, the more she is concerned with regional politics, the less likely her regional vote is a reaction to the national political arena.

A principal factor is voter positions. When the federal government consists of a party or a coalition of parties from one side of the political spectrum, voters whose opinions are between the government's position and the median voter, or on the other side of the median voter, might try to pull policy in their direction and thus support the opposition parties in regional elections. But, of course, voters on the opposite pole from the government probably did not support the government in the national elections either. Switchers are likely to be found among relatively centrist voters. Therefore, the more centrist a voter is, the more likely she is to prefer a split partisan control of the federal and regional arms of the government (given that one arm is already controlled by one side). It is important to remember, though, that unlike in the U.S. two-party system, voters in multi-party systems have many more options and many opportunities to switch their votes either to parties on the same ideological side of the party (parties) in power or to parties on the other side, whether for compensatory or other reasons.

Two additional factors affect the likelihood of a voter deserting the party she supported in federal elections. First is partisanship. Loyal partisans are more likely to vote consistently, while weak or non-partisans are more prone to switching. In general, the more a voter is attached to a party, the less likely she is to switch her party support between national and regional elections.

Second is voter sophistication. Undoubtedly, few Swiss voters understand the detailed distribution of power and division of responsibilities between the federal government and the cantons, few Spanish voters understand the (different) relations between Madrid and each of the regions, few Canadian voters are experts on Canadian federalism, and so on. However, just as British voters in parliamentary environments have hardly ever experienced a coalition government and Israeli voters always have, voters in federations have repeatedly experienced their political reality shaped by both their regional and federal governments. Nonetheless, some voters might be better aware of the vertical division of power than others. Voters who are politically sophisticated are more likely to understand the compromise between the two levels of government and use their ballot to work around it. Therefore, among moderate voters, the more politically sophisticated they are, the more likely they are to switch their ballots in regional elections and deviate from their federal choices.

2.2.3 Prospective Voters

Unlike the parliamentary version of my model, the federal and presidential contexts introduce a temporal component. While voters in parliamentary contexts assess the likely developments after election night, in presidential and federal systems they look back and plan forward. In the case of non-concurrent elections, they assess the likely developments after election night while keeping in mind who was elected in the most recent presidential (federal) race. This does not imply that voters are retrospective. They are still prospective; they vote with expectations of policy formation in mind.

A seemingly similar conceptualization, Governing System as a Thermostat, is offered by Erikson, MacKuen, and Stimson (hereafter

EMS) (2002, 326–8). Using the metaphor of a thermostat, the authors describe two groups of university department faculty – soft-hearted liberals and tough-minded conservatives. Each member of the faculty has a preference for a particular room temperature. Members of the liberal group wish to have the thermostat set to high temperature, while the conservatives prefer to have it set to low. Members of the faculty in EMS's model offer feedback in response to past policy; they monitor the temperature and instruct the engineer in charge of the furnace toward a warmer or colder one when it deviates from the desired temperature. EMS write: "Residents . . . pay attention to the current temperature, and (at least as a collectivity) give negative feedback so that the engineer can readjust the furnace to avoid overshooting" (326).

In spite of the similar language, it is important to note the difference between this metaphor and compensatory voting. Voters in EMS's model monitor the status quo and attempt to shift it by changing the actual temperature to a target temperature. Compensatory voters, on the other hand, expect that a new status quo will be preceded by compromise, and thus they exaggerate their stated target temperature. Relatedly, the target temperature of EMS's voters does not depend on the status quo, while compensatory voters base their stated target temperature on how big a shift from the status quo temperature they want to achieve, and how much dilution of their target temperature they expect.

2.3 CAN VOTERS REALLY COMPENSATE?

Whether in directing one's ballot to compensate for compromise among competing parties in a single institution (parliament) or for different arms of policy making against one another (in presidential and federal systems), the compensatory logic might seem highly demanding at first glance. Can voters really figure it all out?

As I will demonstrate, voters need not be especially knowledgeable nor terribly sophisticated to pursue this logic. They need not have a detailed model of bargaining in parliaments, they need not know whether the Chilean president has decree power or only authority to introduce referendums, nor do they need to have command of the intricacies of German federalism. Often, the discourse in the media sets the debate in terms intuitive to the inattentive potential voter. The discussion in the Netherlands in the 1990s is a good example. Dutch voters regularly heard about the "purple coalition" – the coalition of the Dutch Labour Party (red) and the conservative liberal party, the VVD (blue), along with the progressive liberals, D66. A red vote, then, makes the purple coalition redder, while a blue vote pulls it in the opposite direction. British voters, on the other hand, can safely expect that, as has been the case repeatedly since World War II, when a (single) party is in power, it (and solely it) is in power.

Several additional factors make the compensatory logic easy for voters to follow. First is campaign rhetoric employed by politicians themselves. In parliamentary environments in particular, when a particular party is expected to win a large fraction of the votes, other parties often use balancing language to attract voters. The 2006 Israeli elections in which, as expected, the center party Kadima secured a plurality of the votes and later became the senior member of the coalition, serve as a good example for such rhetoric. Yossi Beilin, the leader of the liberal party Meretz, called on prospective voters to support his party with the following argument: "This time the elections are not about who wins, but what the coalition will look like . . . we want to be in the coalition as a factor that will affect the manner in which the land will be divided."[5] Even more explicit was Jack Layton, the head of the NDP, in the days leading to the 2006 Canadian elections: "Give us your vote this time, in this election, and we'll balance the Conservatives in the next parliament."[6] And although the Canadian parliamentary system is not one in which we would expect compensatory vote in great numbers, even there party leaders sent a clear message to voters: vote for us, and we'll balance them.

These messages from leaders do not fall on deaf ears. Voters use cues from parties as a compass helping them to navigate their way in a complicated political world (Druckman 2001). Moreover, even poorly informed voters are able to follow their better informed counterparts and, emulating them, make choices they would have made had they been better informed (Lupia 1994, 2002) or take cues from various other sources (Lupia and McCubbins 1998).

---

[5] *Haaretz*, February 8, 2006. My translation.
[6] *Globe and Mail*, January 23, 2006.

2.4 THE COMPENSATORY VOTE MODEL: A GENERAL FORMAL VERSION

The empirical motivation of this study is accounting for regularities such as those presented in Figures 1.1–1.3. The theoretical motivation is providing a general framework for understanding the way political paths set by institutions are incorporated into and reflected in voter choice. Inspired by Downs, the compensatory model highlights the importance of policy for voter choice. Voters in the model receive intrinsic value by expressing support for a party ideologically similar to them, yet they are also policy minded.

My approach to modeling compensatory vote takes a middle road. On the one hand, I allow for voters to incorporate considerations that go beyond representation of their views and imply longer time horizons and a choice that reflects at least basic institutional principles of post-electoral bargaining. In doing so, I attribute to voter choice a degree of sophistication greater than previous theories – namely, directional and proximity – do. On the other hand, I employ a decision-theoretic rather than a game-theoretic framework. Although, as will become clear, voter decision in my model is affected by impressions of what others might do, voters in my model do not coordinate their behavior with all other voters, and their behavior is not derived from general equilibrium. Indeed, the individual voter behaves as if she is pivotal, assuming away the turnout question. Given these considerations, I employ a simple decision-theoretic model. A game-theoretic extension to the model presented here, however, is, of course, possible, and would present an interesting opportunity for further exploration.

In focusing on how institutional environments shape voter choices, I leave party strategy out of my conceptualization domain and zero in on voter motivation given party positions. Party strategy is, of course, important, but it is not the focus of my study. In the last chapter, however, I explore party strategy in light of the insights about voter motivations produced here.

Recall our voter in Westland watching the evening news and comparing expected policy with a counterfactual policy. The counterfactual policy takes different forms depending on the institutional context. When evaluating a party in a unicameral parliamentary system, the counterfactual is the absence of the party from parliament, holding the distribution of power of the other parties fixed. In presidential and federal systems it is various institutions that provide policy inputs; thus the counterfactual is the absence of the party from the particular institution in question. In the former, the president and the legislature both shape policy. In legislative elections in presidential systems, the counterfactual policy is, then, the one that would have evolved under a different legislature, holding authority and position of the executive constant. In federal systems, state and federal governments are assigned relative weights depending on the distribution of authority between the two. Therefore, in regional elections in federal environments, the counterfactual can be a different regional government, holding the federal government fixed.

In its most general form, my compensatory-vote model juxtaposes expected policy (P) and the counterfactual policy (P_C). The compensatory voter compares her ideological distance from each:

$$U_{ij} = -\beta_1 \left[(v_i - P)^2 - (v_i - P_C)^2 \right] \tag{2.5}$$

where U_{ij} is the utility of voter i for party j and β_1 is a weight. Policy, its counterfactual parallel, and thus the gap between them depend on a variety of factors, domestic and international. First, and most obvious, policy is affected by the parties involved in policy formation, their positions and impact. Additionally, it depends on a variety of domestic factors such as effectiveness of the bureaucracy in implementing legislation, discrepancy between positions of the bureaucracy and the legislative ranks, and bureaucracy independence (Huber and Shippan 2002). In the formation of particular policies, additional bodies have their impact: the military on defense policy, the central bank on economic policy, interest groups on particular policy areas, and so on. Lastly, in an open globalized economy, policy depends on international markets and economic conditions, as well as on exogenous shocks, economic (e.g., energy crisis) or political (e.g., war). My conceptualization focuses on partisan and electorally related institutional factors in the formation of policy. Empirically, diffusion of power caused by these factors is likely the most relevant and visible to voters. Voters are probably more likely to be aware of repeated compromise among parties of the governing coalition than of more remote and less visible effects such as that of governmental agencies or the bureaucracy, their importance not withstanding. Such factors beyond the electoral sphere are not within the scope of this study.

I model policy as a weighted average of policy positions of the various partisan and institutional inputs. Similarly, the counterfactual policy assigns each input except the one in question a weight. The formation of policy (and counterfactual policy) by partisan and other institutional actors obviously varies by institution, as I elaborate later.

Recall the proximity model, under which the utility of voter i ($i=1,\ldots,n$) for party j ($j=1,\ldots,J$) is inversely related to the ideological distance between i and j. In one dimension:

$$U_{ij} = -\beta_2 (v_i - p_j)^2 \tag{2.6}$$

Of course, issue voting is unlikely entirely policy oriented. As the proximity model assumes, voters may simply prefer the party whose position is most similar to theirs, as presented in Equation 2.6. Combining the two motivations and setting the two weights to sum to one, voter motivation can be characterized by:

$$U_{ij} = -\beta (v_i - p_j)^2 - (1-\beta)\left[(v_i - P)^2 - (v_i - P_C)^2\right] \tag{2.7}$$

To find the position of the party that maximizes the voter's utility, I differentiate Equation 2.7 with respect to p_j:

$$\frac{\partial U_{ij}}{\partial p_j} = 2\beta(v_i - p_j) + 2(1-\beta)(v_i - P)\frac{\partial P}{\partial p_j} \tag{2.8}$$

and set the result to zero:

$$p_j^* = v_i + \frac{1-\beta}{\beta}(v_i - P)\frac{\partial P}{\partial p_j} \tag{2.9}$$

Policy and counterfactual policy are formed differently under different institutional environments. In the next step, I introduce specific institutional context into policy and the counterfactual policy in each environment. With them, the solution will take specific and more intuitive shapes.

2.4.1 Compensatory Vote in Parliamentary Elections

Under the proximity model described in Equation 2.6, a voter evaluates parties based on her ideological distance from each party. Voter motivation under this framework is expressive: she prefers party A to party B if A better represents her views.

How do voters perceive policy? One possibility is that voters have a somewhat naïve understanding of democracy: policy is an average of policy positions of parties in parliament, weighted by the relative impacts of the different parties:

$$P = \sum_{j=1}^{J} s_j p_j$$

where p_j is the ideological position of party j and s_j is the relative impact of party j, such that $\sum_{j=1}^{J} s_j = 1$ and $s_j \in [0,1) \ \forall j$.

Utility from policy-motivated voting can be represented as:

$$U_{ij} = \beta_1 \left[(v_i - P_{-p_j})^2 - (v_i - P)^2 \right] \tag{2.10}$$

Where P_{-p_j} is the counterfactual policy – the policy that would be formed if all parties with the exception of party j were included in the policy-formation process:

$$P_{-p_j} = \left(\frac{1}{\sum_{k \neq j} s_k} \right) \sum_{k \neq j} s_k p_k$$

The policy impact of party j can be expressed by the difference between P and P_{-p_j}. As can be seen in Equation 2.10, given a weight of the party, the impact increases as the difference between the position of the party and the policy increases; or, similarly, given the policy input of the party, the impact increases with the weight the party carries.

The intuition behind the bracketed term in Equation 2.10 is a counterfactual analysis comparing the voter's utility from policy produced by a parliament in which j is a member with that voter's utility from policy produced by a parliament from which j is absent.

If party j pulls policy closer to the voter, this term is positive. If, on the other hand, j pulls it away from the voter, it is negative. The voter's utility for party j approaches maximum when P is close to the voter's bliss point and P_{-p_j} is far from it. Since the model describes a policy-oriented yet naïve voter, I assume that in j's absence, other parties do not change their ideological placement to fill in the vacuum. Relatedly, while each party's absolute impact increases in j's absence, I assume that parties' relative impacts do not change.

The counterfactual analysis is in line with Downs's notion of party differential, which I mentioned earlier. Importantly, the difference $P - P_C$ is the impact of the party, not that of the voter. Of course, it would be unreasonable to claim that the impact of a voter's participation is the presence or disappearance of the party from the political map. Rather, $P - P_{-p_j}$ is the impact of party j in the policy space, and hence $\left[\left(v_i - P_{-p_j}\right)^2 - \left(v_i - P\right)^2 \right]$ is the policy benefit of voter i for party j.

As in the general case, combining the two motivations in the parliamentary context and normalizing the sum of the weights β_1 and β_2 to 1 results in the following utility function:

$$U_{ij} = -\beta \left(v_i - p_j\right)^2 - (1 - \beta)\left[\left(v_i - P\right)^2 - \left(v_i - P_{-p_j}\right)^2\right] \qquad (2.11)$$

where $\beta \in [0, 1]$ is a mixing weight on the two components of the utility such that the more compensatory the voting is, the smaller is β.

The bracketed term in Equation 2.11 implies that the voter's utility for each party depends on characteristics of other parties, and in particular their policy positions and relative weights. While at first glance this might seem in tension with the decision making of rational actors (why would voter evaluation of party A depend on characteristics of party B?), the two are compatible once policy-oriented choice is acknowledged. Policy – as well as counterfactual policy – is a function of the positions of (all) other parties. The degree and direction of policy pull a voter seeks to accomplish, and thus her utility for each party, depends on her evaluation of ideological placement and the impact of other parties. I will return to this property of voter choice in the concluding chapter.

The mixing weight β represents a summary of a nuanced political reality. In the theoretical model presented earlier, individuals vary in the extent to which they vote out of representational or compensatory considerations insofar as the context in which they vote varies. In particular, party placements relative to their own ideological placements, and their particular expectations as to parties' relative impacts, affect the decision rule they employ. Therefore, two ideologically similar voters making their choice in two different electoral environments – one in which the center of gravity is to her left and one in which it is to her right – might endorse different parties under a compensatory logic.

Under the specification here, β captures the extent to which voter choice, any voter choice in a given system, is motivated by compensatory or representational considerations. But not only institutional environments affect the relative weight of the consideration that voters employ. Voter characteristics *within* a given institutional environment may affect it as well. For example, two ideologically different voters may employ different decision rules; one might wish to pull policy only by a modest amount and thus employ a representational consideration, while the other might choose to "overshoot" in order to achieve a sizeable pull. Even two ideologically identical voters may employ different decision rules because of different perceptions of distribution of power in the parliament, and hence of how much pull is required. An empirical β that lies in the 0–1 interval can therefore be interpreted as an average of a heterogeneous electorate, employing different strategies.

An additional interpretation sees any individual voter as following a mixed decision rule. As I discussed earlier, each individual carries conflicting considerations. While it advances one's preferred policy, compensatory voting also involves endorsement of an object of choice ideologically different from the voter, and hence is expressively costly. Conversely, while carrying representational benefits, proximity voting does not necessarily advance one's policy interests. In consensual systems, the two motivations often translate into two different choices at the ballot booth. The mixing parameter β, then, may represent tension between two motivations and the relative extent to which an individual voter's choice is guided by compensatory versus representational considerations. In a way, it is a summary of multiple selves (Elster 1985).

Even in consensual polities, however, policy formation may not be a product of daily negotiations. Power sharing can produce policy in various ways. Laver and Shepsle (1996) propose a model of coalition and policy formation in which each party is the sole authority of policy formation in some jurisdictions. According to their model, negotiation about the distribution of portfolios (policy dimensions) takes place after the elections, but once the distribution is agreed upon, policy is simply a (multi-dimensional) combination of the parties' ideal points with respect to the portfolios each party holds, rather than a compromise on each such policy area. In other words, under this framework the compromise is across dimensions rather than within them. Compensatory vote is just as likely under this model of policy formation; votes are still watered down in the policy-formation process. However, it may be appropriate, perhaps more than under the assumption of within-dimensions compromise, to break the compensatory logic issue area by issue area, and to have a set of dimension-specific mixing parameters (β^d) rather than a single one.

To illustrate the calculation in Equation 2.11, imagine a three-party legislature with parties A, B, and C, such that $S_A = 1 - S_B - S_C$. In this case,

$$P_{-p_A} = \frac{s_B}{s_B + s_C} p_B + \frac{s_C}{s_B + s_C} p_C.$$

Substituting this expression into Equation 2.11, we get voter i's utility for party A in the three-party case:

$$
\begin{aligned}
U_{iA} &= -\beta(v_i - p_A)^2 - (1-\beta)\left[(v_i - P)^2 - (v_i - P_{-p_A})^2\right] \\
&= -\beta(v_i - p_A)^2 - (1-\beta)(v_i - s_A p_A - s_B p_B - s_C p_C)^2 \\
&\quad + (1-\beta)\left(v_i - \frac{s_B}{s_B + s_C} p_B - \frac{s_C}{s_B + s_C} p_C\right)^2
\end{aligned}
\tag{2.12}
$$

Calculating the utility for party B as in Equation 2.12 and taking the difference between the two gives the net utility of voting for A versus B:

$$
\begin{aligned}
U_{i,A-B} &= U_{iA} - U_{iB} \\
&= \beta\left[(v_i - p_B)^2 - (v_i - p_A)^2\right] \\
&\quad + (1-\beta)\left[(v_i - P_{-p_A})^2 - (v_i - P_{-p_B})^2\right]
\end{aligned}
\tag{2.13}
$$

This is the difference in the expressive value between the two parties and the difference between the policy benefits of the two. When $U_{i,A\text{-}B} > 0$, the voter votes for party A rather than B. This holds when both the ideological similarity of party A is greater than that of party B (the expressive value of A is greater than the expressive value of B) and the impact of party A on policy is more beneficial to the voter than the impact of party B, or when only one of the two holds but the utility of party A over party B is greater than that of B over A.

Differentiating Equation 2.12 with respect to p_A and setting the result to zero, we get the optimal ideological placement of A for voter i:

$$p_A^* = v_i \frac{\beta(s_A - 1) - s_A}{\beta(s_A^2 - 1) - s_A^2} + \frac{(1-\beta)s_A(s_B p_B + s_C p_C)}{\beta(s_A^2 - 1) - s_A^2} \tag{2.14}$$

Interpreting β is key, and while voter behavior is represented here as a combination of the two motivations, with β as a mixing parameter as discussed earlier, examining the two extremes is helpful for interpretation of the entire range. If supporting a party whose position differs from the voter's position bears no psychological/expressive costs such that voting over policy is the sole consideration in mind as far as issues are concerned, β will be arbitrarily close to zero; the voter's only motive is compensatory – to achieve a policy as close as possible to her own bliss point. The solution in Equation 2.14, then, reduces to:

$$p_A^*(\beta) \xrightarrow[\beta \to 0]{} \frac{v_i - (s_B p_B - s_C p_C)}{s_A} \tag{2.14a}$$

That is, when voting is purely compensatory, the ideological placement of party A preferred by the voter is the mirror image of policy produced by the combination of parties B and C alone weighted by the impact of party A. The less impactful party A is (the smaller the denominator in Equation 2.14a), the farther away it has to locate ideologically in order to shift policy outcome in its direction. In addition, the more extreme parties B and C are, the more extreme the voter would like party A to locate in order to balance the other two parties.

When β approaches one, the prediction of the model reduces to the proximity prediction:

$$p_A^*(\beta) \xrightarrow[\beta \to 1]{} v_i \tag{2.14b}$$

Depending on the institutional environment, an empirical β that is arbitrarily close to 1 may stand for different decision rules by voters. In consensual systems, the two motivations diverge, and hence an empirically large β stands for voters giving priority to representational considerations and engaging in proximity voting, contrary to my theoretical prediction. In majoritarian systems with little compromise, the two motivations converge, and thus an empirically high β can be a product of either compensatory or representational consideration; when the process of policy formation does not involve dilution of one's vote, voting for a party and voting for policy are observationally equivalent.

In general, for any $\beta \in [0, 1)$, the optimal party position (p^*_A) is spatially different from the voter's own position. In the case of pure policy-oriented voting, the ideal placement of party A is the point in the policy space that yields a policy compromise P identical to the voter's bliss point. We can see given p^*_A (Equation 2.14a), that compromise is expressed by:

$$P\Big|_{p_A=p^*_A} \xrightarrow[\beta\to 0]{} s_A \frac{v_i - (s_B p_B - s_C p_C)}{s_A} + s_B p_B + s_C p_C = v_i \qquad (2.15)$$

So far, I have presented the logic that leads to compensatory voting. However, I have not yet shown that all else being equal, voters who vote compensatorily in parliamentary elections will prefer extreme parties to parties that are ideologically similar to them. The next section takes up this task. I offer an example of four hypothetical voters employing compensatory and representational decision rules, and demonstrate how their vote choice depends on the decision rule they employ.

2.4.1.a A Simple Example

To get a sense of the predictions of the model, let us consider the following simple example. Imagine four voters in a unidimensional left-right ideological space marked by 1 through 9. The four voters, v_1 through v_4, are placed at 2, 4, 6, and 8, respectively. Further, imagine three parties, A through C, each carrying identical policy impacts, placed at 2.5, 4.5, and 8, respectively. Examining ideological proximity, we can see that v_1 is most similar to party A, v_2 and v_3 to the center party B, and v_4 to party C. We can therefore expect these to be their respective choices.

Compensatory considerations, however, lead voters to vote outwardly and support parties whose positions are more extreme than their own. Given party positions and weights, policy is placed at $(2.5 + 4.5 + 8)/3 = 5$. In the absence of party A, the leftmost party, the counterfactual policy is a compromise between parties B and C ($P_{-p_A} = 0.5 * 4.5 + 0.5 * 8 = 6.25$) and is thus the rightmost of the three counterfactual policies. Applying the same logic, the two other counterfactual policies are $P_{-p_B} = 5.25$ and $P_{-p_C} = 3.5$. Which party pulls policy closest to each voter's position? Comparing each voter's ideological distance between her own position and policy (5) with the distances between her position and the counterfactual policies (6.25, 5.25, and 3.5) according to Equation 2.10 reveals that compensatory considerations alone would lead voters 1 and 2 to support party A, and voters 3 and 4 to support party C.[7] The two moderate voters, then, v_2 and v_3, turn to extreme parties and away from the one ideologically similar (close) to them.

2.4.2 Compensatory Vote in Multi-Office Elections

Recall our voter in Westland watching the evening news. Her implicit assumption about policy takes a different form depending on the institutional context. In presidential and federal systems, the focus is on inter-institutional negotiations that shape policy. Accordingly, the relevant counterfactual is the absence of a party from one of the negotiating institutions. But formation of policy by partisan and other institutional players obviously varies between the two contexts. I begin with presidential systems, and then turn to federations.

2.4.2.a Compensatory Vote in Presidential Systems

Not surprisingly, the executive and the legislature in presidential systems are the main formal agents of policy inputs within the boundaries of the electoral scene. I conceptualize policy input of the legislature as an average of the positions of the legislative parties weighted by some impact coefficient (e.g., seat share). For simplicity, I assume a unicameral legislature. Further, I assume that the position of the executive arm is that of the president herself. Let *leg* denote the legislature. The

---

[7] Take voter 1, for example. $u_{1A} = (2 - 6.25)^2 - (2 - 5)^2 - = 9.0625$. By a similar calculation, her utility for parties B and C are $u_{1B} = 1.5625$, and $u_{1C} = -6.75$.

policy input of the legislature is $P^{leg} = \sum_j s_j^{leg} p_j^{leg}$, where s_j^{leg} is the weight of party j in the legislature and p_j^{leg} is the position of the party. Policy (P), then, is a weighted average of the policy inputs of the two institutions: $P = w^{pres} P^{pres} + w^{leg} P^{leg}$, where w^{pres} and w^{leg} are the relative weights of the presidency and the legislature, respectively, and P^{pres} is the position of the president.

A variety of factors affect the relative weight of the president's position compared with that of the legislature. We can think of w^{pres} as constitutional authorities (legislative or others), personality characteristics, public approval, the stature of the president in her party, or any other factor affecting the power of the president. For the time being, I use presidential impact as a general term standing for either or all of these factors. I will elaborate on this point further in the empirical investigation.

As earlier, I assume that a voter might have two considerations – representation of her views and pursuit of policy – with relative weights (β and 1-β, respectively) on each. The former is represented by the voter's ideological distance from party j, $(v_i - p_j)^2$, and the latter by the difference between her ideological distance from policy and her distance from counterfactual policy, $-[(v_i - P)^2 - (v_i - P_C)^2]$. Thus, voter utility for party j in the legislature is:

$$U_{ij}^{leg} = -\beta(v_i - p_j^{leg})^2 - (1 - \beta)[(v_i - P)^2 - (v_i - P_C)^2] \qquad (2.16)$$

Normalizing $w^{pres} + w^{leg} = 1$, voter utility then becomes:

$$\begin{aligned} U_{ij}^{leg} = &-\beta(v_i - p_j^{leg})^2 - (1 - \beta) \\ &\{[v_i - (wP^{pres} + (1 - w)P^{leg})]^2 - (v_i - P_C)^2\} \end{aligned} \qquad (2.17)$$

where the counterfactual policy is $P_C = P_{-jleg} = wP^{pres} + (1 - w)P_{-jleg}^{leg}$.

I turn now to the examination of a simple example, illustrating how compensatory motivation guides voter choice in presidential environments.

2.4.2.b A Simple Example
Imagine nine voters on an ideological continuum such that the position of the leftmost, v_1, is 1, the second, v_2, is 2, and so on up to v_9=9,

voting in non-concurrent legislative elections in a presidential system (see Table 2.1). The president is placed at 3 ($P^{pres} = 3$), and three parties of equal weight compete in the legislative elections, and are positioned such that $p_{A^{leg}} = 4.5$, $p_{B^{leg}} = 7$, and $p_{C^{leg}} = 9.5$. Voters v_1 through v_5 are thus ideologically closest to party A in the legislature, v_6 through v_8 closest to party B, and v_9 closest to party C.

Assume further that the president and the legislature have equal weights in determining policy, such that $P = 0.5 * P^{pres} + 0.5 * P^{leg}$ $= 0.5(3+7) = 5$. To calculate the counterfactual policies, consider first the legislative policy input in the absence of each of the three parties: $P^{leg}_{-A^{leg}} = 8.25$, $P^{leg}_{-B^{leg}} = 7$, and $P^{leg}_{-C^{leg}} = 5.75$. Combining these with the president's input, the counterfactual policies are: $P_{-A^{leg}} = 5.625$, $P_{-B^{leg}} = 5$, $P_{-C^{leg}} = 4.375$. Given these values, we can now calculate voter utility for each of the three parties according to Equation 2.17. These utilities are given in columns 5 through 7 of Table 2.1, and the highest entry per voter is highlighted in bold. Based on these values, the next column notes for each voter her expected choice based on a compensatory logic, while the last column notes the party that the voter would have supported had she applied a consideration of ideological proximity.

As the table shows, the four leftmost voters, v_1 through v_4, ideologically closest to party A, support party A according to a compensatory logic as well. Indeed, since policy is at position 5, these voters have no incentive to vote for any party to the right of A that will pull policy away from them. Similarly, the rightmost voter (v_9) supports the party ideologically closest to her, party C. However, moderate-right and right voters (v_6, v_7, and v_8), whose positions are ideologically closest to party B, support party C. This is because once their vote is diluted by compromise between the executive and the legislature, the extremity of party C makes it a more effective agent in pulling policy closer to them. Voter 5 is an interesting case of the compensatory logic. While ideologically the legislative party A is most similar to her views, and C is most different, post-electoral compromise between the president (at 3) and the legislature makes both parties A and C equally attractive to her, as if we had shifted the ideological continuum two units to the left.

This simple example illustrates how different decision rules may lead voters to hold different assessments of parties and eventually support different parties. In the example, I juxtapose two decision

TABLE 2.1. *Voter Choice in Presidential Systems: An Example*

Voter	$(v - P_{-A^{leg}})$	$(v - P_{-B^{leg}})$	$(v - P_{-C^{leg}})$	$(v - P_{-A^{leg}})^2 - (v - P)^2$	$(v - P_{-B^{leg}})^2 - (v - P)^2$	$(v - P_{-C^{leg}})^2 - (v - P)^2$	Compensatory Choice	Proximity Choice
1	21.39	16	11.39	5.39	0	−4.61	A	A
2	13.14	9	5.64	4.14	0	−3.36	A	A
3	6.89	4	1.89	2.89	0	−2.11	A	A
4	2.64	1	0.14	1.64	0	−0.86	A	A
5	0.39	0	0.39	0.39	0	0.39	A or C	A
6	0.14	1	2.64	−0.86	0	1.64	C	B
7	1.89	4	6.89	−2.11	0	2.89	C	B
8	5.64	9	13.14	−3.36	0	4.14	C	B
9	11.39	16	21.39	−4.61	0	5.39	C	C

$p^{pres} = 3$; $p^{leg}_A = 4.5$, $p^{leg}_B = 7$, $p^{leg}_C = 9.5$; $p^{leg} = 7$, $P = 5$; $P_{-A^{leg}} = 8.25$, $P_{-B^{leg}} = 7$, $P_{-C^{leg}} = 5.75$; $P_{-A^{leg}} = 5.625$, $P_{-B^{leg}} = 5$, $P_{-C^{leg}} = 4.375$.

rules, proximity ($\beta = 1$) and compensatory ($\beta = 0$). But these are two extremes, and as I discussed earlier, voter choice can be a mixture of expressive (proximity) and compensatory considerations, such that any combination of the two is also possible. The larger β is, the higher the threshold necessary to push voters to support parties ideologically different from them over to those similar to them.

2.4.2.c Compensatory Vote in Federations

As I discussed earlier, the inter-institutional compensation in federal environments is of similar, but not quite identical, logic to that of presidential environments. In federal systems, policy inputs of regional and federal governments are assigned relative weights depending on the degree of centralization of the state and the authorities held by both levels. Unlike presidential systems with two branches – one legislative, one executive – the regional arm in federal environments has multiple extensions: each region has its own government. Policy is thus a function of the policy input of the federal government and each of the regional governments.

The different regions may or may not have the same weight. An obvious example for unequal weights is those polities in which different regions are represented in the upper house in a fashion proportionate or partly proportionate to their population. This is the case for the German länder, each having between three and seven representatives in the Bundesrat. Although not constitutionally a federation, the European Union is another example of a multi-level governance system in which member states are currently represented in the Council by voting weights monotonic (if progressively proportional) with states' populations. Perhaps the most obvious example is Spain, in which some regions have greater degree of autonomy than others, and the state is decentralized to different degrees with respect to different regions.

Regional policy is, of course, not homogenous: different regions might have different interests or voter tendencies. Noting the weight of federal inputs with w^{fed} and regional inputs for each of r regions as w^k ($k = 1 \ldots r$), policy $P = w^{fed} P^{fed} + \sum_{k=1}^{r} w^k P^k$, where P^{fed} is the policy input of the federal government and P^k is the policy input of region k, such that $w^{fed} + \sum_{k=1}^{r} w^k = 1$.

Therefore, in regional elections in region k, the counterfactual policy is the absence of party j, holding policy input of the federal

government, as well as those of other regional governments, fixed:
$P_C = w^{fed} P^{fed} + \sum_{m \neq k} w^m P^m + w^k P^k_{-jk}$, where the policy input and
counterfactual policy input of each region, as well as that of the
central government, is determined according to the institutional
structure of the polity. In parliamentary systems, for instance, we can
think of policy input for each region as a weighted average of the parties
in the region, as I conceptualize it in the previous two sections.

Thus, voter utility for party j in the elections in region k is:

$$U^k_{ij} = -\beta(v_i - p^k_j)^2 - (1-\beta)[(v_i - P)^2 - (v_i - P_C)^2] \qquad (2.18)$$
$$= -\beta(v_i - p^k_j)^2 - (1-\beta)$$
$$\left\{ (v_i - P)^2 - \left[v_i - \left(w^{fed} P^{fed} + \sum_{m \neq k} w^m P^m + w^k P^k_{-jk} \right) \right]^2 \right\}$$

Voters in federations, then, face an inter-institutional policy-formation
process, involving compromise among their own region, all other regions,
and the central government.

***

Is this a reasonable way to model voter choice? When evaluating each
party, the voter assesses the change in policy due to the impact of the
party. The assessment is of the party's impact rather than of her own
impact as a voter. She imagines what policy would have looked like in
the absence of the party compared with what it looks like in its
presence. The policy impact of the party is then defined as change in
policy that can be attributed to the party: $P - P_C$.

One way to examine the counterfactual is by contrasting the impact
on policy it grants to powerful parties with the impact on policy it
grants to less powerful ones. Under a parliamentary regime, given a
certain distance among parties, a party that enjoys substantial weight
for its policy input (e.g., holds a large number of portfolios) has a
greater impact on policy: the difference between policy and counterfactual policy will be great, while the difference between policy and
counterfactual policy for a party whose input weight is small will be
trivial. Under a presidential regime, given a policy distance among
parties in the legislature, a party that occupies more seats or key

positions in the legislature, or the party of the median legislator, is likely to have greater impact on policy. Policy in its absence will differ substantially from policy in its presence. However, the comparable difference for a party holding only a trivial number of seats may not be as large. Under a federal regime, if a particular region is considered of greater political importance, any difference in policy input between the region and the central government (or other regions) results in a greater difference between that policy and a policy that would have been formed without the region. This is also the case for any party input, as in the presidential and parliamentary environments. Thus, as one might expect, different parties might have different policy impacts depending on their input weight. Similarly, one can show (as I do in the final chapter of this study) that party impact depends on the degree to which the position of the party resembles or differs from that of other parties.

2.5 COMPENSATORY, STRATEGIC, AND PROTEST VOTE

Like a strategic vote, a compensatory vote is policy oriented. Under both frameworks, voters are forward looking and pursue a choice that presumably utilizes their votes effectively. Nonetheless, the two differ in both the circumstances under which they are employed and their logic. Sophisticated or strategic voters prefer the party ideologically most similar to them, yet faced with the danger of wasting their vote because of considerations of viability or out of concern of getting their least preferred party in power, they might endorse their second best choice. Unlike strategic voters, compensatory voters, being aware of post-electoral fragmentation of power, do not necessarily prefer the party ideologically similar to them to hold power; indeed, such a party might be less effective than one different from them. Given the constellation of power, they might simply prefer the more extreme party.

Moreover, strategic and compensatory vote are exercised under different electoral circumstances. Strategic voting because of considerations of party viability is particularly relevant in systems in which party entry into the parliament is difficult: under small district magnitude, especially in single-member districts, or in systems with a high threshold. As Duverger's Law states: the simple-majority single-ballot system (i.e., simple plurality rule) favors a two-party system (Duverger 1954, 217). Whether a result of psychological or mechanical motivations, strategic voting under first past the post has been supported empirically in studies of various elections (see, e.g., Alvarez and Nagler 2000 for analysis of the 1987 British elections, and Blais et al. 2001 for analysis of the 1997 Canadian elections). More generally, strategic considerations encourage voters to concentrate their vote on fewer parties, controlling for social cleavages and heterogeneity (Clark and Golder 2006). And although Cox in his seminal work shows how voters in multi-member districts vote strategically as well (this behavior manifests itself in the famous M+1 rule), he adds that "strategic voting ought to fade out in multi-member districts when the district magnitude gets much above five" (Cox 1997, 199). Compensatory vote, on the other hand, is more likely to occur where the institutional environment encourages fragmentation of power and a plethora of parties. As I show in Chapter 3, large district magnitude is important in encouraging fragmentation of power, and hence compensatory vote.

While strategic and compensatory votes are exercised under different circumstances, the constellations under which compensatory and protest votes are likely to emerge are similar. Protest vote is a natural competing explanation for moderate voters' support for extreme parties in parliamentary systems, or for voters' supporting an opposition party in regional or legislative elections. Nonetheless, the phenomenon I identify and conceptualize here is distinct from protest vote. While compensatory vote is associated with parties that, like others, are parties placed on the standard left-right continuum (even if on a different point on the continuum than some of their supporters), protest vote is often an endorsement of anti-system parties. These parties do not necessarily have a clear position on the standard left-right ideological continuum, the continuum I employ and on which my empirical analysis in the next chapter relies, and they often portray themselves as outsiders to the political system.

2.6 CONCLUSION

In this chapter, I have laid out the theoretical foundations for compensatory voting. I started with general principles of policy-minded voter choice. From this principle follows the incorporation of political institutions into voter choice. I then examined what would such a choice look like under three different institutional regimes. The three regimes differ greatly, but the underlying principle is the same. Voters in parliamentary systems compensate for compromise among parties in parliaments, voters in presidential systems compensate for compromise between president and legislature, and voters in federal systems compensate for compromise between federal and regional governments.

I presented a variety of implications of my argument for voter behavior and some well-known electoral regularities. Many of these implications are explored in this study for the first time. Some regularities have been explored in specific settings and theoretical contexts, and here I reexamine them as a manifestation of a more general principle. Lastly, for some well-established regularities I offer a new interpretation.

APPENDIX 2.1 ANALYTIC SOLUTION

Second-order condition on U_{iA} with respect to p_A:

$$\frac{\partial^2 U_{iA}}{\partial p_A{}^2} = \theta[-2\beta - 2(1-\beta)s_A{}^2] \qquad (a1)$$

Rewriting Equation a1, it is easy to see that this is a maximum:

$$\frac{\partial^2 U_{iA}}{\partial p_A{}^2} = 2\theta s_A{}^2(\beta - 1) - 2\theta\beta$$

Since $0 < \beta < 1$ and $\theta > 0$, both expressions are negative, and therefore $\partial^2 U_{iA}/\partial p_A{}^2 < 0$.

Differentiating U_{iA} with respect to p_B, we get:

$$\frac{\partial U_{iA}}{\partial p_B} = 2\theta(1-\beta)s_B(v_i - p_A s_A - p_B s_B - p_C s_C)$$

$$\frac{-2\theta(1-\beta)s_B\left(v_i - \frac{p_B s_B}{s_B + s_C} - \frac{p_C s_C}{s_B + s_C}\right)}{s_B + s_C} \qquad (a2)$$

Setting the result to 0 and solving for p_B:

$$p_B{}^* = -\frac{(1-\beta)s_B(v_i - s_A p_A - s_C p_C) - \frac{(1-\beta)s_B\left(v_i - \frac{s_C p_C}{s_B + s_C}\right)}{s_B + s_C}}{-(1-\beta)s_B{}^2 + \frac{(1-\beta)s_B{}^2}{(s_B + s_C)^2}} \qquad (a3)$$

Second-order condition with respect to p_B:

$$\frac{\partial^2 U_{iA}}{\partial p_B{}^2} = \theta \left[-2(1-\beta)s_B{}^2 + \frac{2(1-\beta)s_B{}^2}{(s_B+s_C)} \right] \tag{a4}$$

Rewriting Equation a4, it is easy to see that this is a minimum:

$$\frac{\partial^2 U_{iA}}{\partial p_B{}^2} = 2\theta(1-\beta)s_B{}^2 \left(\frac{1}{(s_B+s_C)^2} - 1 \right) \tag{a5}$$

Since all elements are positive and $0 < s_B + s_C < 1$, $\partial^2 U_{iA}/\partial p_B{}^2 > 0$. These results are symmetrical with respect to p_C.

APPENDIX 2.II SIMULATIONS – COMPENSATORY VOTE IN PARLIAMENTARY DEMOCRACY

To illustrate the aggregate effect of the compensatory decision rule, I conduct a set of simulations of voter choice under different conditions. For each configuration of conditions, I examine parties' vote share. Specifically, I simulate 10,000 voters whose positions are normally distributed on an ideological continuum with mean zero. Voters choose first among four parties, two centrist and two extreme (marked A through D). I assign the four parties impact weights of 0.15, 0.35, 0.35, and 0.15, respectively.

I vary the degree of compensatory vote, party positions, and the dispersion of voter positions (reported only briefly), and examine party vote-shares under the different configurations. I employ three values of β: 0.2 (strong compensatory motivation), 0.8 (weak compensatory/strong representational motivation), and 0.99 (almost entirely representational motivation). I change party positions to generate three alternative hypothetical party systems. For simplicity, however, I design all three party systems as symmetrical. The first assigns parties A through D positions of $-2, -1, 1,$ and 2, respectively. The second assigns them positions of $-2, -0.5, 0.5,$ and 2, and thereby crowds the two impactful parties closer to the center, and the third assigns them positions of $-1.5, -0.5, 0.5,$ and 1.5, and hence places the four parties closer together. Finally, with respect to voter issue positions, I employ two distributions: the first describes an ideologically dispersed electorate $(v_i \sim N(0,1))$; the second describes a more centrist electorate $(v_i \sim N(0,0.6))$.

To determine party vote-shares, I calculate voter utility for each of the parties according to Equation 2.11. I then calculate for each voter the probability of choosing each of the parties whereby

$$\mathrm{Pr}_{ij} = \frac{\exp(U_{ij})}{\sum_{j=1}^{m} \exp(U_{ij})}.$$

Finally, to calculate parties' vote-share, I add each party's predicted probabilities and divide the sum by the number of voters.

Panel A of Table A.2.1 presents the results of these simulations. The entries in each cell are the vote shares of the four parties. Since the values assigned are symmetrical with respect to zero, my analysis focuses on vote shares of parties B and C (the relatively centrist parties) compared with those of parties A and D (the relatively extreme parties). The table demonstrates several aspects of the predictions of the model. First, comparing entries within each row reveals that the more compensatory the vote, the more voters prefer extreme parties; vote shares of the two extreme parties are largest under β of 0.2, somewhat smaller under β of 0.8, and smallest in the representational case ($\beta = 0.99$). Second, other things being equal, extreme parties do better when all parties are squeezed toward the center, whether under compensatory or representational vote (see the comparison within each column). This conforms with our intuition; when the centrist impactful parties are relatively indistinguishable from one another, the policy incentive for the moderate left (right) to prefer parties on the extreme left (right) increases. Third, the effect of compensatory vote holds across configurations of party placements, but its magnitude depends on party placements and the relative distances among them (see cells (a) and (c) compared with (d) and (f)). It is greatest when the two centrist parties are squeezed at the center and the two extreme ones are far out. Consistent with the pattern discussed earlier, when the centrist parties are crowded together the motivation for moderate ideologues to support the extremes increases, and more so the more policy-motivated they are. Lastly, all these results hold when voter positions are less dispersed ($(v_i \sim N(0, 0.6))$, not reported here).

Panel B repeats this exercise for a five-party system. This allows me to explore the implications of the model for aggregate vote share in systems in which there is a centrist party placed at the position of the

TABLE A.2.1. *Parliamentary Environment: Monte Carlo Simulation of Party Vote Shares*

A. *Four-Party System*

Party Placements	Mixing Parameter		
	$\beta = 0.2$	$\beta = 0.8$	$\beta = 0.99$
−2, −1, 1, 2	(a) A = 0.171 B = 0.332 C = 0.328 D = 0.169	(b) A = 0.120 B = 0.374 C = 0.380 D = 0.126	(c) A = 0.123 B = 0.387 C = 0.376 D = 0.114
−2, −0.5, 0.5, 2	(d) A = 0.216 B = 0.285 C = 0.283 D = 0.215	(e) A = 0.143 B = 0.362 C = 0.356 D = 0.139	(f) A = 0.127 B = 0.369 C = 0.372 D = 0.132
−1.5, −0.5, 0.5, 1.5	(g) A = 0.223 B = 0.270 C = 0.277 D = 0.231	(h) A = 0.196 B = 0.305 C = 0.305 D = 0.194	(i) A = 0.197 B = 0.311 C = 0.306 D = 0.185

Entries are party vote-shares given levels of compensatory vote and party placements. Party impacts are fixed at $s_A = s_D = 0.15$, $s_B = s_C = 0.35$. Voter distribution is $v_i \sim N(0,1)$. Number of simulations = 10,000.

B. *Five-Party System*
I. $\sigma^2 = 1$

Party Placements	Mixing Parameter		
	$\beta = 0.2$	$\beta = 0.8$	$\beta = 0.99$
−2, −1, 0, 1, 2	(a) A = 0.102 B = 0.317 C = 0.172 D = 0.309 E = 0.100	(b) A = 0.089 B = 0.263 C = 0.295 D = 0.256 E = 0.098	(c) A = 0.096 B = 0.240 C = 0.325 D = 0.240 E = 0.099
−2, −0.5, 0, 0.5, 2	(d) A = 0.136 B = 0.258 C = 0.216 D = 0.249 E = 0.140	(e) A = 0.111 B = 0.259 C = 0.258 D = 0.260 E = 0.111	(f) A = 0.115 B = 0.255 C = 0.265 D = 0.256 E = 0.109

TABLE A.2.1 (*cont.*)

| −2.5, −0.5, 0, 0.5, 2.5 | (g)
A = 0.112
B = 0.277
C = 0.232
D = 0.267
E = 0.113 | (h)
A = 0.071
B = 0.288
C = 0.280
D = 0.286
E = 0.075 | (i)
A = 0.074
B = 0.282
C = 0.287
D = 0.286
E = 0.071 |

II. $\sigma^2 = 0.6$

Party Placements	Mixing Parameter		
	$\beta = 0.2$	$\beta = 0.8$	$\beta = 0.99$
−2, −1, 0, 1, 2	(j) A = 0.105 B = 0.302 C = 0.192 D = 0.298 E = 0.103	(k) A = 0.066 B = 0.268 C = 0.340 D = 0.256 E = 0.069	(l) A = 0.066 B = 0.248 C = 0.376 D = 0.242 E = 0.067
−2, −0.5, 0, 0.5, 2	(m) A = 0.129 B = 0.259 C = 0.229 D = 0.251 E = 0.131	(n) A = 0.073 B = 0.278 C = 0.290 D = 0.281 E = 0.078	(o) A = 0.070 B = 0.281 C = 0.302 D = 0.277 E = 0.071
−2.5, −0.5, 0, 0.5, 2.5	(p) A = 0.101 B = 0.281 C = 0.246 D = 0.271 E = 0.101	(q) A = 0.036 B = 0.302 C = 0.312 D = 0.308 E = 0.042	(r) A = 0.035 B = 0.304 C = 0.322 D = 0.302 E = 0.037

Entries are party vote-shares given levels of compensatory vote, party placements, and distributions of voter positions. Party impacts are fixed at $s_A = s_E = 0.05$, $s_B = s_D = 0.375$, $s_C = 0.15$. Mean voter distribution fixed at 0. Number of simulations = 10,000.

median voter. As in the previous analysis, I vary the degree of compensatory vote (with the same values of β as before), party positions, and distribution of voter positions. I assign the parties relative weights of 0.05 for the two extreme parties, A and E; 0.375 for the two moderate ones, B and D; and 0.15 for the center party, C. In terms of party positions, I assign parties the same placements as in the first two configurations, while adding a centrist party at zero: the first configuration, then, assigns policy positions of -2, -1, 0, 1, and 2 for parties A through E, respectively, and the second assigns positions of -2, -0.5, 0, 0.5, and 2. In the third configuration, I stretch the extreme parties outward, with placements of -2.5, -0.5, 0, 0.5, and 2.5. As in the previous analysis, voters' positions are normally distributed around zero ($v_i \sim N(0, 1)$).

My analysis focuses on the vote shares of the two extreme parties, the two moderate parties, and the center party. The simulations reveal several patterns. First, the center party gains support as voting becomes more representational. This effect is strongest in the first configuration of parties ((a), (b), and (c) in Table A.2.1B) where the spatial gap between the centrist party and the moderate ones is the greatest. The mirror image of this pattern shows that the extreme parties lose support as voting becomes representational. This effect is weakest for the first configuration of parties. The differential effect can be explained by the relative positions of the parties. In the first configuration the moderate parties are more distant from the center parties compared with the other two five-party systems, and therefore the vote share of each can vary quite a bit depending on voter strategy. Conversely, in this party system the moderate and extreme parties are idelogically closer to each other, and therefore their respective vote shares can change only to a limited degree. Thirdly, and consistent with the center party's gaining of support, the moderate parties lose support as voting becomes more representational in the first party system. There is, however, no real change in support for the moderate parties in the other two-party systems. This is not because voters do not switch between parties, but rather because voters switching from the moderate parties to the center party cancel out by switching from the extreme parties to the moderate ones.

Section II of the table analyzes party vote shares under the same party-system configurations and voter strategy, but with a less dispersed distribution of voter positions ($v_i \sim N(0, 0.6)$). Under this more compact distribution, the effects of varying party configurations on the vote shares of the center and extreme parties reported earlier are magnified. This is because, other things being equal, a relatively modest shift in party positions affects a bigger share of a densely distributed electorate compared with an ideologically dispersed electorate.

PART II

EMPIRICAL EVIDENCE: HOW VOTERS
COMPENSATE FOR DIFFUSION OF POWER

3

Compensatory Vote in Parliamentary Democracies

3.1 INTRODUCTION

How does voter choice depend on institutional environment? In Chapter 2, I presented a model of voter choice in parliamentary and other democracies. I showed that, other things being equal, in political systems that facilitate bargaining and compromise, a party ideologically similar to the voter may often be less effective in representing her interests than a party placed away from her and away from the center of gravity of the party system. In systems in which policy is determined by a few political actors, on the other hand, policy formation involves little compromise, and thus voter motivation to turn to extreme parties is diminished.

In this chapter, I test the implications of the compensatory model in parliamentary environments. Before turning to the details of the empirical analysis, let us review these implications and preview the findings. The implications are clear. The more compromise and power sharing facilitated by parliamentary norms and procedures and by the electoral system, the more voters will compensate for such expected compromise that threatens to dilute their vote after it is cast. The more compensatory voters are, the more likely they are to support parties whose positions differ from and are often more extreme than their own. This principle may help us understand regularities such as the one presented in Figure 1.1 in which relatively moderate voters often support relatively extreme parties.

My findings support these claims. First, contrary to what current theories predict, I demonstrate that the proportion of voters supporting the party ideologically most similar to them is *smaller* in polities characterized by power sharing. In fact, it is majoritarian cases such as the UK and Canada that have higher rates of proximity voting. Second, across fourteen parliamentary democracies, I find that voters employ some mixture of proximity vote and compensatory vote, with a relative weight on each. On the one hand, they derive expressive value from supporting the party ideologically most similar to them. On the other hand, they are instrumental in supporting a party that will effectively guard their interests in the post-electoral political process. Third, the weight on the compensatory component of the vote is correlated with diffusion of power. Taking into consideration the political cleavages specific to each polity, voters living in polities characterized by power-sharing arrangements such as multi-party government, permissive electoral systems, agenda-setting power by the opposition, or consociational democracy are directed by compensatory considerations more so than are their counterparts living in polities characterized by arrangements that leave little room for compromise. Thus, for example, voters in countries such as Belgium or Switzerland are substantially more compensatory than voters in the UK or Canada. Lastly, coming full circle, I demonstrate that compensatory vote is strongly correlated with a low rate of proximity voting. In other words, in those countries in which power sharing is the norm, voters are compensatory *and* support parties whose views differ from their own views in great numbers. Accordingly, the less compromise allowed by the institutional apparatus, the less voters are guided by compensatory considerations, and the higher the rate of proximity voting.

The argument here integrates national-level factors into the analysis of individual choice. The empirical analysis has to do so as well. Thus, I first turn to micro-level data in a variety of parliamentary democracies, and estimate an empirical model of voter choice. I then utilize macro-level data on institutional diffusion of power and further investigate how variation in the logic voters employ in different polities estimated in the first step is explained by institutional mechanisms. The first step of my analysis, then, will focus on voters, and the second on institutions in which voter behavior is embedded.

Empirically, a cross-national individual-level analysis walks a fine line. On the one hand, we are in search of a cross-country generalization about the principles that guide voter decisions. The institutional argument of the compensatory vote model aims exactly at that. On the other hand, the context in which voters make their decisions differs across countries. Not only do the parties on the ballot among which voters choose differ across countries, but so do the social and political cleavages that lead voters to support different parties. Being of Maori origin is likely to affect voter choice in New Zealand; living in the industrial north is likely to have an effect in the UK; being a farmer is relevant in Norway; Basque origin matters in Spain, and so on. Any cross-national empirical analysis at the individual level will have to acknowledge these differences and allow for causal heterogeneity across countries. My estimation approach allows me to establish a general relationship between institutional diffusion of power and voter decision rule across polities while allowing the individual-level model of voter choice to vary across countries, depending on the political context.

The chapter is structured as follows. I begin with individual-level analysis. I present evidence regarding voter decision rule in various parliamentary systems, focusing on distances between voters and parties in general and compensatory vote in particular. Building on these results, I then shift the discussion to the national arena, examining different mechanisms that facilitate compromise and diffusion of power. Finally, I connect the two levels of analysis.

3.2 DATA AND SELECTION OF CASES

The institutional hypothesis implied by the compensatory vote model guides my selection of cases. To review, the argument predicts that the more institutional mechanisms encouraging compromise are built into policy formation, the more voters will compensate for the expected dilution of their vote, and thus will endorse parties whose positions are more extreme than their own. The empirical analysis in this chapter draws on fourteen Western parliamentary democracies that vary greatly in their institutional mechanisms: Australia, Belgium (Flanders), Canada, Denmark, Iceland, Ireland, The Netherlands, New Zealand, Norway, Portugal, Spain, Sweden, Switzerland, and Great Britain.

TABLE 3.1. *Lijphart's Two-Dimensional Scale of Power Sharing*

Polity (Election)	Executive-Parties Dimension	Federal-Unitary Dimension
Australia (1996)	−0.67	1.72
Belgium (1999)	1.42	0.21
Canada (1997)	−1.07	1.88
Denmark (1998)	1.45	−0.38
Great Britain (1987)	−1.39	−1.19
Iceland (1999)	0.66	−1.03
Ireland (2002)	0.12	−0.42
The Netherlands (1998)	1.16	0.35
Norway (1989)	0.92	−0.65
Portugal (2002)	0.36	−0.70
Spain (2000)	−0.59	0.42
Sweden (1998)	1.04	−0.79
Switzerland (1999)	1.87	1.61
25th percentile	−0.90 (Malta)	−0.65 (Norway)
75th percentile	1.04 (Sweden)	0.28 (Venezuela)

Note: New Zealand is missing from the table. The 1996 election is the first New Zealand election after the 1994 electoral reform, and thus Lijphart's coding of it does not apply.

An examination of how these cases score on Lijphart's (1999) famous two-dimensional map of power sharing demonstrates their diversity. The first dimension, the executive-parties dimension, summarizes the arrangement of executive power, the party system, the electoral system, and interest groups. The second, the federal-unitary dimension, summarizes centralization, cameral structure, rigidity of constitutional amending, judicial review, and central bank independence. On both dimensions, low values stand for high levels of centralization. Table 3.1 presents the value of each of the fourteen polities on Lijphart's two dimensions (measured in the 1971–1996 interval), along with the 25th and 75th percentiles. As the table indicates, the cases represent a wide range of institutional mechanisms. Canada, Great Britain, Australia, and Spain have a relatively high concentration of power on the executive-parties dimension, with the first two scoring among the lowest, while Switzerland, Belgium, and The Netherlands, with a particularly high level of fragmentation, are in the upper quartile. On the federal decentralization dimension, Great Britain, Iceland, and Sweden represent systems with particularly low levels of decentralization, while Australia, Canada, and Spain are in the upper quartile.

In the analysis that follows, I draw on Lijphart's measures of power diffusion and modify them in accordance with my theoretical argument. I elaborate on my measures later, but I will mention here a few details about institutional arrangements in the set of polities under study. First, the cases vary greatly in their district magnitude. In fact, of all parliamentary democracies, my sample includes three with district magnitude of one (Great Britain, Canada, and Australia), and the one with the highest parliamentary district magnitude, the Netherlands (150). Second, two of the cases, Switzerland and Belgium, scoring among the highest on the executive-parties dimension, represent an extreme arrangement of power sharing: consociational democracy. Third, Belgium, Canada, Switzerland, and to a certain degree Spain represent federal systems, while Iceland is among the most centralized polities on this dimension.[1] Finally, Belgium represents an extreme case of party-system fragmentation.

The cases vary in an additional aspect relevant to voter behavior. Issue voting has become an increasingly important predictor of voter choice during the 1990s (e.g., Barnes 1997). Utilizing data from the late 1980s, the 1990s, and the first decade of the twenty-first century allows me to mitigate a potential concern that my findings are specific to cases in which issues were of particular importance to voters.

3.2.1 Measurement

For most cases, individual-level data are drawn from the Comparative Study of Electoral Systems (Modules I and II). Great Britain and Norway are exceptions; results for my analysis of Great Britain draw on data collected by the 1987 British Election Study, and the analysis of Norway draws on the 1989 Norwegian Election Study. Measurement of all micro-level concepts relies on self-reported data from the relevant surveys. I elaborate on these measures next.

Voter position. Like the theoretical model, the empirical analysis is unidimensional. For all cases but Great Britain, the surveys offer a general left-right placement scale. The British Elections Study offers

[1] The process of devolution in the UK is not much reflected in Lijphart's measure, which averages values between the 1970s and the mid-1990s. This is not a concern here since the election under study is the 1987 British elections.

seven issue items for self-placement instead. However, since in the 1987 British elections the three main parties aligned in the same order across all seven items, with Labour being the leftmost party and the Conservatives the rightmost, a single summary dimension can provide a good representation of the policy space. For a detailed description of party placements on the issues in the British case, see Appendix 3.I.

Party position. Students of electoral politics have grappled extensively with the measurement of party positions. Two different approaches are found in the literature. The first warns against potential projection by voters, whereby respondents are likely to view the parties they endorse as ideologically similar to them. If this is the case, according to this approach, party positions should be measured independently of voter position. Thus, this approach uses measures exogenous to the perception held by the individual voter – such as the average of individually perceived party position (Rabinowitz and Macdonald 1989), party position as perceived by experts (Laver and Benoit, 2005), or party position extracted from the party manifestos (Gabel and Huber 2000). An additional consideration mentioned by Rabinowitz and Macdonald in favor of this approach is that our theories require that each party has a single position on every issue. However, as Westholm explains, while the researcher ought to be able to identify a single position for each party, it is not essential that all voters have an identical perception of parties' positions (1997, 870).

The second approach is less concerned with such potential endogeneity. Rather, it contends that a study whose focus is voter choice should measure party positions as they are perceived by individual voters. This is the approach Blais et al. (2001), Westholm (1997), and others follow. In particular, Westholm writes: "Not only do we need to know each voter's own views of the issues but also his or her beliefs as to where the parties are located. Although voters may at times be mistaken about these locations, it is their personal beliefs about these locations, whether right or wrong, that will guide preference formation. The best source for both types of information is therefore the individual voter" (1997, 870). Similarly, Blais et al. write about the use of aggregate measures of party position: "This does not make theoretical sense because there is no reason to believe that voters react to an aggregate score of which they are unaware"

(2001, 85). Since voters are the focus of both this study and the theories from which this study departs, I conduct most of the analysis measuring party position as perceived by the individual voter.

The skeptic, however, might still be concerned with projection bias. Voters, it is often argued, tend to view parties they support as ideologically more similar to them than these parties actually are (Brody and Page 1972; Krosnick 2002). Two considerations mitigate this concern. First, accounting for such a tendency by including background variables in the estimation, I reduce the risk of projection bias. For example, including union membership that is likely to make one feel close to the Labour Party or church attendance that fosters closeness to the Christian Democrats hinders potential bias of the estimation results (see also Blais et al. 2001 for a similar argument). Second, under the worst-case scenario, to the extent that projection bias still exists, using this measure simply means a conservative test for my theory: the empirical analysis is less likely to yield support for compensatory voting and more likely to support the restricted model – the proximity model ($\beta = 1$). In line with previous studies (Merrill, Grofman, and Adams 2001), I have neither theoretical nor empirical reason to suspect that this choice tilts the results in different directions across systems in a way correlated with their institutional design.[2]

It is important to establish that voters' perceptions of party placements are not substantially, and especially not systematically, distorted (Aldrich and McKelvey 1977). Table 3.2 examines respondents' perceptions of party ideological positions in two sample cases: Denmark and the Netherlands. For each party, the table compares its ideological position as perceived by all respondents, by respondents who supported that party, by the educated (high school degree and higher), and by the less educated. Examining perceptions of party placement across these four groups allows me to focus on two comparisons. The first is between party placement as perceived by all voters and by supporters of that party alone, checking for projection

---

[2] In a study comparing voter placement of party positions in the United States, France, and Norway, Merrill, Grofman, and Adams (2001) report no systematic differences across the three systems (the authors note that Republicans perceive the Democratic candidate to be substantially more liberal than the Democrats do, and that this bias is greater than all other comparisons in their study, but their findings do not suggest any systematic difference across systems, such as the United States and France compared to Norway).

TABLE 3.2. *Party Positions as Perceived by Respondents*

	All respondents	Respondents supporting this party	Education < high school	Education > high school
Denmark				
Socialist People	2.5 (1.6)	2.8 (1.5)	2.5 (1.6)	2.5 (1.6)
Social Democrats	4.4 (1.5)	4.5 (1.6)	4.2 (1.6)	4.4 (1.5)
Center Democrats	5.5 (1.3)	5.5 (1.4)	5.4 (1.5)	5.6 (1.2)
Conservatives	7.2 (1.6)	7.5 (1.2)	7.3 (1.6)	7.2 (1.7)
Liberals	7.5 (1.9)	7.6 (1.8)	7.7 (1.8)	7.5 (2.0)
Danish People	8.6 (2.2)	8.2 (2.1)	8.6 (2.2)	8.7 (2.2)
The Netherlands				
Green Left	2.0 (1.8)	1.6 (1.4)	2.3 (2.1)	1.9 (1.6)
Labour	3.6 (2.0)	3.4 (2.2)	3.7 (2.4)	3.6 (1.7)
Dem. 66	4.5 (1.7)	4.3 (1.5)	4.5 (1.8)	4.5 (1.6)
CDA	5.8 (1.7)	6.2 (1.9)	5.9 (2.0)	5.8 (1.6)
VVD	6.9 (1.9)	7.0 (1.7)	6.4 (2.1)	7.1 (1.8)

Note: Standard deviations in parentheses.

bias. The second is a comparison by education, checking whether the less educated tend to place parties closer to the center of the scale, simply opting for a default category. Several patterns emerge from the table. First, the four groups hold similar perceptions of party placements. The order of perceived party placement from left to right is identical, regardless of respondent education and party choice. Second, voters who support a particular party do not differ in their perception of its position from the electorate as a whole. The average perception of all respondents (first column) and the perception of party supporters alone (second column) are almost identical, with standard errors of these averages sometimes eight times larger than the difference in point estimates. Even examining the average perceived positions on their own, a non-systematic picture emerges, especially with respect to the rightmost and leftmost parties, the ones most susceptible to projection bias. While in Denmark the Socialists are perceived by the general sample (public) as slightly more extreme compared with the perception of their own supporters, in the Netherlands the Green Left is perceived by the respective sample as slightly more moderate. Similarly, while in Denmark the Danish People's Party is perceived by the general sample as more extreme than it is perceived by its own voters, the opposite is true in the Netherlands with respect to the VVD. There is no systematic pattern, therefore, on either end of the scale.

Lastly, a comparison of respondents holding a high school degree and above with those with fewer years of formal schooling shows no systematic differences. As the table indicates, in Denmark there is no such pattern. In the Netherlands, although a small difference with respect to the rightmost and leftmost parties emerges, that difference is statistically insignificant. Nonetheless, to mitigate potential remaining concerns, all my analyses here include respondents' level of education, such that even if a difference in perceptions of party placement existed, it would be controlled for empirically.

Party Impact. Along with party positions, party impact determines policy as well as the counterfactual policy. The choice of measure of party impact in the context of a model of voter choice is in fact a reflection of a theory of diffusion of power in the parliament that presumably voters intuit, or with which their behavior corresponds. In the past three decades, the neo-institutional research tradition has produced numerous insightful analyses regarding bargaining in parliaments, cabinet formation, and portfolio allocation.[3] This line of research greatly enhances our understanding of various political processes in legislatures, such as coalition formation and durability, and portfolio allocation. This project does not offer a new theory of bargaining in parliaments. Instead, I utilize four different measures of power sharing, accounting for different ways in which voters might perceive distribution of power in the parliament.

In Chapter 2, I introduced a middle-of-the-road view of policy formation that voters might hold. According to this view, while voters' time horizon spans beyond election night into the following months of policy formation, voters have a relatively straightforward intuition about policy formation. Based on past experience, they have a general sense of whether their polity is usually characterized by fragmentation or concentration of power, and they adapt their votes accordingly. Nonetheless, the compromise they assume is a simple one, involving an average of the position of the different parties, with a relative weight for each one.

---

[3] Among others, various works by Austen-Smith, Banks, Bawn, Huber, Laver, Lupia, Schofield, Shepsle, Strøm, and Tsebelis have contributed to this extensive body of literature.

My first measure uses a simple (perhaps the simplest) approximation of impact: party seat-share in the parliament. According to this logic, the greater the seat share of the party, the greater the party's impact. And while game-theoretic models have argued that party impact may not always reflect its size (e.g., Austen-Smith and Banks 1988), empirical work since Gamson's study (1964) has repeatedly shown that contrary to predictions of bargaining models, a party's share of portfolios is often proportional to its seat share in the coalition.[4]

It is often the case that public opinion polls prior to the elections predict the popular vote rather than predicted seat share, either in the country as a whole, or sometimes, as in Canada, in each region. In these cases, voters' expectations regarding the results of the elections are probably based on the average of these reports. And while in highly proportional systems the vote-share and seat-share predictions are similar, in less proportional systems the two diverge. My second measure of party impact, then, is the actual popular vote, which, I assume, is a proxy for the average public opinion poll prior to the election.

Although all members of the legislature have an impact on policy formation, members of the opposition, it might be argued, are not as influential as their colleagues in the coalition, even controlling for the smaller number of seats they usually hold. Similarly, coalition parties that hold the lion's share of portfolios may be more powerful than their junior partners. To account for the differential impact of coalition partners versus opposition members, I employ two measures combining seat share in parliament and portfolio share in cabinet. The first weighs them equally, and the second in a 3:1 ratio. By both measures, parties in the opposition score zero on the portfolio scale, and so their seat share is down-weighted, while parties in the governing coalition have their seat share in parliament weighted more heavily. This allows me to assign more weight to every seat a coalition member occupies compared with those of the opposition benches. Both measures incorporate the distribution of seats in the

---

[4] Gamson's Law does not provide us with insights as to the impact of members of the opposition. The broad empirical support for its predictions regarding allocations of portfolios in the coalition, however, shows the relevance of seat-share as a resource for impact in the cabinet.

chamber. The first measure weighs each such seat much more heavily than each opposition seat, and the second somewhat more heavily.

One might wonder why *all* parties in parliament are assigned an impact greater than zero. After all, some parties on the extreme right or the radical left are unlikely to participate in the governing coalition and have a direct effect on policy. There are several motivations for not entirely discounting the role of the opposition in general and of small non-governmental parties in particular. First, opposition parties are often partners in ad hoc pacts with factions of the governing coalition, creating unlikely alliances, and thereby enable parts of their agendas to be implemented. This is particularly common in polities in which minority governments are prevalent. Among stable parliamentary democracies, minority governments have consisted of about one-third of all governments between 1945 and 1987, with Canada, France, Ireland, and Spain having more than 40 percent of their governments as minority governments, and Denmark, Norway, and Sweden having an average parliamentary basis of governments smaller than 50 percent (Strøm 1990, 58).[5] While some minority governments survive by external support to which members of the opposition commit themselves prior to the formation of the government, others survive by leaning on shifting majorities, hopping from issue to issue and from one majority to another, leaning on, and compromising with, different segments of the opposition (Strøm 1990, 97). Second, whether by norm or a set procedure, some parliamentary systems enable the opposition to have authority via the committee system, including committee chairmanship (Laver and Hunt, 1992), a practice that allows the opposition to have partial control over policy formation. Third, different systems have idiosyncratic mechanisms that allow the opposition to have a direct effect on policy. Strøm (1990) describes two such mechanisms in Norway. First is the Board of Presidents, composed of the president and vice-president of each of the two divisions of the Storting along with the president and vice-president of the entire legislature. This body, in which the opposition is represented by three of the six members, serves

---

[5] Strøm's sample includes Belgium, Canada, Denmark, Finland, France (IV Rep.), Iceland, Ireland, Israel, Italy, the Netherlands, Norway, Portugal, Spain, Sweden, and the UK.

as a communications center and a facilitator of compromise, particularly under circumstances of minority government. Second is conferences among parliamentary leaders of the various parties. In these meetings, taking place relatively frequently in the post-war period, party leaders discuss compromises on various issues. While the meetings are not institutionalized, they cover a variety of topics depending on political circumstances, such as economic and defense issues, and even negotiations of coalition formation (Strøm 1990, 207–209). Lastly, in addition to using these official mechanisms, even uninvolved in the policy process itself, opposition parties affect policy outcomes by shaping the discourse, placing issues on the agenda, and forcing established parties to address these issues (see Avakumovic 1978 for a discussion of the effect of the CCF-NDP in Canada, and Meguid 2005 for the impact of rising parties on policy in Western Europe). These mechanisms are consistent with Warwick's (2001) finding that the stated positions of coalition governments are biased toward the parliamentary center of gravity and toward the positions of parties that support the government but are not members of it, as well as with McDonald and Budge's (2005) work, which finds an effect of the median voter and median parliamentarian on policy (150–152).

Appendix 3.II presents the four measures in each of the fourteen polities/elections. As can be seen in the table, the four alternative measures are strongly correlated across polities. Nonetheless, by implicitly making different assumptions about bargaining in the parliament, the four measures yield somewhat different potential distributions of party impacts. The vote-share measure assumes the greatest fragmentation of power, the seat-share measure assumes a somewhat less diffused power, and the two-seats portfolio averages assume the greatest concentration of power, with the simple average advantaging governing parties the most. Consistently, in the highly proportional systems, the measures are empirically similar and even identical (e.g., the vote-share and seat-share measures in the Netherlands), yet in the highly disproportional systems they vary substantially (e.g., Great Britain).

Once measuring voter position, party position, and party impact, both expected policy and expected counterfactual policy are calculated as weighted averages, as illustrated in the theoretical model. With these measures in hand, I turn to the empirical analysis.

3.3 PROXIMITY VOTING

I begin by examining the degree of proximity voting across the polities in my sample. Figure 3.1 presents the proportion of voters supporting the party they perceive as ideologically most similar to them in each of the fourteen elections. The proportion varies substantially, with as few as 25 percent of voters in Ireland and as many as 67 percent in the UK. Given the small cross-party compromise facilitated by the Westminster system, that the proportion in the UK is the highest is hardly surprising. In fact, one might expect it to be even higher. However, tactical or strategic voting, common in the UK (Cain 1978; Niemi et al. 1993), likely accounts for the fact that the level of proximity voting is not higher.

A comparison of Australia with the UK and Canada, the other two single-member-district systems included in the sample, reveals an additional difference. Although the Australian system is highly disproportional, having district magnitude of one, often governed by a single party, and characterized by a small number of parties – all nearly identical to the British and Canadian cases – unlike the UK and Canada, the Australian system is characterized by a low level of proximity voting. The Alternative Vote system used for the Australian House of

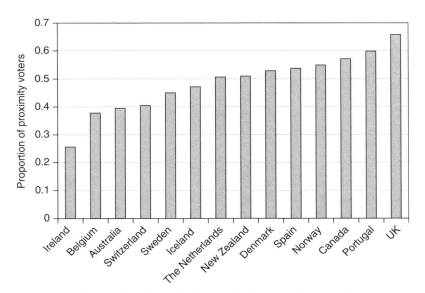

FIGURE 3.1. Proportion of proximity vote in fourteen democracies

Representatives may account for the difference. Australian voters rank all candidates on the ballot. After an initial count of first preferences, if none of the candidates secures a majority, the votes of the candidate with the least number of first-ranked votes are reallocated according to the second preference on these ballots. This method of preference aggregation allows voters to support small parties even though they cast their ballots in a single-member district environment; they might still be influential when their votes are reallocated. In fact, Cox refers to this non-exclusive electoral system as one that "mitigates concentrating tendencies of simple plurality rule . . ." (Cox 1997, 92). Similarly, the Single Transferable Vote system in Ireland (along with societal/religious cleavages) may partly account for the low proportion of proximity votes there. Having an opportunity to rank multiple candidates, voters are easily swayed away from the candidate most similar to them on their first-rank vote.

3.4 COMPENSATORY VOTE IN PARLIAMENTARY DEMOCRACIES

To estimate the degree of compensatory voting, I first derive a statistical model of voter choice for each polity/election. The systematic component of the statistical model is in line with the theoretical model, including the representational and compensatory motivations weighted by a mixing parameter (β), along with an issue salience parameter θ. For each polity, the analysis includes background variables established in the literature as socio-political cleavages relevant for voter choice in that polity.[6] The systematic component of the empirical model, then, is:

$$
\begin{aligned}
\mu_{ij} &= \theta \left[-\beta \cdot representational_{ij} - (1 - \beta) \cdot compensatory_{ij} \right] + \delta_j Z_i \\
&= \theta \left\{ -\beta (v_i - p_j)^2 - (1 - \beta) \left[(v_i - P)^2 - (v_i - P_{-p_j})^2 \right] \right\} + \delta_j Z_i
\end{aligned}
$$

$$(3.1)$$

The probability of voter i $(i = 1, \ldots, n)$ voting for party j $(j = 1, \ldots, m)$, then, depends on her utility for that party and her utility for all

---

[6] Thus, for an election with m parties, the model produces $m-1$ vectors of coefficients (δ_j) of background variables (Z_i). This implies that the model varies across countries; each election/country has idiosyncratic factors affecting voter choice. As I elaborate later, in spite of the differences in model specification, my estimation technique will allow me to draw comparisons across polities.

other parties:

$$\pi(vote_i = j) \equiv \pi_{ij} = \frac{f(\mu_{ij})}{\sum_{k=1}^{m} f(\mu_{ik})} \tag{3.2}$$

where $\sum_{j=1}^{m} \pi_{ij} = 1$. Once I compute the probabilities as in Equation 3.2, I derive a likelihood function for the multinomial choice model into which I substitute the systematic component and the probabilities in Equations 3.1 and 3.2:

$$L \propto \prod_{i=1}^{n} \pi_{i1}^{y_{i1}} \pi_{i2}^{y_{i2}} \dots \pi_{im}^{y_{im}}, \quad \text{or} \quad \log L \propto \sum_{i=1}^{n} \sum_{j=1}^{m} y_{ij} \log \pi_{ij} \tag{3.3}$$

such that $y_{ij} = 1$ if the ith voter votes for party j and 0 otherwise.[7]

I estimate Equations 3.1 through 3.3 in each of the fourteen country/elections. The issue component of the model is identical across systems. To illustrate the country-specific estimation, Table 3.3 presents a sample result – the full set of estimates from the 1998 Dutch elections, with party impact measured as seat share. Model specifications of all fourteen country/elections are presented in Appendix 3.III.

The dependent variable is voter choice, and the reference category is the Dutch Labour Party. As the table shows, background variables have different effects on the likelihood of supporting different parties. Examine, for example, the effects of education, income, and gender. The highly educated are likely to support the liberal party D66 or the Green Left, and are somewhat likely to support the VVD or the Christian Democrats compared with the Labour Party. The wealthy are likely to endorse the VVD and D66 compared with Labour, yet income does not distinguish statistically between the other two parties and Labour. Finally, women are more likely to support the Labour Party than the Christian Democrats or the VVD.

---

[7] I reparameterize β using logistic transformation such that $\beta \in [0,1]$: $\beta = 1/(1 + \exp(-a))$. This reparameterization will allow me to compare voter-decision rule across polities. To separately identify β and θ, I multiply through and rearrange terms. I rewrite the bracketed term in Equation 3.1 as:

$$\theta[-\beta PRX_{ij} - (1 - \beta)CMP_{ij}] = \theta(-\beta PRX_{ij} - CMP_{ij} + \beta CMP_{ij}) = \theta[\beta(CMP_{ij} - PRX_{ij}) - CMP_{ij}] = \theta\beta(CMP_{ij} - PRX_{ij}) - \theta CMP_{ij}$$

TABLE 3.3. *Compensatory Vote in the Netherlands (1998)*

| Compensatory/Representational (β) | | 0.543 (0.016)* | | |
| Salience (θ) | | 0.208 (0.011) | | |

	VVD/PA	CDA/PA	D66/PA	GL/PA
Age	0.001 (0.006)	0.022 (0.006)	−0.008 (0.006)	−0.014 (0.007)
Education	0.201 (0.073)	0.151 (0.075)	0.458 (0.064)	0.305 (0.065)
Income	0.455 (0.076)	−0.076 (0.083)	0.233 (0.072)	0.020 (0.076)
Woman	−0.545 (0.183)	−0.487 (0.188)	0.140 (0.173)	−0.082 (0.166)
Catholic	−0.168 (0.134)	0.403 (0.142)	−0.125 (0.159)	−0.472 (0.175)
Church attendance	−0.081 (0.062)	0.636 (0.057)	−0.104 (0.068)	0.117 (0.068)
Married	−0.101 (0.127)	0.582 (0.157)	0.052 (0.116)	−0.190 (0.143)
Union member	−0.836 (0.180)	−0.505 (0.194)	−0.146 (0.166)	−0.264 (0.182)
Unemployed	−1.386 (0.200)	0.750 (0.192)	1.710 (0.329)	0.364 (0.315)
Constant	−1.965 (0.546)	−4.151 (0.534)	−3.456 (0.444)	−1.676 (0.456)

Log likelihood = 1198.20, N = 1152

Note: Standard errors in parentheses. VVD–People's Party for Freedom and Democracy, CDA–Christian Democratic Appeal, D66–Democrats 66, GL–Green Left Party, PA–Labour Party.

* This coefficient is calculated via logistic parameterization (as explained in footnote 7). Standard errors are calculated via simulations (1,000 random draws) from the multivariate normal distribution, with the vector of estimated coefficients as the mean and estimated variance-covariance matrix as variance.

My main quantity of interest and the focus of the discussion here is the extent to which voting is proximity-driven or compensatory, as captured by the parameter estimate $\hat{\beta}$. Recall that higher values of β signify representational vote and lower values signify compensatory vote; holding voter policy preferences constant, the smaller β is, the greater is the proportion of voters who support parties whose positions differ from, and are often more extreme than, their own. Table 3.4 focuses on the estimated β across polities. Each row presents the results of a different polity, and each of the four columns indicates the measure of party impact used (vote share, seat share, and the two seat-share portfolio-share averages). The table reveals several patterns. First, examining each column reveals a substantial cross-country variation in the degree of compensatory vote. I elaborate on and explain this variation later, but notice for now that the estimated mixing coefficient varies from less than 0.1 (highly compensatory) in Belgium to about 0.9 (highly representational) in Canada. Second, the value of the mixing coefficient is similar, yet not identical, across the four measures. The vote-share measure produces the most compensatory results, results produced by the seat-share measure are slightly less compensatory, and the two portfolios/seats measures produce the most representational results, with the simple average measure being more representational than the weighted average measure ($\bar{\hat{\beta}} = 0.56$, 0.60, 0.65, and 0.70, respectively). The different theoretical assumptions about diffusion of power underlying each of the four measures contribute to this empirical variation. Shifting the center of gravity toward the government, the seat/portfolio averages assume more concentration of power than the other two. Similarly, since almost no electoral system is perfectly proportional, the vote-share measure assumes more dispersion of power than the seat-share measure, and thus produces more representational results. These differences across measures vary in magnitude with the proportionality of the system. In highly disproportional systems, the gap between the results produced by the vote-share measure and those produced by the portfolios/seats measure is greater than the gap in highly proportional systems (e.g., Canada vs. Iceland). Again, this is because in proportional systems, the different assumptions about diffusion of power are empirically similar (albeit not identical to one another). Nonetheless, the point estimates are strongly correlated across the four measures (see the correlations at the bottom of the table), suggesting that compensatory decision rule holds under varying

TABLE 3.4. *Voter-Decision Rule ($\hat{\beta}$) in Fourteen Polities, Utilizing Four Impact Measures*

Election	$\hat{\beta}$ (Impact as votes)	$\hat{\beta}$ (Impact as seats)	$\hat{\beta}$ (Impact as 1:3 portfolios/seats)	$\hat{\beta}$ (Impact as 1:1 portfolios/seats)	N
Australia 1996	0.393 (0.031)[a]	0.507 (0.027)	0.548 (0.034)	0.602 (0.017)	963
Belgium 1999	0.039 (0.025)	0.054 (0.025)	0.038 (0.031)	0.100 (0.037)	1088
Britain 1987	0.733 (0.058)	0.834 (0.034)	0.850 (0.043)	0.893 (0.051)	1716
Canada 1997	0.614 (0.044)	0.769 (0.047)	0.882 (0.026)	0.925 (0.101)	429
Denmark 1998	0.748 (0.051)	0.746 (0.052)	0.800 (0.045)	0.836 (0.043)	1166
Iceland 1999	0.478 (0.039)	0.483 (0.042)	0.471 (0.063)	0.544 (0.029)	666
Ireland 2002	0.460 (0.066)	0.522 (0.067)	0.561 (0.061)	0.621 (0.066)	662
The Netherlands 1998	0.543 (0.016)	0.543 (0.016)	0.596 (0.016)	0.655 (0.034)	1152
New Zealand 1996	0.675 (0.036)	0.679 (0.034)	0.743 (0.035)	0.794 (0.028)	1824
Norway 1989	0.645 (0.052)	0.673 (0.050)	0.782 (0.020)	0.863 (0.020)	1345
Portugal 2002	0.660 (0.042)	0.737 (0.095)	0.753 (0.083)	0.802 (0.075)	359
Spain 2000	0.652 (0.079)	0.709 (0.075)	0.692 (0.078)	0.661 (0.084)	373
Sweden 1998	0.610 (0.036)	0.620 (0.037)	0.757 (0.038)	0.850 (0.046)	748
Switzerland 1999	0.553 (0.016)	0.573 (0.021)	0.606 (0.029)	0.650 (0.048)	866
$\bar{\hat{\beta}}$	0.557	0.604	0.649	0.700	

Note: The table presents the estimate of the mixing parameter $\hat{\beta}$ in each of the fourteen polities using each of the four impact measures. Each such coefficient is one of a full model of voter choice estimated, as generally presented in Equations 3.1 through 3.3.
[a] Standard error.
Correlations of results across the four measures: $r\left(\hat{\beta}_{seats}, \hat{\beta}_{votes}\right) = 0.97$, $r\left(\hat{\beta}_{seats}, \hat{\beta}_{3:1-seats:portfolios}\right) = 0.98$, $r\left(\hat{\beta}_{seats}, \hat{\beta}_{1:1-seats:portfolios}\right) = 0.95$, $r\left(\hat{\beta}_{votes}, \hat{\beta}_{3:1-seats:portfolios}\right) = 0.95$, $r\left(\hat{\beta}_{votes}, \hat{\beta}_{3:1-seats:portfolios}\right) = 0.93$, $r\left(\hat{\beta}_{3:1-seats:portfolios}, \hat{\beta}_{1:1-seats:portfolios}\right) = 0.99$.

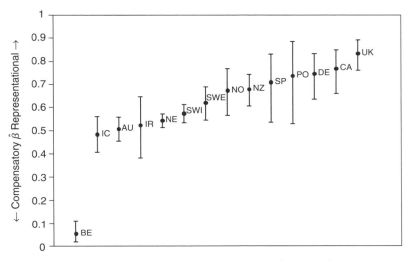

FIGURE 3.2. Compensatory/representational vote in fourteen democracies
Note: The figure presents the mixing parameter (produced by the seat-share measure) along with 95% confidence intervals in the fourteen polities. Uncertainty is computed via simulation (Herron 2000; King, Tomz, and Wittenberg 1998).

assumptions about the policy-formation process reflected by the various measures.

To further examine cross-country variation in voter decision rule, Figure 3.2 presents the mixing parameter $\hat{\beta}$ capturing the degree of compensatory/representational vote produced by the seat-share measure in the fourteen cases along with 95 percent confidence intervals. The figure further demonstrates the differences in voter strategy, with voters in Belgium (Flanders) and Iceland being the most compensatory, and in the UK and Canada the most representational. The figure presents several interesting comparisons. As it shows, the estimate for Belgium is substantially lower than that in other polities. A comparison of the two consociational systems, Belgium and Switzerland, is instructive. The two are decentralized federal systems, with both the Belgian regions and the Swiss cantons carrying substantial authority. The Belgian system grants both Wallonia and Flanders representation in the cabinet. The Swiss golden formula assures that the four main parties in parliament are represented in the seven-member Swiss executive. In spite of these similarities, voting is substantially more compensatory in the former. A comparison of Belgium with (semi-federal) Spain and with Iceland reveals a similar pattern. The three share a proportional electoral system with a similar average district magnitude, yet voting in Belgium is substantially more compensatory. Why are voters in Belgium more compensatory than both voters in similarly federal and consociational Switzerland, and voters in electorally similar Spain or Iceland? The high fragmentation of the Belgian party system (ENPP = 7.6) may account for this finding. The four main parties, Liberal, Socialist, Christian Democratic, and Ecologist in Wallonia each have a parallel party in Flanders, and a nationalized party system is wanting. Policy formation in Belgium is highly fragmented, even compared with these other polities. And although the fragmentation of the party system may itself be a product of the Belgian power-sharing arrangement along regional lines, one still wonders how it affects the strategy voters employ within each region.

A second interesting comparison is that of Australia with the two other single-member-district systems, Canada and the UK. As discussed earlier, the three systems are characterized by similar political outcomes. Nonetheless, compensatory voting is substantially more prevalent in Australia than in the other two. Here, too, the Alternative Vote system is an immediate suspect. Having an opportunity to reveal a preference profile rather than a first choice only, Australian voters may first rank a small, ideologically remote party. Thus, while the initial analysis reveals a potential effect of the extreme result in Belgium on empirical grounds simply by scoring substantially lower than the rest of the cases on the dependent variable, it also reveals a potential effect in Australia on theoretical grounds.

Finally, the figure demonstrates that the uncertainty with which compensatory vote is estimated is not constant across countries. In some cases (e.g., the Netherlands), there is little uncertainty around the point estimate, while in others (e.g., Portugal) it is estimated with a larger cloud of error. The different levels of uncertainty about voter strategy can largely be accounted for by the varying sample size across macro units (see the last column of Table 3.4).[8]

---

[8] Importantly, the uncertainty is not correlated with the size of the point estimate $\hat{\beta}$ itself: our ability to estimate voter strategy does not depend on the strategy itself. The estimates with the largest error (Spain, Portugal, and Ireland) are of various sizes.

3.5 HOW VOTER DECISION RULE VARIES BY INSTITUTION

So far, I have established that voters employ a mixed decision rule, and that the relative weights of the mixture vary across polities. What explains the variation in the degree of compensatory vote across countries? The model predicts that voters will be more compensatory (β will be smaller) the more institutional mechanisms facilitating compromise are in place. Thus, as I turn to estimating the effect of arrangements of power-sharing on voter strategy, empirically small β in polities characterized by diffusion of power will lend support for my theory. Conversely, empirically large β in systems with a high level of power sharing, and in particular estimated βs that are as large as or larger than β in systems with little power sharing leads me to infer that the data do not support my hypothesis.

3.5.1 Measuring Power Sharing in Parliaments

The literature offers numerous measures of power sharing. Given the motivation of this study, an appropriate measure of power dispersion should satisfy two conditions. First, while institutional diffusion of power takes various forms, my focus here is on dispersion of power in the parliament itself. Second, the mechanism of power dispersion captured should be exogenous to voter choice. In particular, I depart from Lijphart's strategy of averaging institutional dispersion of power throughout the post-war period (1945–1996) and instead measure it in the five elections immediately preceding the election under study for each polity. I turn now to a description of these measures.

Single-Party Cabinet.[9] This indicator measures the average period of time a single-party government has been in power during the five electoral cycles that preceded the election under study. The greater the proportion of time the executive consists of only one party, the less dispersed is power in the legislature. This measure ranges from 0 in

---

[9] Data used to construct this measure are disaggregated data used in Lijphart's Patterns of Democracy and available at: http://64.233.167.104/search?q=cache: P_iDHQdvuvQJ:www.tamuk.edu/geo/Urbana/Database/POD-DATA.DOC+lijphart+ POD+patterns+ of+democracy&hl=en&ie=UTF-8. I thank Professor Lijphart for making his data available publicly.

Belgium, Denmark, the Netherlands, and Switzerland to 1 in Australia, Canada, and the UK.

Effective number of parliamentary parties.[10] An additional potential factor diffusing power in the parliament is the number of parties. Here, too, I employ the average effective number of parliamentary parties in the five electoral cycles preceding the election studied. This measure ranges from 2.16 in the UK to 7.65 in Belgium.

District magnitude. The number of seats in the parliament with which each district is represented is commonly considered a mechanism affecting party viability. I employ the (logged) average district magnitude per system. The higher the district magnitude, the more likely is power to be dispersed. The measure ranges from 0 in Australia, the UK, and Canada to 5 in the Netherlands.

Control over plenary agenda. A key component in controlling the discourse is setting the order of the day. Döring offers a measure that captures different aspects of the degree of priority given to the government in setting the plenary agenda and controlling time on the legislature floor, ranging from an arrangement by which the government alone determines the plenary agenda (1) to an arrangement whereby the chamber determines the agenda (7).[11] The more control the government has, the more concentrated power is, with Ireland and the UK having the minimum score of 1 and the Netherlands the maximum score of 7.

Table 3.5 presents correlations among the various measures across the fourteen cases. The table reveals several patterns. First, the four aspects of power sharing are correlated with each other in the expected direction. Polities characterized by an effective plethora of parties are less likely to have single-party governments (r = −0.78), as are polities with a high district magnitude (−0.60), and polities in which the chamber, as opposed to the government, controls the plenary (−0.35). Consistently, the effective number of parliamentary parties is positively correlated with high district magnitude, although less than one might expect (0.44), and with the agenda controlled by the chamber (0.33). Lastly, the latter two are strongly and positively correlated (0.85). Thus, although some aspects of power sharing do go together, the variation in the strength of the correlations demonstrates the value

---

[10] I thank Matt Golder for sharing his data, which allowed me to construct this measure.
[11] For a discussion of those aspects, see Döring 1995, 224–5.

TABLE 3.5. *Measures of Institutional Power Dispersion – Correlations*

	Single party government	Effective number of parliamentary parties	ln(DM$_{Avg.}$)	Plenary control (Döring)
Single-party government	1	−0.78	−0.60	−0.35
Effective number of parliamentary parties		1	0.44	0.33
Ln(DM$_{Avg.}$)			1	0.85
Plenary control (Döring)				1

The table presents correlations across the institutional measures of parliamentary power dispersion. Low prevalence of single-party governments, large effective number of parties, large district magnitude, and high plenary control (by the chamber) indicate high levels of diffusion.

in examination of various aspects of power sharing and their reflection in voter choice.

Of course, these are only a subset of a range of parliamentary mechanisms that diffuse and concentrate power. Among the many additional mechanisms are procedures for the introduction of bills by opposition members, committee chairmanships, and frequency of minority governments. It is unlikely that all mechanisms affect voter strategy to the same degree, and even that they all affect voter strategy. It is possible that some mechanisms have a greater effect on voters, while others have little effect. The analysis of the extended range of mechanisms, parliamentary and beyond, and their effect on voter behavior is beyond the scope of this study.

3.5.2 Institutional Effect on Voter Choice

I turn now to the second step of my analysis: how do institutional mechanisms of power sharing affect voter decision rule? This step presents two estimation challenges. First is the small number of observations. Although the results within each polity are based on a large number of respondents, the number of macro-level units is still only fourteen, and in some cases, due to data limitations, even smaller.

In fact, even if we knew the "true" β in each polity, we would still have only fourteen polity/elections observations. Second, what we seek to explain, the mixing parameter of compensatory/proximity vote, is not known with certainty but is instead estimated, and therefore an additional level of uncertainty should be introduced into the analysis. Each of these constraints, and in particular the combination of them, calls for cautious interpretation of the results (Achen 2005).

To visually examine the relationship between institutional mechanisms and voter decision rule, Figure 3.3 presents scatterplots of the $\hat{\beta}$'s presented in Figure 3.2 on the vertical axis against each of the four measures of institutional dispersion of power described earlier, as well as a fifth one, a composite index, standardizing and adding the four indicators. Given the two challenges and the danger that a single (estimated) point drags the regression line and produces misleading results, the figure includes three (and where data are limited, two) OLS trendlines exploring the effects of two potentially influential observations: Belgium and Australia.[12] The solid line is the default line based on all observations, the long-dashed line omits Australia from the analysis, and the short-dashed line omits both Australia and Belgium.

Panel A of the figure presents the relationship between voter decision rule and the prevalence of single-party governments. The (small) cluster of observations takes a general shape consistent with the prediction of the model: the more prevalent a single-party government is, the more representational (less compensatory) is the vote. Panel B presents voter-decision rule and the effective number of parliamentary parties in the five previous elections. As predicted by the model, the greater the number of parties, the more compensatory is the vote. Similarly, (logged average) district magnitude presented in Panel C is negatively correlated with $\hat{\beta}$: the greater the district magnitude, the more compensatory is the vote. Panel D presents Döring's measure of control of the plenary agenda. Here, too, as predicted, a negative, although not strong, relationship evolves: the more control the

[12] Döring's measure of control of the plenary is available only for the western European cases. Also, since the 1996 New Zealand election was the first under the new electoral system, it is included only in the district magnitude analysis, where the 1996 (not the averaged lagged) district magnitude is calculated. For the other measures, I did not employ the 1996 values of NZ out of concern for endogeneity.

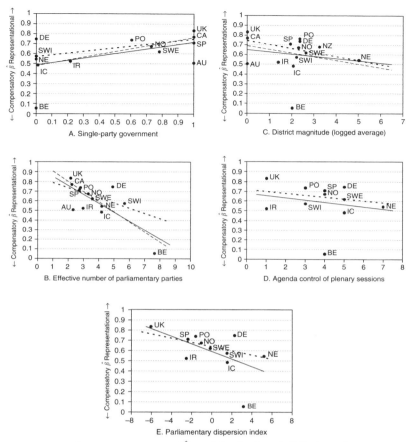

FIGURE 3.3. Compensatory vote $(\hat{\beta})$ and institutional diffusion of power
Note. The figure presents the mixing parameter (β) estimated in the first step as a function of institutional measures of dispersion of power. OLS lines are included. The solid line incorporates all data points, the thin long-dashed line omits Australia, and the thick short-dashed line omits Australia and Belgium.

chamber has (and less the government has), the more compensatory is voter behavior.

Panel E presents a composite index in which the previous four are standardized, recoded so that high levels indicate dispersion of power, and summed. The figure shows a negative relationship between the summary measure of power diffusion and $\hat{\beta}$: the more diffused is power in the parliament, the more compensatory is the vote.

As is seen in the figure, the relationships generally hold under the three specifications, where omitting Australia enhances the results marginally, and omitting Belgium in addition attenuates them somewhat in the first two panels and does not make a substantial difference in the others. Nonetheless, and in line with the earlier discussion, Belgium is an outlier among polities with multi-party governments, and Australia among the ones with single-party governments (Panel A). Accordingly, district magnitude does not account for voter strategy in these two cases as much as it does in others, and the degree of chamber control of the agenda does not account well for voter strategy in Belgium.

After visually examining the relationship between voter decision rule and institutional mechanisms, I turn to estimating it with greater precision. As in the visual analysis, given the small number of cases, I conduct the analysis for three different data configurations: all cases, all cases omitting Australia, and all cases omitting both Australia and Belgium.[13] Consistent with the results in Figure 3.3, I present the extremes here: the strong and the weak sets of results among the three (the former excluding Australia and the latter excluding both Australia and Belgium).

Empirically, I expect β to decrease with institutional diffusion of power. In particular, let β^l be voter taste for compensatory/representational choice in polity/election l $(l = 1 \ldots r)$. The prediction can be represented by a simple linear relationship:

$$\beta^l = W^l \gamma + \eta^l \tag{3.4}$$

where W^l is a vector capturing institutional mechanisms of power dispersion, γ is a vector of coefficients, and η^l is a random error with zero expectation. The macro model predicts that if high values of W indicate high levels of diffusion of power, then γ will be negative.

As mentioned earlier, the dependent variable for the second step is not known with certainty. To account for the uncertainty in $\hat{\beta}$, I simulate the sample distribution $\hat{\beta}$ from each of the fourteen models. I then estimate the second step on each of the simulated sets of $\hat{\beta}$ and average the results.[14]

---

[13] Of course, if more cases were available, one would want to conduct a systematic examination of what is behind the Australian and the Belgian cases.

[14] I start by estimating the micro model and computing the variance of $\hat{\beta}$ in each country using a simulation approach (see Herron 2000; King, Tomz, and Wittenberg

Results of the estimation are presented in Table 3.6. Each column presents a simple regression that corresponds with a panel of Figure 3.3. Each cell in the table includes two entries. The first is the simulated Least Squared omitting Australia alone, and the second is the simulated regression omitting both Australia and Belgium. A few things emerge from the table, all of which should be considered with caution given the small number of macro units. First, the signs of all measures are in the predicted direction. Single-party government is positively correlated with $\hat{\beta}$. Similarly, the effective number of parliamentary parties and district magnitude are negatively correlated with $\hat{\beta}$, as are opposition control over plenary agenda, and the composite index of power diffusion. Not surprisingly, the relationships reach standard levels of statistical significance only in some of the cases. The effect of the prevalence of single-party government is statistically significant for both case specifications, the effect of the number of parliamentary parties is significant in the absence of Australia, and the composite index of power diffusion is statistically significant. This is consistent with the pattern presented in Panel B of Figure 3.3, where the gap in the estimation between the two case specifications is greater for the number of parties than for other indicators of power fragmentation.

These results shed light on the effect of contextual factors on voter choice. The path leading from votes to policy, a path determined by institutional arrangements, accounts for variation in the decision rules that guide voters across polities. Mechanisms that affect the degree of compromise and bargaining in policy formation, such as the number of parties in government and the number of parties in

---

1998). This produces T simulated estimates of $\hat{\beta}$ in each polity ($T = 1000$ here). I then stack the simulated estimates from the different polities such that I have T sets of r $\hat{\beta}$s. Finally, I estimate Eq. 3.4 using OLS for each of the T sets of $\hat{\beta}$. The overall estimate of γ is the average $\hat{\gamma}$ across the T dataset. To calculate the uncertainty in $\hat{\gamma}$, I follow the procedure described in Rubin (1987):

$$SE(\hat{\gamma})^2 = \frac{1}{T}\sum\nolimits_{t=1}^{T} SE(\hat{\gamma}_t)^2 + S_{\hat{\gamma}}^2\left(1 + 1/T\right)$$

where $S_{\hat{\gamma}}^2 = \sum_{t=1}^{T}\left(\hat{\gamma}_t - \bar{\hat{\gamma}}\right)^2 / (t-1)$. (The correction $1 + 1/T$ is negligible when T is big as in this case.) The standard error of $\hat{\gamma}$ combines the average of the variance of $\hat{\gamma}$ across runs with the sample variance of the point estimate $\hat{\gamma}$.

TABLE 3.6. *Institutional Mechanisms and Voter Decision Rule*

	Predicted Sign	Model (a)	Model (b)	Model (c)	Model (d)	Model (e)
Single-party government (lagged)	+	0.281 (0.124) – – – 0.177 (0.085)				
Number of parliamentary parties (lagged)	–		−0.104 (0.027) – – – −0.052 (0.035)			
District magnitude	–			−0.038 (0.047) – – – −0.041 (0.027)		
Opposition control	–				−0.022 (0.040) – – – −0.019 (0.024)	
Dispersion of Power Index*	–					−0.037 (0.019) – – – −0.020 (0.013)
Constant		0.479 (0.075) – – – 0.569 (0.054)	1.006 (0.113) – – – 0.839 (0.132)	0.690 (0.116) – – – 0.743 (0.068)	0.675 (0.168) – – – 0.717 (0.102)	0.590 (0.059) – – – 0.637 (0.040)
N		12 / 11	12 / 11	13 / 12	11 / 10	11 / 10

Note: In each cell, the first entry omits Australia and the second omits Australia and Belgium. Standard errors in parentheses.
* High values represent diffusion.

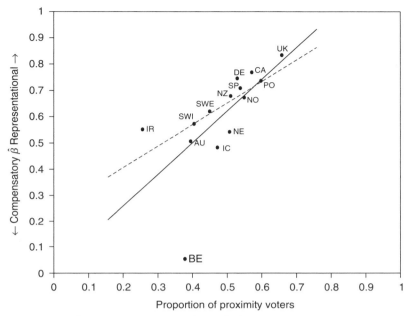

FIGURE 3.4. Compensatory vote and proximity vote

parliament, can be traced in voter choice. In fact, voter choice reflects them.

In the simulations presented in Chapter 2, I showed that as voting becomes more compensatory, the vote share of extreme parties increases holding voter and party positions fixed. The empirical analysis in this chapter showed that voters are more likely to engage in compensatory vote when parliamentary procedures and norms facilitate compromise and power sharing. This does not automatically imply, however, that extreme parties are stronger in, say, Ireland, than they are in, say, Denmark or the Netherlands. In fact, they are not. What it implies, however, is a relationship between institutional mechanisms, support for parties ideologically remote from the voter, and compensatory vote.

Figure 3.4 takes another step in the examination of this relationship. The horizontal axis presents the proportion of voters supporting the party ideologically most similar to them (the rates reported in Figure 3.1). The vertical axis is the familiar $\hat{\beta}$ (reported in Figure 3.2), with low values marking a high degree of compensatory vote. The relationship between the two is clear: the more compensatory the vote is, the fewer voters support the party most similar to them ideologically. The relationship holds with or without Belgium (expressed by the solid and dashed lines, with correlations of 0.68 and 0.80, respectively). Compensatory vote, then, captures the general voting decision rule in the electorate.

Of course, the proportion of voters following proximity voting might be explained by additional variables other than compensatory voting. Ireland, the polity with the lowest degree of proximity voting in the sample, in which other allegiances are central to voter decisions, is but one example in which a multi-reason explanation is undoubtedly in order. Nonetheless, the strong correlation of proximity voting with compensatory vote, along with the correlation of compensatory vote with institutional mechanisms, support compensatory vote as a main reason for systematic differences in proximity voting across polities.

3.6 CONCLUSION

The empirical analysis in this chapter considers voter behavior under parliamentary systems. Voters, it is argued, recognize when policy is a function of more than one player and, indeed, when it is a product of a compromise among multiple agents. They then take into account the degree to which institutional mechanisms dilute their vote when converting votes to policy, and thus their vote choice reflects likely post-electoral developments. In other words, voters use parties as instruments to attain their preferred policy.

The theoretical model I introduce in Chapter 2 is consistent with the basic intuition communicated in Downs (1953), but breaks with the vast majority of the voting literature. The notion that voters actually behave as if they engaged in a policy–counterfactual policy comparison, not to mention actually engage in one, may not seem palatable at first. In this chapter, I estimated a realization of the model, and found solid support for it. No test alone is definite support for the compensatory model, but a combination of the findings reported here and those in the upcoming chapters makes the possibility of policy-oriented choice hard to ignore.

The analysis in this chapter implicitly makes an important simplifying assumption. It assumes that given a set of institutional mechanisms or norms, all voters in a given polity/election employ the same voting strategy. In practice, however, it is unlikely that, for instance, all Swiss voters are compensatory to a given degree, and similarly, all Britons employ the same decision rule. The extent to which different voters incorporate the post-electoral institutional game and are therefore compensatory is likely to depend on voter characteristics. While I do not analyze such individual-level variation here, two factors stand out as suspects. First is partisanship. As I mention earlier, compensatory vote bears a cost. In particular, supporting a party with different views from the ideologically closest party detracts from the expressive value of voting. Thus, it is probable that those attached to a party are less likely to endorse a party with different views from their own than those not attached to one; the support of an ideologically remote party is more difficult for the partisan. Second is political sophistication. Although I do not assume that voters are aware of the nuances of all parliamentary procedures, compensatory vote assumes some intuitive understanding of the path leading from votes to policy, and is thus more cognitively demanding than proximity voting. Thus, other things being equal, I expect the politically sophisticated to be more compensatory than the less sophisticated. I leave the exploration of these effects for future research.

APPENDIX 3.1 1987 BRITISH PARTY SYSTEM

TABLE A.3.1 *Average Placements of the Three Main Parties on Each of Seven Issues*

	Labour	Liberal Democrats	Conservative
Welfare	2.5	4.3	8.1
Crime	5.5	6.2	7.6
Redistribution	2.9	4.9	8.6
Nationalization	2.9	5.7	9.3
Taxation	2.9	4.4	7.4
Phillips Curve	2.2	3.8	6.7
Defense	2.0	5.0	8.1

APPENDIX 3.II PARTY IMPACTS

TABLE A.3.2 *Party Impacts*

	% Votes	% Seats	Seats: Portfolios (3:1)	Seats: Portfolios (1:1)
Australia				
Labour	0.41	0.35	0.26	0.17
Liberal	0.41	0.53	0.65	0.76
National	0.09	0.13	0.10	0.06
Australian Democrats	0.07	0.00	0	0
Green	0.02	0.00	0	0
Belgium (Flanders) out of Flemish total vote				
The Flemish Greens	0.12	0.10	0.16	0.15
Liberals and Democrats	0.24	0.25	0.40	0.37
Socialists	0.16	0.15	0.24	0.22
Christian Democrats	0.23	0.24	0.02	0.13
Flemish Block	0.16	0.17	0.16	0.09
People's Union	0.09	0.09	0.01	0.05
Canada				
Liberals	0.39	0.52	0.64	0.76
Reform	0.20	0.20	0.15	0.10
Progressive Conservatives	0.19	0.07	0.05	0.03
New Democrats	0.11	0.07	0.05	0.04
BQU	0.11	0.15	0.11	0.07
Denmark				
Socialist People	0.09	0.08	0.06	0.04
Social Democrats	0.41	0.41	0.55	0.70
Center Democrats	0.05	0.05	0.04	0.03
Conservative People	0.10	0.10	0.08	0.05
Liberal	0.27	0.27	0.20	0.14
Danish People	0.08	0.08	0.06	0.04
Iceland				
Left Green	0.09	0.10	0.07	0.05
Alliance	0.27	0.27	0.20	0.14
Liberal	0.04	0.03	0.02	0.02
Progressive	0.19	0.19	0.27	0.35
Independence	0.41	0.41	0.44	0.46

TABLE A.3.2 (*cont.*)

	% Votes	% Seats	Seats: Portfolios (3:1)	Seats: Portfolios (1:1)
Ireland				
Sinn Fein	0.07	0.03	0.03	0.02
Labour	0.12	0.14	0.10	0.07
Green	0.04	0.04	0.03	0.02
Fine Gael	0.25	0.20	0.15	0.10
Progressive Democrats	0.04	0.05	0.07	0.09
Fianna Fail	0.47	0.53	0.62	0.70
The Netherlands				
Labour	0.33	0.33	0.34	0.34
People's Party for Freedom and Democracy	0.28	0.28	0.30	0.33
Christian Democratic Appeal	0.21	0.21	0.16	0.11
Democrats 66	0.10	0.10	0.14	0.18
Green Left	0.08	0.08	0.06	0.04
New Zealand				
Labour	0.30	0.31	0.23	0.16
Alliance	0.11	0.11	0.08	0.06
NZ First	0.14	0.14	0.12	0.10
National	0.35	0.37	0.51	0.66
ACT NZ	0.06	0.07	0.05	0.03
Norway				
Labour	0.36	0.38	0.48	0.57
Progress	0.14	0.13	0.10	0.07
Center	0.07	0.07	0.07	0.07
Christian Democrats	0.09	0.09	0.08	0.08
Conservative	0.23	0.23	0.19	0.16
Socialist Left	0.11	0.10	0.08	0.05
Portugal				
Block of the Left	0.03	0.01	0.01	0.01
Unitarian Democratic Coalition	0.07	0.05	0.04	0.03
Socialists	0.39	0.42	0.31	0.21
Social Democrats	0.42	0.46	0.56	0.67
People's Party	0.09	0.06	0.08	0.09
Spain				
Popular Party	0.50	0.55	0.67	0.78
Socialists	0.39	0.38	0.28	0.18

TABLE A.3.2 *(cont.)*

	% Votes	% Seats	Seats: Portfolios (3:1)	Seats: Portfolios (1:1)
United Left	0.06	0.02	0.02	0.01
Convergence and Union	0.05	0.05	0.03	0.02
Sweden				
Social Democrats	0.39	0.39	0.55	0.70
Left	0.13	0.13	0.10	0.07
Center	0.05	0.05	0.04	0.03
Christian Democrats	0.13	0.13	0.10	0.06
People's Party	0.05	0.05	0.04	0.03
Moderate	0.25	0.25	0.19	0.12
Switzerland				
Social Democrats	0.26	0.28	0.22	0.28
Green	0.06	0.05	0.04	0.03
Christian Democrats	0.18	0.19	0.22	0.24
Free Thinking Democrats	0.23	0.24	0.25	0.26
Swiss People's Party	0.26	0.24	0.22	0.19
UK				
Labour	0.32	0.37	0.27	0.18
Conservatives	0.44	0.60	0.70	0.80
Liberals	0.24	0.04	0.03	0.02

APPENDIX 3.III MODEL SPECIFICATION

Australia

Parties included: Labour, Liberal, National, Australian Democrats, Green.

Background variables: age, gender, education, union membership, family income, church attendance, employment status, rural/urban, denomination.

Belgium (Flanders)

Parties included: Flemish Greens, Liberals and Democrats, Socialists, Christian Democrats, Flemish Block, People's Union.

Background variables: age, gender, education, union membership, family income, church attendance, denomination.

Canada

Parties included: Liberals, Reform, Progressive Conservatives, New Democratic Party.

Background variables: age, education, family income, gender, province, denomination, family status, union membership, employment status.

Denmark

Parties included: Socialist People, Social Democrats, Center Democrats, Conservative People, Liberal, Danish People.

Background variables: age, gender, education, family income, employment status, rural/urban.

Iceland

Parties included: Left Green, Alliance, Liberal, Progressive, Independence.

Background variables: age, gender, education, union membership, family income, employment status, rural/urban.

Ireland

Parties included: Sinn Fein, Labour, Green, Fine Gael, Progressive Democrats, Fianna Fail.

Background variables: age, gender, education, union membership, family income, church attendance, denomination, employment status, rural/urban.

The Netherlands

Parties included: Labour, People's Party for Freedom and Democracy, Christian Democratic Appeal, Democrats 66, Green Left.

Background variables: age, education, family income, gender, denomination, church attendance, family status, union membership, employment status.

New Zealand

Parties included: Labour, Alliance, New Zealand First, National, ACT New Zealand.

Background variables: age, gender, education, union membership, family income, belief in Christ, religion membership, employment status, rural/urban, Maori.

Norway

Parties included: Labour, Progress, Center, Christian Democrats, Conservative, Socialist Left.

Background variables: region, class, age, gender, religiosity, education.

Portugal

Parties included: Block of the Left, Unitarian Democratic Coalition, Socialists, Social Democrats, People's Party.

Background variables: age, gender, education, family income, church attendance, employment status, rural/urban, public/private sector employee.

Spain

Parties included: Popular Party, Socialists, United Left, Convergence and Union.

Background variables: age, gender, education, family income, employment status, region.

Sweden

Parties included: Social Democrats, Left, Center, People's Party, Christian Democrats, Moderate.

Background variables: age, gender, education, union membership, family income, church attendance, employment status, rural/
urban.

Switzerland

Parties included: Social Democrats, Green, Christian Democrats, Free
Thinking Democrats, Swiss People's Party.

Background variables: age, gender, education, union membership,
family income, rural/urban, religiosity, denomination.

United Kingdom

Parties included: Labour, Conservative, Liberal-Democrats.

Background variables: region, union membership, public/private
sector employee, blue collar, gender, age, home ownership, family
income, education.

4

Balancing Strong (and Weak) Presidents

4.1 INTRODUCTION

In Chapter 3, I investigated the way citizens vote in parliamentary democracies. Parliaments consisting of multiple parties, split control over the plan of the day, and coalition governments are commonly characterized by fractionalized power. Another obvious sign of power sharing is a variety of viewpoints represented by parties that participate in policy formation. But this is only one form in which policy is produced by multiple inputs. An explicit separation of power between an executive and a legislature is yet another form that voters often encounter. How voters vote when power is diffused *across* institutions, and particularly between the executive and the legislature, is the focus of this chapter.

Before delving into the details of the analysis, let me review the implications of the compensatory model for presidential systems, and preview my empirical results. The implications of the argument for presidential democracies are straightforward. While in parliamentary democracies it is parties in parliament that negotiate and compromise, in presidential democracies the compromise is cross-institutional, between the executive and the legislature. If voters are concerned with policy, they may not necessarily support individual politicians whose views are similar to their own, but rather those who, given the expected compromise, will produce policy as close as possible to their own views. Thus, when elections are staggered and only the legislature is up for election, voters, knowing the position of the president, will often turn in the direction of the opposition in legislative elections, seeking to create a legislative–executive combination that will produce a moderate policy. The party of the president will thus perform poorly in non-concurrent legislative elections. Furthermore, the degree to which voters turn away from the executive depends on the relative impacts of the executive and the legislature. The more impact the executive has, the stronger the pull in the opposite direction voters may seek to achieve, and thus the greater the loss for the party of the president in non-concurrent legislative elections. Under concurrent elections, on the other hand, both governmental arms are up for election, and thus voters do not have information about post-electoral compromise. Therefore, the power of the executive will not necessarily be associated with vote loss (even if voters are more likely to split their ballot under a strong executive).

My empirical analysis supports these predictions. First, consistent with previous work analyzing Congressional elections in the United States, I find that the party of the president almost always performs poorly in midterm elections. The bulk of my analysis, however, spans thirty-four democracies during most of the post-war period. These cases vary not only in their economic development and level of democratic stability, but also in the timing of their legislative elections in the presidential cycle, voter turnout, turnout gap between the two types of elections, and their electoral systems. Analyzing presidential and legislative elections, I show that across countries and across time, the party of the president suffers loss of public support in non-concurrent legislative elections more than it does in concurrent elections. I then utilize a measure of the constitutional power of presidents, and demonstrate substantial variation in the authorities of the executive across my cases. Most importantly, I find that the stronger the executive, the greater the loss suffered by her party in non-concurrent elections. This finding holds when controlling for competing factors such as differential turnout and the economy.

Let us begin with a simple example. On November 7, 2006, the United States held elections for the 110th Congress. In these elections, the Republican Party lost its majority in both houses, with Democrats gaining no less than twenty-eight seats in the House of Representatives and six seats in the Senate. An obvious candidate explanation of the change in public mood was the war in Iraq. President George W. Bush was in his second tenure, the United States had been involved in Iraq for over three years, and comparisons in the American media between the Iraq War and the Vietnam War, a trauma engraved in the American collective memory, had been made time and again. The number of U.S. casualties in the war was increasing daily, the costs of the war were mounting, public spending was ever increasing, and the GOP was criticized by Democrats for lack of strategy in Iraq, on the one hand, and lack of fiscal responsibility, on the other. Although a superpower, the United States found itself with few allies and a spreading sense of resentment among intellectuals in the Western world. Media reports of sex scandals in which Republican leaders were involved breaking out only weeks before the elections did not add to the party's standing. It is only natural to imagine that the American public reacted strongly to these events (Page and Shapiro 1992). Perhaps it did. But while current events often affect voter choice, the results of the 2006 elections are the norm, not the exception.

Figure 4.1 presents the results of midterm elections compared with on-year Congressional elections in the United States since 1918. Each bar represents the change in vote share from the preceding general election for the party in control of the White House. As the figure shows, in almost all midterm elections in the past eighty years the party holding the presidency lost seats in the House. This was the case during both terms of Clinton's presidency, in George H. W. Bush's presidency, in Reagan's two terms, in Carter's term, and so on. On only two occasions – the 1926 and 2002 elections – did the party in power increase its support. In the 2006 elections, the Republican Party experienced a 3.6 percent withdrawal of support in its vote share compared with 2004. These results, then, are consistent with almost all midterm elections in the United States.

This regularity extends beyond the United States. As Figure 1.2 demonstrates, in almost all presidential democracies, average support for the party *winning* the presidency is greater than average support for the party *in control* of the presidency. This difference can be seen more clearly by examination of pairs of elections, each part of an electoral cycle. Defining an electoral cycle as bounded between two presidential elections, I examine two differences in voter support of the

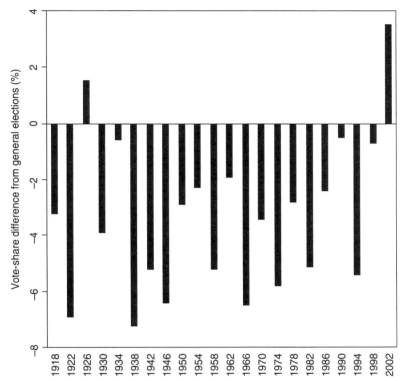

FIGURE 4.1. Midterm vote change for the party in control of the White House, 1918–2002

president's party between presidential and legislative elections. In non-concurrent elections, I examine the gap between the president's vote share in the presidential elections and the vote share of her party in the subsequent legislative elections. Similarly, in concurrent elections, I examine the gap between the vote share of the president and the vote share of her party. For convenience, I define change in voter support in terms of loss of support: the greater the loss, the bigger the number.

Comparing voter support across institutions, presidency and legislature, allows me to examine voter compensatory considerations in presidential systems in a way substantively analogous to the ones I examine in the parliamentary context in Chapter 3. Figure 4.2 presents the gap in voter support in concurrent and non-concurrent elections

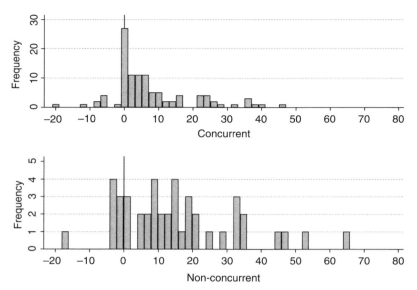

FIGURE 4.2. Vote-share loss of the president's party

(top and bottom panels, respectively) in almost all elections in presidential democracies between 1945 and 2000. The figure reveals several patterns. First, in almost all concurrent elections, the party of the president lags behind the president herself. And while the modal gap is zero, a substantial mass of the distribution is greater than zero, and the average gap in these paired elections is 7.6 percentage points. Second, a similar pattern, albeit of substantially higher magnitude, can be seen in non-concurrent elections. Although fewer elections are held non-concurrently, the data present a clear pattern. The party holding the presidency almost always experiences withdrawal in public support in off-year elections. The average gap is substantially (and statistically) greater than it is in concurrent elections: support for the party of the president is 15.4 percentage points lower than support for the president in the presidential elections immediately preceding the legislative ones. The drop in support, then, is twice as large in non-concurrent elections compared with concurrent elections.

Dozens of electoral cycles in numerous presidential democracies show a similar pattern, then – similar, but not identical. In some polities, the electoral gap between presidential and legislative races is minor, while in others it is quite large. What explains the off-year electoral cycle in presidential democracies? And what explains variations in it? Is there an underlying principle that can help us understand cross-national commonalities and differences in the logic voters across presidential democracies employ?

In this chapter, drawing on the argument of compensatory vote, I explain cross-polity similarities and differences of electoral cycles in presidential democracies. In particular, I draw on institutional and other variation across cases to untangle potential explanations. At the heart of the variation, I argue, is the way voter positions on issues translate to vote choice. To reiterate, my answer conceptualizes voters as endorsing a party such that the resulting policy will be as ideologically (spatially) close to their own views as possible. Voters cast their ballots for a party given the menu of parties on the ballot, but they vote for policy. In other words, their vote choices depend on their expectations with regards to compromise between the executive and the legislative branches.

Recall the implications of the compensatory argument I laid out in Chapter 2. The list is long, and in this chapter I focus on only two such implications. First, if voters are concerned with policy, given that policy is formed by compromise between the executive and the legislature, in non-concurrent elections, when the identity of the president is known, voters will often shun their party and support the opposition. The president's party will then incur losses in off-year legislative elections. This implication has been previously investigated in the American context, although, to the best of my knowledge, not examined against competing explanations in any other presidential democracy. Second, if voters are policy motivated, their votes will reflect the balance of power between the executive and the legislature. In those polities in which the president is strong, they might vote in large numbers for a counterweight in the legislature. Where the president has limited power, they have little incentive to compensate for her authority. In particular, the more powerful the presidency is, the more voters will balance against the executive in non-concurrent legislative elections. Therefore I expect to find vote loss of greater magnitude in systems in which the president is stronger.

The chapter is organized as follows. The next section discusses a sample of the literature about policy balancing in the United States.

I then discuss the advantages of a comparative analysis of electoral cycles. The next section presents the empirical analysis, elaborating on presidential powers as a key explanatory factor. The last section offers a conclusion.

4.2 POLICY BALANCING IN THE UNITED STATES

The advantages of studying compensatory vote in a variety of presidential systems beyond the United States are numerous. It is important to note, however, that the balancing hypothesis has been examined extensively with respect to Congressional elections in the United States. While it is impossible to review all the studies that have analyzed policy balancing in the United States, I mention a few here.

Fiorina (1996) proposes that divided government results from voters' balancing the president and Congress against one another. Policy following general elections can be made in one of four combinations – a Democratic or a Republican Congress and a Democratic or a Republican president – such that two policies are produced by unified government ("extreme policies") and two by divided government ("moderate policies"). Middle-of-the-road voters, and in particular those who are ideologically positioned between the two moderate policies and a subset of those between the moderate and the extreme policies, will likely split their ticket *as if* they are "in search of moderation" (72).

Alesina and Rosenthal (1995) develop a model for the United States in a similar spirit, incorporating economic policy and specifying how party positions and presidential power affect voter choice. Among other things, the authors use the policy-moderation hypothesis to explain why the party in control of the presidency loses seats in midterm Congressional elections. They argue that "the midterm cycle is always expected to occur, as long as the presidential elections are not completely certain" (84). Scheve and Tomz (1999) test Alesina and Rosenthal's hypothesis about the effect of uncertain outcomes in presidential elections on voter choice in subsequent legislative elections in the United States. Using panel data, they show that the more moderate a voter is, and the more surprised she is by the results of the most recent presidential election, the more likely she is to switch her vote between the presidential elections and the consecutive legislative ones.[1] Studying general rather than off-year elections, Mebane (2000) develops and tests an empirical realization of a model of coordination among voters, as well as policy moderation of the president and the House of Representatives. He shows that a small but significant group of voters both moderate and coordinate in general elections. An additional study of voter choice in the United States puts forth a discounting hypothesis. Lacy and Paolino (1998) argue that voters in separation-of-power systems differentiate between candidate positions and policy. Testing their hypothesis on data from a 1996 survey conducted in Texas, they show that ideological distance between voter position and policy predicts vote choice better than distance between voter position and party platforms. Burden and Kimball (1998), on the other hand, find that voter choice in general elections does not reflect intentional policy balancing.

One exception to the U.S.-specific literature is Shugart's comparative study (1995) of divided government in separation-of-power systems.[2] Shugart asks "why ... patterns of divided, unified, and no-majority government vary" across presidential systems (327). His explanation focuses on institutional differences among presidential systems. According to Shugart, factors such as concurrent vs. non-concurrent elections, the number of parties, and the degree to which legislative elections are localized or nationalized affect the likelihood of divided government. Toward the end of his study, Shugart also examines whether presidential veto power affects the likelihood of an oppositional majority in the legislature, but finds no significant effect, concluding that there is "no support in a data set on comparative presidential systems for the balancing hypothesis that has been developed with respect to the specific conditions of the United States" (337).

---

[1] Other particularly interesting studies are Adams, Bishin, and Dow (2004); Frymer et al. (1997); and Jacobson (1990).

[2] In a conceptual article, Samuels and Shugart (2003) discuss how institutional variation across presidential democracies affects different aspects of representation. They argue that separation of power between government branches, on the one hand, and separation of purpose, on the other, affect both mandate and accountability representation. The more constitutional powers the president has over the legislature, the better voters are able to hold her accountable. Similarly, the more separation of purpose exists by design (e.g., electoral incentives for representatives to campaign separately rather than under the party label), voters are better able to identify who is responsible. The authors do not address policy balancing directly.

This is the only comparative empirical study I am aware of that systematically studies electoral patterns of divided government in presidential democracies. Its focus, however, is on understanding the circumstances that bring about divided government rather than on understanding the micro foundations of voter choice leading to it. My focus here, on the other hand, is on understanding the logic of voter choice leading to a decline in support of the president's party between presidential and legislative elections rather than to an oppositional majority per se.

4.3 ELECTORAL CYCLES IN PRESIDENTIAL DEMOCRACIES: A COMPARATIVE PERSPECTIVE

Conducting a comparative analysis of a variety of presidential systems gives me explanatory leverage in mitigating potential explanations specific to the United States, as well as untangling other candidate explanations. Whether as a result of the U.S. political culture, the strength of its democratic regime, the high level of industrialization, the size of the government, the size of the country, the particular federal structure, the strength of interest groups, the age of its democracy, the authorities of the president, the timing of legislative elections, the electoral system, the low turnout, or any other characteristic of the United States, extending the analysis regionally, contextually, and institutionally to cases that vary on these dimensions substantially lowers the risk that the results are caused by a characteristic specific to the American system unconsidered by the analyst. I next elaborate on some of the possible key factors.

Political business cycles. While the United States holds its legislative elections at midterm, other polities hold their legislative elections at different points in time during their presidential cycles. This difference might have implications not only for the magnitude of the electoral loss but also for its potential cause. That off-year legislative elections all take place at this particular point in the cycle makes inferences about them perilous. Electoral loss in legislative elections at midterm in the United States can be associated with a political business cycle. In particular, as Alesina et al. (1997) describe, Democratic administrations often engage in expansionary policies in the first half of their tenure, and thus experience inflation in the economy by midterm, and Republican administrations, engaging in anti-inflationary policies, often experience a slowdown of the economy by midterm. Loss of support of the presidential party, then, can be the result of a vulnerable economy at midterm. Thus, if business cycles are the cause of withdrawal of support, then the loss will be greatest at midterm.

Electoral systems. Different polities employ different electoral systems for both presidential and legislative elections. The principal underlying factor that might affect the magnitude of the electoral cycle in both electoral systems is the presence or absence of mechanisms that have concentrating effects and pull voters toward rallying around fewer and bigger parties or candidates. Other things being equal, the drop in vote share will be minimal when the presidential electoral system has few such mechanisms and the legislative system has many of them, and will be maximal under the opposite institutional combination. In the presidential race, the relevant factors are whether a majority or a plurality is needed for winning, and, relatedly, whether a runoff among the two leading candidates is required in case a majority is not secured in the first run. A required majority or a runoff mechanically encourages voters to support the two leading candidates and thus increase the baseline presidential vote from which the gap is calculated. In the legislative race, large district magnitude and proportion of upper-tier seats are natural candidates for mechanisms that encourage/enable voters to diffuse the vote and support smaller parties. Controlling for social cleavages, the bigger the district magnitude and the greater the proportion of seats in parliament allocated via upper tier, the greater the number of parties in parliament (Clark and Golder 2006) and therefore the smaller the number of seats each party is likely to receive. Thus, under an institutional effect of the electoral system, the combination of a required runoff in the presidential race with high district magnitude or high proportion of seats allocated via an upper tier in the legislative race will lead to an artificially large drop of voter support between presidential and legislative elections, and, all else being equal, the opposite combination will lead to a relatively minor drop in voter support. This rationale holds both for concurrent and nonconcurrent legislative elections.

Turnout differential. The United States is notorious for its low turnout in presidential elections and for an even lower turnout in nonconcurrent legislative elections. This turnout differential is relevant for two central alternative explanations: second-order elections, and surge and decline.

(a) **Second-order elections.** A principal candidate explanation of the off-year gap in the United States is that legislative elections share many characteristics with the general category of second-order elections. Second-order elections (Reif and Schmidt 1980) are usually considered elections for offices that are not at the national political level, but rather are either supra-national (e.g., elections for the European parliament, as in van der Eijk and Franklin 1996; Marsh 1998) or sub-national (Dinkel 1977). And while these elections are not for national office, second-order elections in voters' minds are *about* the national, first-order, arena. These elections are characterized, among other things, by low turnout and, importantly, by loss of support for the parties in power nationally.[3] Although legislative elections are for a national institution, the second-order elections framework, and particularly the turnout differential, is a natural alternative explanation: if legislative elections are of second order, turnout in them will be substantially lower than the turnout in first-order elections.

(b) **Surge and decline.** In the American case in particular, scholars have argued that the midterm loss is due to the notoriously large differential turnout between general and off-year elections (17.6 percentage points in my dataset). In his famous study, Angus Campbell argues that the set of voters in general elections consists of two groups: those who turn out in Congressional elections, and peripheral voters whose partisanship and political attention are weaker. The partisanship profiles of midterm and general election voters are different, creating waves of surge and decline – systematically high support for the party winning the presidency in general elections, and low support of the presidential party at midterm (Campbell 1966). Examining turnout rates both among partisans and among independents, James Campbell (1987) modifies the argument somewhat to account for the midterm loss. In addition, analyzing eighty years of presidential and Congressional elections, Campbell (1991) contends that in addition to

---

[3] Among other characteristics of second-order elections are high degree of support for small parties and high rate of spoiled ballots. I elaborate further on second-order elections in Chapter 5.

surge and decline, performance evaluation of the incumbent administration affects the midterm loss in the United States. The surge and decline hypothesis, then, suggests that a bigger turnout differential between presidential and legislative elections will be associated with a bigger loss of support for the party of the president in legislative elections.

Results of the presidential race. The results of the presidential race might be related to the results of subsequent legislative elections in several ways. On the one hand, statistically, a landslide victory is likely to be followed by a modest success or even a loss. On the other hand, an unexpected victory by a certain candidate – usually following a close race and thus a small margin of victory – might encourage voters to correct for the unexpected outcome and thus compensate in subsequent legislative elections. I elaborate on this next.

(a) **Regression to the mean.** It is perhaps reasonable to expect that after a victory in the presidential race, the party of the president is bound to experience a natural withdrawal of support in the following legislative elections. By this argument, the result of each particular election is a draw from a distribution of possible outcomes. A draw of a landslide victory in the presidential race is a draw from the upper tail of the distribution, and is likely to be followed by a draw from the lower tail simply because most of the distribution is to the left of that draw. Therefore, we are likely to observe a loss after a victory, and more subtly a less successful performance after a successful electoral performance.

(b) **Predictability of presidential elections.** Alesina and Rosenthal's (1995) theoretical work suggests that the predictability (or lack thereof) of the presidential election outcome affects the off-year electoral loss of the party of the president. In particular, they contend that the greater the surprise in the presidential race, the bigger the loss in the off-year elections, when voters are given an opportunity to correct policy input. Building on this argument, Scheve and Tomz's (2000) empirical work on the United States shows that unexpected results yield the most vote switching at midterm among centrist voters as an attempt to balance policy. And although some voters might have a more accurate perception of the race than others, on average, the less predictable the winner, the smaller the margin. Thus, if voters use legislative elections to correct for unexpected results in the presidential race, then the smaller the margin of victory in the presidential race, the greater the loss in the legislative elections.

Performance. An additional competing explanation is the performance of the president. Simply put, parties of poorly performing presidents might be penalized more heavily than parties of well-performing, successfully governing presidents. The effect of performance can manifest itself via several routes. I examine two here.

(a) **Over-promising/capital spending.** One might argue that any candidate running for office makes promises in her campaign, of which she later fulfills only a subset. This discrepancy causes resentment and even disappointment among voters, as the president's actions fall short of her words. A similar argument is that a president might enter office with some political capital, which she gradually spends when making unpopular decisions. Both these reasons would cause voters to withdraw their support from the party of the president in non-concurrent elections. If this is the case, voter disappointment is likely to increase as the time since the presidential elections passes, with further disappointments and further negative assessments of the president, and thus we are likely to observe a positive monotonic relationship between the timing of legislative elections in the federal cycle and drop of support for the party of the president.

(b) **The economy.** Perhaps the most obvious candidate explanation is the state of the economy. If voters use legislative elections as a referendum on the performance of the administration in power, then the state of the economy is an important criterion they might use for their evaluation. Notice that this approach implicitly assumes a retrospective evaluation of the government whereby voters punish or reward it depending on the state of the economy, while, as I discuss in Chapter 2, compensatory vote assumes prospective evaluation. If non-concurrent legislative elections are indeed a referendum on the administration's performance, the party in power will do better when the economy is fast growing.

Presidential power. Most important for the compensatory hypothesis is the degree of presidential power vis-à-vis the legislature. While the U.S. president has various constitutional powers vis-à-vis Congress, she is also limited in many ways. If voters balance the executive and the legislature against one another, the relative weights of the presidency and the legislature should affect voter strategy.

Voters might react to a strong executive differently from the way they react to a relatively weak one. The variation in executive strength provides me with empirical leverage for testing the compensation argument against others.

4.4 EMPIRICAL ANALYSIS: ELECTORAL LOSSES BY STRONG PRESIDENTS

My analysis includes almost all presidential democracies in the post-war period.[4] I exclude from the analysis semi-presidential systems, which, although their presidents are popularly elected, also have fully functioning parliaments. The president in semi-presidential systems is one of two executives, and works side by side with the prime minister. Furthermore, the authority of the president vis-à-vis the parliament in semi-presidential systems is substantially limited in comparison to presidents in pure presidential systems. Thus it is reasonable to expect that these hybrid regimes will have their own electoral logic and dynamics, different from that of pure presidential systems.

4.4.1 Data

Table 4.A.1 in Appendix 4.I presents a summary of the country-year observations in the dataset. As the table shows, the data span across the Americas, Africa, Asia, and Europe, with 34 polities altogether. They include almost all democratic electoral cycles in the post-war period, where the starting point of an electoral cycle is defined by the presidential elections and the ending point by subsequent (or concurrent) legislative elections. Of the 199 legislative elections, 133 are concurrent with presidential elections and 66 are non-concurrent. The majority of polities hold both concurrent and non-concurrent elections with Bolivia, Costa Rica, Guyana, Honduras, Malawi, Mexico, Nicaragua, Nigeria, Panama, Peru, Sierra Leone, Uruguay, Venezuela, and Zambia holding concurrent elections only (in the period sampled), and Cyprus, Namibia, and Russia holding non-concurrent elections.

---

[4] I limit the analysis to cases with Polity scores equal to or greater than zero.

The number of electoral cycles per polity varies between 1 and 28,[5] with an average of 5.2.

The cases included in my dataset represent a wide array of electoral arrangements. Of the 66 non-concurrent legislative elections in my data, 30 took place at midterm and 36 did at other points in the cycle. In addition to the United States, only Ecuador, the Dominican Republic, and Cuba in the 1940s held all their non-concurrent elections at midterm. Fifty-seven percent of the elections in the dataset (including the United States) did not require a presidential runoff by law, while 43 percent did require one. As for the legislative electoral system, only 32 percent are of district magnitude of one, with an average median of 5 and a mean of 6.5. Lastly, 18 percent of the cases have some proportion of the seats in the lower House allocated via upper tier. Cross-sectional examination of the turnout gap between general and legislative elections shows a picture different from that of the United States. While the turnout gap between general and legislative elections in the United States is on average 17 percent, across all polities and elections the turnout gap between on- and off-year elections is 8.3 percentage points, and merely 4.5 when the United States is excluded. Finally, the analysis includes a range of presidential authority levels, from systems with a relatively weak president (e.g., Peru, United States) through ones with a moderately strong president (e.g., El Salvador, Indonesia) to ones with a particularly strong president (e.g., Bolivia).

Conducting a comparative analysis across countries and over time comes with a cost. While most studies of the United States I mention here utilize individual-level data, my analysis of voter behavior in presidential democracies relies on aggregate data. An important caveat is the infamous pitfall of making a micro-level inference based on aggregate data. On its own, an electoral gap in concurrent elections does not necessarily imply a high rate of ticket splitting, and is certainly not solid evidence of compensatory vote. At the extreme, 50 percent of the voters can split their ticket between parties A (presidency) and B (legislature), and the rest in the opposite direction. The vote-share gap will be nil. Similarly, an electoral gap of X percent in

[5] The dataset includes fourteen concurrent and fourteen non-concurrent Congressional elections in the United States.

staggered elections does not necessarily imply that X percent switched their votes from the party of the president to another. It does imply, however, a decline of support of X percent for that party.

With this caution in mind, I turn to some of the potential sources of the off-year vote-share gap, beginning with my key variable of interest, presidential powers.

4.4.2 Analyzing Electoral Cycles

A first step in my analysis is a comparison of the vote share of the winning presidential candidate with the vote share of her party in legislative elections. The circumstances under which voters support a candidate but withdraw their support from her party may shed light on the reasoning behind such behavior. Table 4.1 presents a summary of the vote shares in presidential and legislative elections. The average vote share of the leading presidential candidate is 50.8 percent.[6] The winner's average vote share is only slightly greater than 50 percent since the data include both systems in which a majority and systems in which only a plurality is needed for victory. Support for the winning presidential party in legislative elections is lower (41.3 percent). Broken down into concurrent and non-concurrent elections, this rate increases somewhat in concurrent elections (42.9 percent) and decreases in staggered elections (37.5 percent). The difference between the two figures is statistically significant (t statistic $= -2.31$). Consistent with these two quantities, the average drop in vote share within dyads of presidential and legislative elections is 9.8 percent (this difference, too, is statistically significant, with p value < 0.01). This gap is more than twice as large in non-concurrent elections (15.4 percent) than in concurrent elections (7.6 percent) (p value < 0.01).[7]

---

[6] This figure is slightly higher when presidential elections are held alone (51.7 percent) compared with when they are held concurrently with elections for the legislature (50.4 percent), although the two are not statistically different.

[7] The average gaps for dyads of elections are slightly different from the gaps when calculated for all presidential and all legislative elections alone. This is because of a few cases in which elections are not neatly staggered. Thus, for example, the gap between pairs of presidential and non-concurrent legislative elections is 15.4 percent, slightly different from 14.2 percent (51.7–37.5). These differences are quite small.

TABLE 4.1. *Vote Shares – Comparison of Means*

Presidential vote share (N = 189)	50.8%
Concurrent (N = 129)	50.4%
Non-concurrent (N = 59)	51.7%
Legislative vote share of presidential party (N = 151)	41.3%
Concurrent (N = 105)	42.9%
Non-concurrent (N = 45)	37.5%
Vote share gap (presidential – legislative) (N = 150)	9.8%
Concurrent (N = 105)	7.6%
Non-concurrent (N = 44)	15.4%

4.4.3 Presidential Powers

Presidential power is determined by a variety of factors. Principally, the constitution grants the president a variety of authorities and limits her with respect to others. Furthermore, within a given polity, some presidents are considered stronger than others by virtue of their personality and charisma. In addition, within the term of a president in some periods, the executive enjoys greater public support than in others depending on current events, her performance, and the level of unity of her party. Finally, as in parliamentary systems, interest groups, bureaucracy independence, and global economic factors all affect the relative power of the president. While all these factors are important, I focus here on the first aspect of presidential power mentioned, authority granted by the constitution.

The use of constitutional powers has both theoretical and empirical advantages. Theoretically, unlike many alternative measures such as the volume of legislation the president passes through the legislature, or the nature of the party system (or the party of the president itself), powers granted to the executive by the constitution are exogenous to electoral results. And while it would be tempting to employ less abstract measures or measures that might be more intuitive to a non-specialist ("everybody knows X was a weak president"), it is crucial, given the focus of this study, to employ a measure that temporally precedes election returns.

To measure constitutional powers, I follow Shugart and Carey's (1992) coding of constitutions. For most cases where available, I employ Shugart and Carey's data. For others, however, I rely on independent coding of constitutions, extending Shugart and Carey's coding both in time and space.[8] The measure contains ten indicators of presidential powers. The first six are legislative powers, and include package veto/override, partial veto/override, decree power, exclusive introduction of legislation (in reserved policy areas), budgetary powers, and proposal of referenda. The other four indicators are non-legislative powers: cabinet formation, cabinet dismissal, censure, and dissolution of the assembly. Each indicator is coded between 0 (minimal presidential authority) and 4 (maximal presidential authority).

Table 4.A.2 in Appendix 4.II presents the indicators and their coding. As the table shows, the power of the president is shaped both by the range of her authority and the degree of restrictions under which she can exert her authority. The former simply refers to how far her authority can reach. Budgetary powers are a good example. Budgetary powers of the president range from minimal authority, by which the assembly has complete authority to prepare and amend the budget, to extended authority, by which the president prepares the budget with no amendments permitted. The latter refers to how restrictive are the conditions under which the president's authority can be exerted. For example, the extent of package veto authority depends on the majority required for the assembly to override the president's veto, from weak presidents having a veto power with only a simple majority required for override to strong presidents having veto power with no override.

Figure 4.3 presents the distributions of the ten aspects of presidential powers in the sample across the thirty-five constitutions in the dataset. As the figure shows, although in all aspects of power there is a clear modal category, the entire range is relevant. The majority of aspects of constitutional authorities – partial veto, decree, introduction of legislation, budgetary power, and dissolution of the legislature – are granted only at a minimum level. On the other hand, most presidents are granted maximal authority to form cabinets, to dismiss them, and to censure. Finally, most presidents are granted moderate authority to introduce the package veto. Correlations

---

[8] I am indebted to Allen Hicken for his permission to use these data, collected in collaboration. I gratefully acknowledge the superb research assistance of DeAundria Bryant, Kim Dorazio, and Dan Magleby in coding constitutions.

among the ten indicators (not reported here) are surprisingly low, suggesting that the ten indeed capture different aspects of power sharing.

Figure 4.4 presents the distribution of a constitutional power index composed of the ten indicators. I follow Shugart and Carey

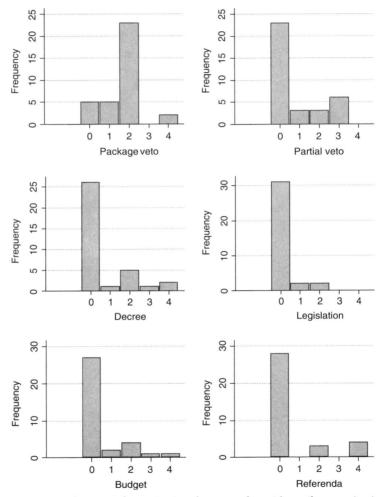

FIGURE 4.3. Indicators of constitutional power of presidents (by constitution)

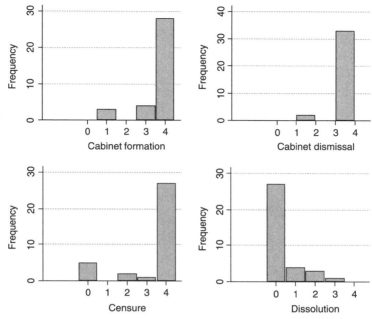

FIGURE 4.3. (continued)

(1992) in assigning each indicator an equal weight and creating an additive index. Although the hypothetical range varies form 0 to 40, we can see that, in practice, presidential powers vary between 9 and 22. Polities with relatively weak presidencies are Peru (with a score of 9) and Colombia in the mid and late 1990s (with a score of 10). Bolivia has the highest score of 22. The median score is 15. For comparison, it is worth mentioning that the commonly analyzed American presidency has a score of 13 on the presidential power scale. Almost all constitutions are constant over time, but vary across polities. Only three cases – Argentina, Colombia, and Zambia – had constitutional changes that affected the powers of the presidency over this period (Argentina from 14 to 21, Colombia from 13 to 10, and Zambia from 14 to 19). And while it is quite probable that voters would react to a constitutional change by changing their patterns of behavior, my analysis speaks first and foremost to cross-polity differences.

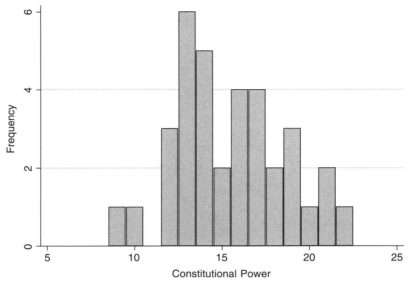

FIGURE 4.4. Presidential powers (by constitution)

As I show here, the loss of support in non-concurrent elections varies greatly from a few percentage points to a few dozen. I next explain this variation.

4.4.4 Explaining Electoral Cycles

Let us begin with a basic, bivariate analysis which I will refine in the following steps. Figure 4.5 presents the electoral loss on the vertical axis against presidential powers on the horizontal axis. The top panel presents the relationship for non-concurrent elections and the bottom panel for concurrent elections. A regression line is superimposed on the cluster of observations. The figure shows a positive relationship between the constitutional power of the president and vote loss of the party in power in staggered elections but not in concurrent ones. These results are statistically supported in Table 4.2. As the table shows, while presidential powers do not correlate with drop in vote share in concurrent elections, the two correlate well in non-concurrent elections. In the non-concurrent case, every unit increase in presidential authority is associated with an electoral loss of 3.1 percentage points. This is

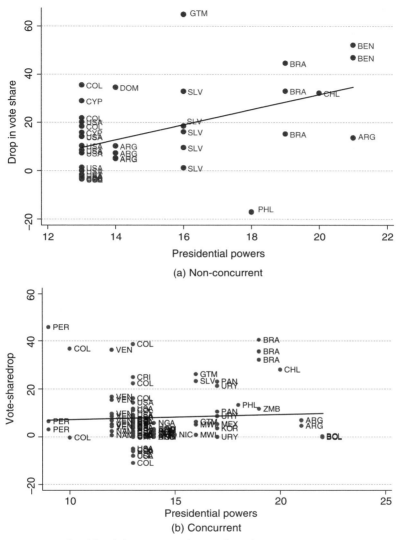

FIGURE 4.5. Presidential powers and vote-share loss

an appreciable effect; recall that each of the ten presidential powers ranges from 0 to 4. Therefore, every additional area in which the authority of the president increases by, say, two degrees, from moderately weak (1) to moderately strong (3), increases the vote loss by 6.2 percentage points.

TABLE 4.2. *Vote-Share Gap, Simple Regression*

	Concurrent	Non-concurrent	Entire sample
Presidential powers	0.23 (.585)	3.13 (<.001)	1.11 (.006)
Constant	4.50 (.458)	−31.13 (.001)	−5.83 (.318)
R^2	0.003	0.24	0.05
N	90	40	131

P-values in parentheses.
Panel-corrected standard errors.

This pattern suggests possible support for the compensatory hypothesis. When the presidential arm of the policy seesaw is clearly identified, as it is in off-year elections, the more weighty it is, the more voters turn the other way in legislative elections to balance the seesaw. In concurrent elections, on the other hand, when the location of the presidential arm is unknown at the time of the elections, presidential strength is irrelevant.

The gap in support of the president's party may be explained by other factors. In the analysis here, I consider several potential factors, aiming at untangling the main competing explanations. I first consider economic performance. Economic performance is a usual suspect affecting support for the incumbent (see, e.g., Alvarez and Nagler 1995, Lewis-Beck 1990, Powell and Whitten 1993). Voters might penalize the incumbent president's party for poor economic performance and reward her for prosperity. Some might argue that this is particularly relevant in Latin America, where most presidential democracies are found. In her study of economic policies and democracy in Latin America, Stokes (2001) shows how often presidential candidates in Latin America abandon their mandate once in office. In particular, when there is a discrepancy between voter preferences and what candidates think is favorable to the markets, candidates often promise policies emphasizing economic security, and, once in power, pursue neo-liberal policies. According to Stokes, candidates are often concerned that liberalization of the economy is much needed, and if not pursued, the economy will stagnate, for which voters will punish them at the polls. My analysis, then, includes economic growth as a general indicator of economic performance.

The methods by which both the president and the legislature are elected might affect the degree to which voters rally around leading candidates, and thus the level of support for both the president and her party. For the legislature, I include in the analysis district magnitude and proportion of seats allocated via an upper tier. For the presidency, I distinguish between systems requiring a majority/run-off and those in which a plurality of the vote suffices for victory. Table 4.3 presents these analyses. In it, I examine different models, starting with the most sparse specification, and gradually moving to a more comprehensive one (given constraints set by the limited number of cases). Since the compensatory logic applies to non-concurrent elections, and preliminary results suggest, as the theory predicts, that presidential powers are relevant for non-concurrent but not for concurrent elections, the analysis examines the effect for non-concurrent elections. In the last column of the table, however, I present the results for concurrent elections, examining the differences between the two, and in particular the difference in the effect of presidential powers. I repeat this practice in Tables 4.4 and 4.5. To reiterate, my expectation is to find an effect of presidential powers in non-concurrent elections but not in concurrent ones.

As Table 4.3 indicates, the effect of presidential power is positive, and varies between 1.1 and 3.2 for a unit increase in power. However, the effect loses statistical significance when a presidential runoff is added to the analysis. The two mechanisms increasing fragmentation of power in the legislative arena – district magnitude and seats allocated via an upper tier – do not have a systematic effect, while a required majority/run-off in the presidential race increases the gap in support. Economic performance in the last electoral reference point is not systematically associated with loss of support for the party of the president. I also conducted the analysis with economic growth measured at the year of the legislative elections – the results are almost identical to those reported here. In concurrent elections, as expected, presidential power does not have an effect on loss of support. Run-off elections for the presidency, however, have a significant effect of over 7 percentage points on the vote-share gap. In other words, in systems that require a run-off in the presidential race, there is a greater vote-share gap between the president and her party both in concurrent and in non-concurrent elections. This effect is not surprising; an electoral

TABLE 4.3. *Vote-Share Gap, Incorporating Electoral Rules*

	Model 1	Model 2	Model 3	Model 4	Model 4
	Non-concurrent				Concurrent
Presidential power	3.22 (<.001)	3.21 (<.001)	1.58 (.876)	−1.05 (.900)	−0.06 (.917)
Legislature electoral system					
Upper-tier seats		0.57 (.201)		−0.24 (.625)	0.27 (.003)
Avg. DM		0.48 (.518)		0.46 (.170)	0.01 (.751)
Presidential run-off			24.76 (.004)	29.35 (<.001)	7.86 (.003)
Growth (lagged)	0.55 (.365)	0.58 (.273)	0.34 (.469)	0.35 (.428)	−0.24 (.334)
Constant	−33.14 (.003)	−38.22 (<.001)	5.57 (.715)	4.61 (.670)	4.76 (.514)
R^2	0.25	0.39	0.46	0.57	0.17
N	33	30	33	30	73

P-values in parentheses.
Panel-corrected standard errors.

system requiring a run-off between two candidates encourages voters to rally around the two leading candidates. Since no such powerful mechanism exists in legislative elections (even a single-member district system is penetrable to third and other parties), the vote-share gap is artificially increased.[9]

One might wonder whether an appropriate economic indicator affecting the electoral fortunes of the incumbent party is the state of the economy in a given region rather than in the nation as a whole. This may be particularly relevant since the majority of the cases I examine are federations. Unfortunately, sub-national economic indicators across countries and over time are difficult to obtain. Additionally, to make use of such indicators, the entire analysis, including the election returns of presidential and legislative elections, would have to shift to the sub-national level, and these data are again, at best, difficult to obtain cross-sectionally and over time. Lastly, while refined data are almost always preferable, it is important to keep in mind that the constitutional power of presidents, my main explanatory variable, varies at the national rather than the sub-national level. A preliminary analysis, however, is reassuring. An examination of the national-level analysis in the most decentralized federations and the least decentralized federations suggests that there is no systematic deviation from the regression line correlated with the level of decentralization. The pattern of electoral behavior in the highly decentralized federations is predicted by the model just as well as the pattern of electoral behavior in centralized polities.

It might seem as though the institutional structure of presidential and legislative elections – namely, a required runoff if a certain vote share is not reached in the first round of the presidential elections, and district magnitude in the legislative elections – have explanatory power that overshadows the compensatory effect. A comparison of the effect of runoff requirements for concurrent and non-concurrent elections is revealing. Not surprisingly, the requirement of a runoff in the presidential race has an effect on the electoral gap between the president and her party even in concurrent elections. The average gap in voter support (7.6 percentage points altogether, as mentioned earlier) is greater when a runoff is required than in those cases in which it is not (10.4 percentage points compared with 6.1, respectively, n = 105,

---

[9] I thank Carles Boix for highlighting this point.

p-value for one sided test = 0.035). The effect of a runoff is even greater in non-concurrent elections. The average 15.3 percent drop of support mentioned here is more than three times greater in cases in which a runoff is required compared with those cases in which it is not (27.5 percentage points compared with 7.7, respectively).

Reviewing the same comparisons within institutional category highlights the contingent effect of concurrency. The effect of concurrency is substantial among the cases requiring a runoff (a statistically different drop of 27.5 percent in staggered elections compared with 10.4 in simultaneous ones). When a runoff is not required, however, the effect of concurrency disappears (a drop of 7.1 percent compared with 6.1, statistically indistinguishable).

District magnitude, as I discussed earlier, is expected to affect the number of parties and hence the vote share of each party, and, by extension, the gap in vote share between the president and her party; the larger the district magnitude, the bigger the gap. What is the effect of district magnitude contingent on concurrency? I split my sample into two groups, those having district magnitude of one and those having a district magnitude greater than one. The former group consists of 31 percent of the legislative elections in my dataset, and the latter of 69 percent averages a magnitude of nine. Larger district magnitude for legislative elections results in greater loss of support in concurrent elections (a gap of 4.8 for district magnitude of one compared with 8.8 for district magnitude greater than one, with p-value = 0.057 for a one-sided test). Similar to the effect of the presidential runoff, the effect is substantially greater in non-concurrent elections, with a drop of voter support of 4 percentage points in single-member district elections compared with 22 percentage points in electoral systems with larger districts. Consistently, the effect of concurrency depends on district magnitude. The effect is statistically indistinguishable in cases in which district magnitude is one (drop of 4.0 and 4.8 percentage points for non-concurrent and concurrent cases, respectively), but is appreciable in electoral systems with district magnitude greater than one (drop of 8.8 percentage points in concurrent elections compared with 21.9 in non-concurrent elections). Thus, while the small number of cases makes it harder to achieve standard levels of significance in the more comprehensive analysis, a systematic effect is observed when raw data are examined.

Next, I consider the effect of the predictability of the presidential race and the timing of the legislative elections. Following Alesina and Rosenthal's (1995) theoretical work, and Scheve and Tomz's (2000) empirical work in the United States, I examine how the predictability (or lack thereof) of the presidential elections outcome affects the off-year loss. Recall that the hypothesis put forth by Alesina and Rosenthal is that the greater the surprise, the bigger the loss in the off-year elections when voters are given a chance to "correct" policy input. To measure the surprise, I include in the analysis the margin of victory of the winning presidential candidate over the candidate who came in second. And although some voters might have a more accurate perception of the race than others, on average, the more uncertain are the results of the elections, the smaller is the margin of victory.

The margin of victory also allows me to mitigate the concern that the non-concurrent withdrawal is a natural regression to the mean. Since electoral success (i.e., vote share) of the president in itself is affected by the electoral system (e.g., through the number of candidates competing), I focus instead on the margin of victory in the presidential race. If regression to the mean is the cause of the loss of support, the greater the margin of victory, the greater the loss.

Timing of the legislative elections with respect to the presidential elections might affect withdrawal of support. The timing variable borrowed from Golder (2004) is coded as proximity to presidential elections, such that its minimum value (0) is halfway between two presidential elections, and its maximum (1) is concurrent. In Golder's terms:

$$2 * \left| \frac{L_t - P_{t-1}}{P_{t+1} - P_{t-1}} - \frac{1}{2} \right|$$

where L_t is the year of the legislative elections, P_{t-1} is the year of the previous presidential election, and P_{t+1} is the year of the next presidential election (see Golder 2004, 11).

Table 4.4 presents the results of the analysis incorporating the presidential margin of victory and the timing of the legislative elections (non-concurrent elections in the first four columns). The timing of the non-concurrent legislative election does not have a significant effect on

TABLE 4.4. *Vote-Share Gap, Incorporating Timing and Surprise*

	Model 1	Model 2	Model 3	Model 1
	Non-concurrent			Concurrent
Presidential power	3.30 (<.001)	2.37 (.014)	2.57 (.009)	0.17 (.683)
Presidential margin of victory	0.51 (.001)		0.49 (.001)	0.33 (.005)
Timing		22.96 (.201)	19.66 (.149)	
Growth (lagged)	0.58 (.285)	0.55 (.321)	0.58 (.223)	−0.05 (.823)
Constant	−43.64 (<.001)	−24.51 (.064)	−35.82 (.006)	1.25 (.826)
R^2	0.46	0.31	0.51	0.17
N	33	33	33	76

P-values in parentheses.
Panel-corrected standard errors.

the off-year loss. As for the margin of victory, the bigger the gap, the greater the off-year loss, suggesting that a regression to the mean is potentially at work. This result, however, is not necessarily in tension with Scheve and Tomz's analysis. As those authors carefully explain, a test should focus on moderate voters – those prone to switching if surprised by the result of the presidential elections. Such a test requires individual-level data, and is beyond the scope of my analysis. Most importantly, the effect of presidential powers holds once the presidential margin of victory is included in the model. The stronger the president, the greater the loss, with an effect of similar magnitude as in the preliminary analysis, between 2.4 and 3.3 percentage points per unit of authority. Again, this is not the case in concurrent elections in which presidential power has no effect.

Before incorporating turnout into the analysis, it is important to examine the turnout gap between presidential and legislative elections itself, as well as how it varies with presidential power. A comparison of turnout in the two types of race yields an interesting picture. The average presidential turnout in the data is 70.1 percentage points. Legislative turnout is statistically lower in nonconcurrent elections (61.5 percent) and, predictably, it is practically identical to presidential turnout in concurrent elections (69.7 percent). Is turnout in legislative elections lower in those polities where the president is granted more authority? If this is the case, and the ones who turn out to vote in legislative elections are an uneven subset of those turning out in presidential elections, it is possible that the stronger the president, the lower, and hence more uneven, is turnout in legislative elections. If so, then particularly low and uneven turnout (i.e., of voters who are especially discontent with the president) will be associated with a strong executive, and potentially challenge the compensatory hypothesis. A quick glance at the data provides an answer to the question. Turnout in non-concurrent legislative elections is *positively* correlated with presidential power (0.37, p-value = .01) and, moreover, the gap between presidential and legislative turnout is *negatively* correlated with presidential power (−0.36, p-value = .02). Therefore, although voters turn out in lower numbers in legislative elections than in presidential elections, the gap is not necessarily greater in systems with a stronger executive.

Table 4.5 presents the results of the analysis incorporating turnout gap. As the table shows, turnout gap has a positive effect on vote loss. The bigger the gap, the greater the vote loss in legislative elections. This does not detract from the effect of presidential powers, which continues to be positive and of appreciable magnitude (between a 3.3 and 4.5 percentage drop for every unit increase of constitutional power). An exception to this pattern is Model 4, in which neither presidential powers, turnout, the presidential electoral system, nor economic performance affects the electoral results. It seems that this is a case of a nearly saturated model with a plethora of explanatory variables and only thirty observations, pushing against limited information encapsulated in the data. Once more, as the theory predicts, the effect of presidential powers dissipates once concurrent cases are examined.

One might wonder if loss of voter support in off-year legislative elections is merely a reflection of a more general trend in voter sentiment. Voters might elect a challenger in the following elections anyway, such that the legislative elections are simply an opportunity to measure a secular trend taking shape in the months leading up to the next presidential elections. An examination of vote shares in the United States, the longest series of presidential elections available, sheds light on this possibility. My data include all general and legislative elections between 1946 and 2000, fourteen concurrent and fourteen non-concurrent elections overall. Seven of the concurrent elections led to reelection of a

TABLE 4.5. *Vote-Share Gap, Incorporating Turnout Differential*

	Model 1	Model 2	Model 3	Model 4	Model 5	Model 2
	Non-concurrent					Concurrent
Presidential power	4.10 (.001)	4.53 (<.001)	3.30 (.004)	0.94 (.977)	3.83 (.001)	0.49 (.231)
Turnout gap	0.39 (.230)	0.55 (.081)	0.54 (.053)	0.20 (.756)	0.67 (.011)	0.56 (.202)
Presidential margin of victory		0.56 (<.001)			0.53 (<.001)	0.38 (.004)
Timing			31.83 (.090)			
Legislative electoral system					27.21 (.035)	
Upper-tier seats				-0.33 (.640)		
Avg. DM				0.77 (.377)		
Presidential run-off				30.90 (.113)		
Growth (lagged)	0.52 (.399)	0.54 (.355)	0.49 (.329)	0.28 (.549)	0.52 (.253)	0.07 (.759)
Constant	-49.77 (.017)	-68.17 (.001)	-44.00 (.022)	-26.00 (.402)	-62.48 (<.001)	-4.52 (.439)
R^2	0.29	0.54	0.40	0.61	0.62	0.20
N	32	32	32	29	32	72

P-values in parentheses.
Panel-corrected standard errors.

president or a president's party (1948, 1956, 1964, 1972, 1984, 1988, and 1996), while in the other seven, a different party took control of the presidency. A comparison of the legislative elections preceding these two sets of general elections is revealing. The average drop in voter support in those non-concurrent legislative elections preceding the elections leading to reelection of the president or a different candidate from the president's party is 4.6 percentage points (S.E. $= 2.5$) compared with 7.3 percentage points (S.E. $= 3.2$) in those non-concurrent elections preceding a change of the party holding the presidency. The two are not statistically distinguishable (p-value $= 0.26$), yet the small number of observations makes standard levels of statistical significance unlikely a priori. The comparison, therefore, yields no definite conclusion.

My dataset includes almost all presidential democracies and almost all electoral cycles in these polities since World War II, yet, as the tables show, after separating elections into concurrent and non-concurrent cases, and controlling for important variables, the number of cases per model drops rather quickly, and often comes down to only slightly over thirty in the non-concurrent subsample. Since constitutions rarely change, some of these cases are constant on my key variable of interest. And although the effect of presidential powers is consistently positive, when all or almost all control variables are included in the analysis, that effect loses its statistical significance. The results, however, are qualitatively stable across model specifications.

To summarize the results so far, my analyses reveal several points. Most importantly, constitutionally powerful presidencies suffer electoral losses more than their weaker counterparts do in non-concurrent legislative elections – voters turn away from strong presidents more than they do from weak ones. This relationship is contingent upon two additional institutional factors: runoffs, which mechanically reduces the number of candidates competing for the presidency; and large district magnitude, which mechanically increases the number of parties competing in legislative elections. This loss of voter support is positively correlated with the margin of victory in the presidential race: the wider the margin of the presidential victory, the greater the subsequent electoral loss. Several factors do not affect the magnitude of the loss. Neither closeness of the legislative elections to the midpoint of the presidential cycle, nor the amount of time since the presidential elections which can cause segments of the public to be alienated by unfulfilled promises at various different points, nor poor performance, make a difference: strong presidents lose more in different points in the cycle. Lastly, turnout differential has no systematic effect: the electoral gap between presidential and legislative elections is not a product of different sub-groups of the population turning out for the two types of elections.

4.4.5 Additional Tests

The empirical analysis I presented here involves multiple decisions regarding case selection, measurement, and model specification. I describe here how the results persist or change with these decisions.

Democracies. The analysis presented here includes all polities whose Polity score is 0 or greater. One might argue that this approach errs on the inclusive side – perhaps a more strict inclusion criterion is in order. I therefore conducted the analysis by including only cases whose Polity score is greater than 2, and then those whose score is greater than 4. The former step omits 12 percent of the cases (e.g., Honduras, Uruguay, Guatemala, Zambia, and the Philippines in some years), and the latter an additional 8 percent (e.g., Chile in some years, Ecuador and the Philippines in other years.) The results of these analyses are similar to the original results. Separately, I also eliminated the United States from the analysis. The omission of the United States – the longest data series in the analysis, the highest scoring democracy in the data, and the most industrialized – verifies that the United States does not drive the results of the comparative analysis. The results of the analysis without the United States are qualitatively similar to the original results reported, although standard levels of statistical significance are slightly harder to reach given the smaller number of cases.

Election timing. The analysis so far assumed a particular structure to the effect of the timing of the legislative elections in the presidential cycle: legislative elections were measured by their distance from the midpoint of the cycle, assuming that halfway through a president's tenure is a particularly vulnerable point. This specification, borrowed from Golder (2004), follows the second-order elections literature, which finds that the midpoint in the electoral cycle is a particularly vulnerable one (van der Eijk and Franklin 1996). Further, I repeated all analyses with a linear time specification, allowing the effect to increase or decrease monotonically over time. This specification guards against the competing explanation of political capital spending or reneging on promises made during the campaign. As I mentioned earlier, presidential candidates may spend their political capital on unpopular programs once in office. This spending is not free – it costs the president in electoral support. According to this logic, the electoral loss should monotonically increase with time as the president spends more and more of her political capital and as the public's patience reaches its limit. However, in all model specifications parallel to the ones in Tables 4.3 through 4.5, I found no effect of the timing of the legislative elections on the drop of support for the party of the president.

Electoral support. In many cases, several parties endorsed a particular presidential candidate. In my analysis, I assign each party its vote share only, irrespective of the presidential candidate it endorsed. However, I also conduct the analysis taking into consideration preelectoral alliances. In those cases in which parties formally coalesced behind a candidate in a pre-electoral alliance, I calculate the vote-share gap as the gap between the president and that of the electoral alliance. In cases in which a party supported a candidate of another party but did not enter an official electoral alliance, I conduct the analysis with each party assigned its own vote share, as before. The results of this analysis are similar to the original results, with presidential powers systematically affecting the magnitude of the electoral cycle in non-concurrent elections, joined by turnout gap.

Presidential Powers. Recall that Shugart and Carey's constitutional powers measure includes both legislative and other powers of the president. And although legislation is only one aspect in which presidential authority can be realized, it is clearly an important one. I therefore examine how presidential power regarding legislation alone (the combination of Shugart and Carey's first six indicators) explains the off-year electoral cycle. The results are similar to the results produced by the more general presidential powers index. In other words, when presidents' legislative authorities alone are considered, voters still shun strong presidents more than they do weak presidents.

4.5 A FEW POTENTIAL EXTENSIONS AND IMPLICATIONS

Why does the party of the president do poorly in off-year elections? The analysis in this chapter is, to the best of my knowledge, the first comparative study of the causes of the off-year electoral decline in separation-of-powers systems. I showed that the institutional distribution of power between the executive and the legislature is reflected in voter behavior. The stronger the presidency, the weaker the performance of her party in legislative elections taking place nonconcurrently with presidential elections. In concurrent elections, however, presidential power is not associated with the electoral performance of the president's party. This finding, I argue, is an indication in support of the compensatory hypothesis: voters use their ballots in legislative elections to compensate for compromise between the president and the legislature, and thus they compensate more when the president is stronger.

Nevertheless, I would like to point to several potential extensions to the analysis beyond the ones I explored here. The first extension has to do with presidential power. Although widely accepted, the measure of presidential constitutional power offered by Shugart and Carey and used here is not uncontested. In two recent papers, Tsebelis and Alemán (2005) and Tsebelis and Rizova (2007) point at an aspect of presidential authority that is often overlooked – the authority to offer positive modifications to vetoed bills. Since a presidential proposal sometimes becomes the default alternative, this authority substantially increases the impact of the president in the legislative process. This is, in a way, a form of conditional agenda-setting power, since the president is authorized to introduce a last proposal. At the same time, if the president's proposal is not accepted, the amendatory power dissipates. An analysis of the relationship between this aspect of presidential power and off-year electoral loss can be particularly illuminating.

The second extension is government position. In Chapter 2, I mention presidential extremity as one of the factors affecting the magnitude of the off-year cycle. The expectation is that the more extreme the president is, the greater is the off-year electoral shift in the direction of the ideological opposition. Measuring presidential extremity and opposition ideology within countries over time and in a manner comparable across countries is beyond the scope of this study. In the next chapter, however, analyzing multi-office elections in the federal context within a single case over time, I am able to take steps in this direction.

While the first two extensions touch on policy formation, the third extension is related to voters. Using aggregate data, I am able to examine only some implications of the argument. Complementing the analysis conducted here, a micro-level analysis would allow me to determine who are the voters switching their ballots between presidential and legislative elections. According to the compensatory hypothesis, other things being equal, voter moderation along with political sophistication should be correlated with vote switching. A complementary study focusing on individual-level behavior in a single country, and differentiating voters according to relevant characteristics, can shed light on this aspect of the argument.

Beyond explaining electoral cycles in presidential democracies, the analysis in this chapter points to the importance of incorporating institutional context into our understanding of voter choice. Current accounts for issue voting – namely, proximity and directional models – have devoted great attention to understanding the way voters evaluate parties and party positions, and have indeed given us important insights. In fact, it is hard to imagine a comprehensive model of voter choice that does not take at least one of them into account. But focusing on the way individuals assess parties, political scientists have neglected to ask what voters wish to maximize, and given what they wish to maximize, what decision rule they might use to assess parties. Changing our assumption about the ultimate object of voter choice from parties to policy gives us analytic leverage in accounting for regularities currently unexplained. And after examining voter motivation through this lens, the role of the institutional context in shaping voter strategy becomes hard to ignore.

This insight brings up an old issue: how institutions are designed to meet certain goals, and how often these goals are not met. Attempts to constitutionally strengthen the executive so that "she gets more done" might result in higher rates of divided government and, depending on one's view, stalemate or moderated policy. A weaker executive, on the other hand, might often have the legislature on her side, and thus get more done. While policy makers design institutions to assist in attaining certain goals, voters often work around institutional mechanisms and turn the designers' efforts on their head. This pitfall is a product of analysts' reifying voter behavior and ignoring the role that institutions have in producing the behavior we observe. It is only when we have a better understanding of the way the behavior we observe is shaped by the institutions we observe, only when we refrain from analyzing behavior as if it were stripped down from an institutional context, that we will be able to successfully understand behavior and successfully design political institutions.

APPENDIX 4.1

TABLE 4.A.1. *Polities and Electoral Cycles Included in the Analysis*

Polity	Legislative election years	Total
Argentina	1973, 1983, 1985, 1987, 1989, 1991, 1993, 1995, 1997, 1999	10
Benin	1991, 1995, 1999	3
Bolivia	1985, 1989, 1993, 1997	4
Brazil	1947, 1950, 1954, 1958, 1986, 1990, 1994, 1998	8
Chile	1949, 1953, 1957, 1961, 1965, 1969, 1993, 1997	8
Colombia	1947, 1958, 1960, 1962, 1964, 1966, 1968, 1970, 1974, 1978, 1982, 1986, 1990, 1991, 1994, 1998	16
Costa Rica	1948, 1953, 1958, 1962, 1966, 1970, 1974, 1978, 1982, 1986, 1990, 1994, 1998	13
Cuba	1946, 1948, 1950	3
Cyprus	1970, 1976, 1981, 1985, 1991, 1996, 2001	7
Dominican Republic	1978, 1982, 1986, 1990, 1994, 1998	6
Ecuador	1952, 1954, 1956, 1958, 1960, 1979, 1984, 1986, 1988, 1990, 1992, 1994, 1996, 1998	14
El Salvador	1985, 1988, 1991, 1994, 1997, 2000	6
Ghana	1979	1
Guatemala	1950, 1953, 1966, 1970, 1990, 1995, 1999	7
Guyana	1992, 1997	2
Honduras	1971, 1985, 1989, 1993, 1997	5
Indonesia	1999	1
Malawi	1994, 1999	2
Mexico	2000	1
Namibia	1994, 1999	2
Nicaragua	1990, 1996	2
Nigeria	1979, 1983, 1999	3
Panama	1956, 1960, 1964, 1989, 1994, 1999	6

TABLE 4.A.1. *(cont.)*

Polity	Legislative election years	Total
Peru	1956, 1962, 1963, 1980, 1985, 1990	6
Philippines	1946, 1949, 1953, 1957, 1961, 1965, 1987, 1992, 1995, 1998	10
Russia	1993, 1995, 1999	3
Sierra Leone	1996	1
South Korea	1992, 2000	2
Ukraine	1994, 1998	2
United States of America	1946, 1948, 1950, 1952, 1954, 1956, 1958, 1960, 1962, 1964, 1966, 1968, 1970, 1972, 1974, 1976, 1978, 1980, 1982, 1984, 1986, 1988, 1990, 1992, 1994, 1996, 1998, 2000	28
Uruguay	1946, 1950, 1954, 1958, 1962, 1966, 1971, 1989, 1994, 1999	10
Venezuela	1963, 1968, 1973, 1978, 1983, 1988, 1993, 1998, 2000	9
Zambia	1991, 1996	2

APPENDIX 4.II: CODING OF PRESIDENTIAL POWERS

The coding here was originally created by Shugart and Carey (1992) and modified by Hellman and Tucker (changes from Shugart and Carey are in italics). Hellman and Tucker analyzed semi-presidential systems and included authorities of the prime minister in their coding. Since my analysis here includes pure presidential systems only, I omit the parts of their coding modification that refer to prime ministers.

TABLE 4.A.2. *Constitutional Powers of Presidents*

Legislative Powers	
	Package Veto/Override
4	Veto with no override
3	Veto with override requiring majority greater than 2/3 (of quorum)
2	Veto with override requiring 2/3
1	Veto with override requiring absolute majority of assembly or extraordinary majority less than 2/3
0	No veto; or veto requires only simple majority to override
	Partial Veto/Override
4	No override
3	Override by extraordinary majority

TABLE 4.A.2. *(cont.)*

2	Override by absolute majority of whole membership
1	Override by simple majority of quorum
0	No partial veto

Decree

4 *Unlimited (to defend the Constitution and its laws)*
3 *Decree-making powers for limited time*
2 *Decrees subject to ex-post facto approval*
1 *Only negative decree-making power (i.e. can make decrees to overrule illegal local government action)*
0 No decree-making power, or only to do what is already an executive power (i.e. set an election date; the actual mechanism of doing so is often an executive decree)

Exclusive Introduction of Legislation (Reserved Policy Areas)

4 No amendment by assembly
2 Restricted amendment by assembly
1 Unrestricted amendment by assembly
0 No exclusive powers

Budgetary Powers

4 President prepares budget; no amendment permitted
3 Assembly may reduce but not increase amount of budgetary items
2 President sets upper limit on total spending, within which assembly may amend
1 Assembly may increase expenditures only if it designates new revenues
0 Unrestricted authority of assembly to prepare or amend budget

Proposal of Referenda

4 *Unrestricted, and only president has right to call referenda*
2 *Restricted, or someone else can call referenda as well (most likely parliament)*
1 *President can call referenda, but needs parliamentary approval as well*
0 No authority to propose referenda

Non-Legislative Powers

Cabinet Formation

4 President names cabinet without need for confirmation or investiture
3 President names cabinet ministers subject to confirmation or investiture by assembly
2 *President appoints prime minister, and then both appoint ministers together*
1 President names premier, subject to investiture, who then names other ministers

TABLE 4.A.2. (*cont.*)

0	President cannot name ministers except upon recommendation of assembly

Cabinet Dismissal

4	President dismisses cabinet ministers at will
3	*President can dismiss ministers at will, but not prime minister*
2	*President can dismiss ministers, but it is in some way restricted either by the assembly or, in the case of a president, by the prime minister.*
1	*Either president can dismiss government (or individual minister) but must have a replacement approved by the assembly first or president does not have right to initiate dismissal of a minister or government, but does have to approve the action once initiated by someone else (usually the assembly)*
0	*President plays no role in dismissing government or ministers*

Censure

4	Assembly may not censure and remove cabinet or ministers
2	Assembly may censure, but president may respond by dissolving assembly
1	Constructive vote of no confidence (assembly majority must present alternative cabinet)
0	Unrestricted censure

Dissolution of Assembly

4	Unrestricted
3	*Negative restrictions (president/prime minister is free to dissolve assembly unless certain conditions apply, i.e. within last six months)*
2	*President can dissolve assembly, but it may lead to new presidential elections as well (does not apply to prime ministers)*
1	*Positive restrictions (president/prime minister can only dissolve assembly if certain conditions apply, i.e. assembly has failed to pass budget within certain time period)*
0	No Provisions

5

Compensatory Vote in Federations

Evidence from Germany

5.1 INTRODUCTION

Let us return to the 1998 federal elections in Germany, which I introduced in Chapter 1, and to some of the fifteen land elections following it. Concurrent with the general elections on September 27, the state of Mecklenburg-Western Pomerania held elections for its land assembly. The Social Democrats and the Greens, winning a majority in the Bundestag, received almost identical support in the state in both federal and land elections – only 1.2 percentage points less in the latter compared with the former. Four and a half months later, in February 1999, the state of Hesse held elections for its assembly. The vote share of the national governing coalition was 3.2 percentage points less than it had been in the federal elections in the land. Seven months later, in September 1999, Saarland, Brandenburg, Thuringia, and Saxony held regional elections. The Reds and the Greens lost support in each of the four states by 13.6 percentage points on average.[1] Next were elections in Berlin in October 1999, with a 16.8 percent drop in public support for the governing coalition. Eight additional land elections took place in the coming months, with the governing coalition losing support in all but one, ending with elections in

---

[1] Saarland and Brandenburg held their elections on September 5, Thuringia on September 12, and Saxony on September 19. The vote share of the Red–Green coalition compared with the 1998 federal elections were 10.3, 5.9, 18, and 20.2 percentage points lower, respectively.

Saxony-Anhalt in April 2002, five months before the next federal elections, with 19.4 percentage points less than in the federal elections. It seemed that the Red–Green coalition was doomed.

But it wasn't. Following these recurring losses, the Social Democrats, led again by Gerhard Schroeder and the Greens led again by Joschka Fischer, won the federal elections in September 2002, formed the governing coalition in the Bundestag, and Schroeder again became the Chancellor of Germany. The incumbent national government that had incurred many regional losses was reelected to office.

One might wonder if this was specific to the 1998–2002 cycle. After all, this was a period in which Germany suffered from high unemployment and was still struggling to recover from the economic shock of reunification. Additionally, the 2002 elections were immediately preceded by major floods, which presented an unexpected opportunity for Schroeder to reestablish his leadership and appear on election day with a positive impression fresh in voters minds. Figure 5.1 presents the change in vote share of the parties in control of the Bundestag (in black) for three additional federal cycles. The top panel of the figure presents the combined performance of the CDU/CSU and the FDP in the regional elections following the Bundestag elections of 1994 in which the two formed a coalition and secured a majority. This cycle was chosen in order to examine more closely both cycles in which the left was in power and cycles in which the right ruled. Since the German party system had gone through a transformation after reunification, it is important to also examine elections prior to the 1990s. The middle and bottom panels show the difference in electoral returns for the SPD and the FDP in the 1976–1980 and the 1972–1976 cycles in West Germany in which they held a majority in the Bundestag. The two cycles in the 1970s are difficult cases; they are both followed by an additional victory for the incumbent federal government, and therefore the losses the federal government incurred in them were not simply a signal of future electoral performance.

The black bars represent the difference between the combined vote share of the two parties in power in the state legislative elections and the combined vote share of the two parties *in the same region* in the preceding Bundestag elections. The vote share in each election is measured by the second vote. For expository purposes, I present elections chronologically, where elections that took place in the same month are displayed next to each other. The figure presents a reality consistent with the 1998–2002 cycle. The party in power loses support in almost

all regional elections. In some cases, the greater losses took place early
on or in the middle of the cycle; in others they did toward the end of the
cycle; and in yet others the losses were relatively constant throughout.

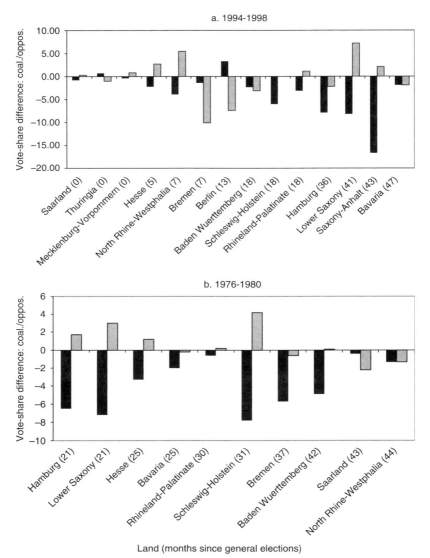

FIGURE 5.1. Vote-share differential: federal and land elections
Note: Black bars represent the change in vote share of the coalition parties between
federal and land elections. Gray bars represent similar change for main ideologically
opposed parties on the other side of the political center of gravity.

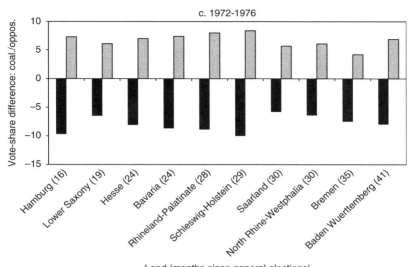

FIGURE 5.1. (continued)

Does this pattern hold beyond the three cycles? Figure 5.2 presents all gaps in vote share between state and federal elections between 1965 and 2002. The length of all federal cycles is normalized to one, such that the zero point on the horizontal axis represents the Bundestag elections and one represents the last month of each of the federal cycles prior to the next federal elections. Therefore, the timing of each election as noted on the chart is the fraction of time since the last Bundestag elections.[2] As in Figure 5.1, the vertical bars represent the difference between the federal and state vote shares of the parties in control of the Bundestag in the relevant cycle, and all cycles are superimposed on one another. Figure 5.2 reveals that the same pattern observed in the three cycles discussed earlier holds true across almost all cycles.[3] The parties of the governing coalition in the Bundestag lose support in the following state elections *in the same regions in which they did well only a few months earlier*, with 6 percent being the average loss.

[2] For presentational purposes, I slightly adjusted the timing of the elections, so that bars representing elections that took place on the same day do not overlap. For this reason the horizontal axis extends slightly past the zero-one interval.

[3] The 1969 federal cycle is an exception to this pattern.

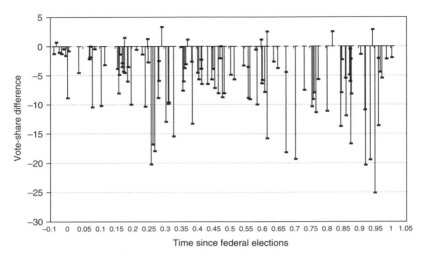

FIGURE 5.2. Electoral divergence: federal and land elections
Note: The bars represent vote-share difference between federal and regional elections. All elections between 1965–2002 are superimposed, and appear according to their timing in the federal electoral cycle.

What can explain this pattern? Why do parties that win voter support in general elections lose electoral ground in subsequent elections, sometimes only weeks later? My analysis here focuses on land and federal elections in Germany as a case study of voter behavior in federal systems. The institutional design of the German system, along with almost forty years of elections that I analyze here (1965–2002), allows for an instructive analysis of voter behavior pertaining to the questions in this study. First, the different schedules of electoral cycles of federal and land elections give me an opportunity to understand voter motivation. Although the vast majority of land elections take place non-concurrently with federal elections, a few are held concurrently. Additionally, different schedules of electoral cycles across länder – regional elections take place at different points in the federal cycle – allow me to examine explanations related to timing. Lastly, comparing years in which the left is in power with ones in which the right is in power, and years of economic prosperity with years of stagnation, enables me to consider various alternative explanations.

The rest of the chapter is organized as follows. In the next section, I examine possible explanations for the documented persistent vertical electoral divergence. I then empirically analyze voter behavior in German land elections, parsing out the potential accounts. I next assess the degree to which my results for Germany can be generalized to other polities. I then review, with a broad brush, vertical electoral divergence in a sample of other mutli-level governance systems. In the final section, I present my conclusions and discuss extensions to the analysis conducted here.

5.2 ELECTORAL CYCLES IN FEDERATIONS: POTENTIAL EXPLANATIONS

By now, my proposed explanation might not come as a surprise. I laid out the argument in detail in Chapter 2, but I will review it briefly here. Voters, I argue, are concerned with policy. In federations, their vote choice reflects the fact that policy is a product of both regional and federal policy inputs, and that the two levels of government share power. Once the composition of federal government is announced, voters are able to use regional elections to balance the federal government in a way that is impossible under concurrent elections: when the federal arm of the seesaw is anchored, voters can use regional elections to pull policy in the opposite direction. Thus, when the federal government is intact, voters often use regional elections to compensate for policy inputs of the federal government; when the Bundestag is controlled by a center-left government, voters often withdraw their support from the left in subsequent land elections and turn to the right, and when the center-right is in power in Berlin, they turn left in their land. They do so such that the combined regional–federal policy is more moderate than the policy the federal government would have pursued had it governed the entire federation on its own.

There are two strongly related, albeit distinct, routes by which compensatory vote in Germany may work. The first, central-regional compromise, is through the relationship between the federal and regional governments. Using this route, since the central government is authorized with setting a general framework for legislation and the regions are responsible for details and implementation, voters may utilize their votes in regional elections to compensate for vertical post-electoral compromise between Berlin and their own land. The second route, the bicameral compromise, works through Berlin politics itself.

Under this route, voters may use their regional votes to affect the composition of the Bundesrat, and thereby the decision making of the central government itself via the representatives sent to the Bundesrat by regional governments. Since the Bundesrat has more power over legislation involving regional issues than over other legislation, this route presents a way by which voters may utilize their regional votes to compensate for bicameral compromise over regional politics.

The logic of both routes works in the same direction, and leads voters to shun parties in control of majority in the Bundestag for compensatory considerations. A priori, the former route offers a more direct effect on policy via policy implementation in the länder, and might seem more plausible. Additionally, the second route implies that loss of support in regional elections should occur only when both chambers are controlled by the same party, and a tipping point of change of majority in the Bundesrat is within reach. Yet as presented in Figure 5.2, loss of support for the parties in power occurs in the vast majority of regional elections. Nonetheless, analyzing land elections in the post-war period, Kern and Hainmuller (2006) show that the loss of voter support is greater when a party (or a coalition) holds a majority in both chambers.[4] Thus, although the former route seems like the more natural one via which voters can compensate, I do not rule out the latter route.

In this context, it is important to mention two particular studies that explore the policy-moderation hypothesis in Germany, albeit in a contained fashion. Inspired by the study of Congressional elections in the United States, Lohmann et al. (1997) examine the effect of party attachment, the state of the economy (retrospective voting in particular), and policy moderation between 1961 and 1989. The authors find support for all three hypotheses. Following Lohmann et al., Gaines and Crombez (2004) examine whether the patterns found in the 1960s through the 1980s persist after German reunification. They find further support for both the moderating-elections hypothesis and economic voting. Neither study, however, finds direct evidence for policy moderation. Rather, they demonstrate how the party in power nationally loses in regional polls.

Compensatory vote, however, is not the only potential explanation. Indeed, different theoretical perspectives have been employed to

---

[4] The authors define loss as difference in vote share from one land election to another in a given land rather than across levels of government, as I do here.

analyze land elections in Germany. Several alternative explanations should be thus considered. Some of these explanations will be familiar from the previous chapter, as they are common to multi-office elections in general. I thus reintroduce them here only briefly; where relevant, I elaborate on the way they apply to vertical, as opposed to horizontal, compensation.

Second-order elections. In a pioneering study of the first direct elections for the European Parliament, Reif and Schmitt (1980) propose that these elections be treated as second-order elections in the national political arena. Voters in these elections, they contend, vote with national considerations in mind, yet apply different decision rules from the ones they apply in national elections. The second-order elections thesis is a key contender explanation for the regional slump of federal incumbents.

The model that Reif and Schmidt use is adapted from a model of second-order elections proposed by Dinkel (1977) to explain land elections in West Germany. Second-order elections are first and foremost elections in which less is at stake in comparison with national elections. They are also (and some would argue, therefore) characterized by low levels of participation, success of small parties, and poor performance of national ruling parties. As for the success that small parties enjoy in second-order elections, Reif and Schmitt argue that voters, being free from strategic considerations that would apply to the national level, vote with their hearts in second-order elections, and this in turn benefits small parties.

This theoretical framework was used further to analyze subsequent elections for the European Parliament (Marsh and Franklin 1996; Marsh 1998). Having limited legislative capabilities, and more importantly, having no effect on the composition of the main executive body, the European Parliament is often referred to as a quasi-parliament. And although its authorities have increased substantially in the past decade (Kreppel 2006), the second-order framework is still particularly appealing for analysis of EP elections.

The framework suggests the examination of land elections as a specific form of second-order elections. According to this approach, voters regard regional politics as having substantially less at stake than national politics, turn against the parties in power in the Bundestag and support the opposition, support small parties more than they do in federal elections, and turn out in lower rates. If land elections are second-order, we should find them characterized by these regularities.

Turnout/surge and decline. An important ingredient of the second-order elections thesis, yet also an explanation on its own, is differential turnout. I elaborated on the potential effect of turnout in Chapter 4, discussing how turnout might affect the divergence in results between general and legislative elections in presidential systems. Briefly, the idea is that the set of voters who turn out in federal elections does not completely overlap with the set of voters turning out in regional elections. In second-order elections, "not only may fewer people vote, but those not voting may be drawn disproportionately from certain groups" (Marsh and Franklin 1996, 24). Therefore, even without any individual shifting her vote choice, different turnout rates can affect second-order election returns. In other words, the parties in power federally do poorly in regional elections since voters who turn out in high rates in these elections vote for change, and voters preferring continuity stay at home at high rates. The discrepancy in returns between the two elections, then, is simply a reflection of differences between two groups of voters that make it to the voting booth.

Trend. We might wonder if the electoral performance of the parties in power is simply a result of a natural change in the climate of opinions of the electorate and is reflected in subsequent federal elections. In other words, any regional election taking place at a certain point in the federal electoral cycle might simply be an opportunity allowing us to measure support for the party holding power in Berlin. If this is the case, then the results of regional elections are not out of the general trend of public support of the incumbent government, and in fact serve as a good predictor of subsequent federal elections.

Divided agenda. In their analysis of electoral divergence between the provinces and Ottawa, Johnston and Cutler (2003) raise the possibility that the two arenas are not linked in Canadians' minds. Voters, they propose, vote on one set of issues in federal elections and on a different set in regional elections. Thus, there may be two separate distributions of voter opinions, each one relevant for a different arena. Relatedly, we might wonder if voters simply prefer some parties to be responsible for national issues and others for regional issues.

If the agendas of the two arenas are indeed separate, we can expect voters to compartmentalize their considerations: when casting their ballots for regional elections, they may weigh regional issues and set aside what happens in Berlin, and when casting a ballot for federal elections, they may ignore their land politics. Furthermore, we are likely to observe some systematic patterns in voter preference over time within each arena, supporting certain parties for particular offices.

The economy. It is not news that the state of the economy might affect voter tendency to support the incumbent government. Whether prospective or retrospective, pocket-book or sociotropic, perceived or objective, in emerging or established democracies, the state of the economy matters (Alt and Alesina 1998; Duch 2001; Duch and Stevenson 2008; Lewis-Beck and Stegmaier 2000; MacKuen, Erikson, and Stimson 1992). Partisan explanations of electoral cycles carry limited weight in this case since each region has little impact on economic policy (exchange and interest rates were set centrally by the Deutsche Bank, and as a part of the transition to a single European market, the German government has lost control over monetary policy instruments). For these reasons and, of course, the small size of some of the länder, most German regions are generally quite vulnerable to trends in the national and global economies.

Nonetheless, one might expect that a prosperous economy in a region would be reflected in support for the incumbent government. In federations, the state of the economy might play a part in several ways. The state of the economy of a region can affect voter satisfaction with the incumbent government directly – voters might simply evaluate the state of the economy in their region. Alternatively, the economy can affect public opinion indirectly via comparison with other regions or with the national economy. Whether we use direct or indirect comparison, we might expect the incumbent party to incur a smaller loss (or even be rewarded) when the economy does well.

Lastly, it is important to note that while compensatory vote or any of the contenders I mention here are potential explanations for drop in voter support, standard models of issue voting – namely, proximity and directional voting – are unable to account for the systematic drop of support for the incumbent parties between federal and regional elections. Simply put, absent institutional context, to account for the repeated loss of support by parties in power, proximity or directional theories would have to argue that voter positions repeatedly shift, each time in the opposite direction from the parties in power, sometimes only weeks after the general elections. Such repeated shifting in the relevant direction may make the arithmetics of loss and victory add up, but it carries little political reasoning. I turn now to an examination of the data in an attempt to parse out the candidate explanations.

5.3 EMPIRICAL ANALYSIS

The aggregate data I analyze consist of all federal and state elections in Germany between 1961 and 2002. They include 117 elections in 12 länder prior to reunification and in 16 post-reunification, as well as 11 federal elections. The vast majority of regional elections in the relevant period were non-concurrent with federal elections; only 6 took place simultaneously. The number of regional elections in each federal cycle (usually four years) varied between 9 and 15 (with the exception of one cycle of five), with a modal category of ten. Most elections took place one land at a time, with a small portion grouped in pairs, and one occurrence of three. With a few exceptions, each land held its elections at the same time in the federal cycle throughout the period.

Who gains from the incumbent's loss? In the previous chapter, I demonstrated how the party of the president loses support in legislative elections. In this chapter, drawing on data from a single country over time, I am able to go one step further and cross support for the ideological (parliamentary) opposition with that of the incumbent federal government.

For each land election in Figure 5.1, next to the drop of support for the parties in power, I present the change in support for the main opposition parties on the other side of the left-right center of gravity (in gray). For 1994–1998, I present the combined change in support for the SPD and the Greens, and in the 1972–1976 and 1976–1980 cycles, I present the change in support for the CDU/CSU. As the three panels show, the parties of the governing coalition at the federal level did poorly in almost all subsequent state elections. Although the degree of withdrawal of support across states varies, the general pattern is overwhelming. The main parties of the ideological opposition to the incumbent government, it is easy to see, usually win a similar portion of the votes lost by the coalition (although, of course, we cannot infer from this aggregate analysis that certain individuals shifted their support from one party to another). Overall, the left did relatively well in state elections in the 1994–1998 cycle, while the right did well in the 1972–1980 cycles, with the 1976–1980 period showing a somewhat looser fit. A majority of those cases in which the loss and gain of support do not match one another are ones in which the electoral system at the regional level – personalized proportional representation with one ballot – is slightly different from that at the national level (Baden-Wuerttemberg, Bremen, North Rhine-Westphalia in Panels a and b, and Hamburg in Panel b).

It is clear, then, that when the left controls Berlin, voters turn right in their region, and when the right rules the federation, voters turn left. In the next stage, I examine possible explanations for this regularity.

Second-order elections. While elections for the European Parliament seem like a natural case of second-order elections, the case of land elections is less obvious. Although the centrality of the Bundestag cannot be denied, the länder affect policy in multiple ways. First, they do so directly through regional politics and implementation of federal policy decisions. Since the states are tasked with policy implementation, the central government has to cooperate with the state governments and their bureaucracies. Putting the formation of German institutions into historical perspective, Lehmbruch (2000) describes regional–national power sharing as characterized by "strong elements of bargaining and quasi-diplomatic accommodation at the executive level" (89). Most obviously, representatives of state governments vote according to instructions from state capitals in the Bundesrat. The states' interests are also represented in most committee deliberations by civil servants (90). In spite of these differences, it is important to allay potential concerns regarding the second-order hypothesis as a contender. I thus examine next whether the characteristics of second-order elections are present in land elections.

One of the characteristics I mentioned earlier is withdrawal of support from the parties in power, and in particular, greater support for small parties at the expense of large parties, compared with their support in the general elections. This withdrawal of support, combined with withdrawal of support for the incumbent coalition, implies that if land elections are second order, then the senior member of the coalition will incur a greater loss of support than the junior member.

Empirical Evidence

Figure 5.3 compares the change of support for the senior coalition member with change of support for the junior member in black and gray, respectively (CDU/CSU compared with FDP in Panel a, and SDP

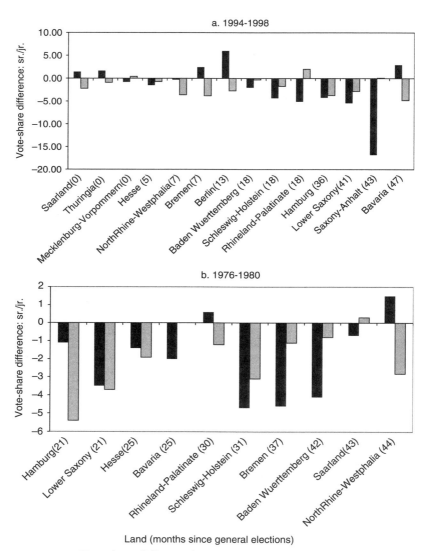

FIGURE 5.3. Vote-share differential: senior and junior coalition partners
Note: The black bars represent the difference in vote share between federal and regional elections of the senior coalition partner. The gray bars represent the same quantity for junior coalition partner.

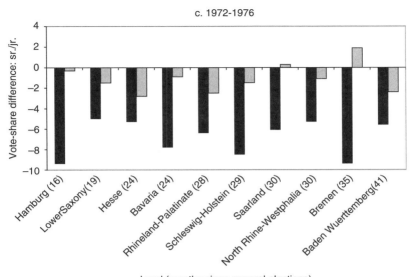

FIGURE 5.3. (continued)

compared with FDP in Panels b and c). As in Figure 5.2, change of
support is calculated in the form of differences: the fraction of votes the
party received in the land elections minus its vote share in the preceding
federal elections. The figure reveals no systematic pattern with regard to
the difference between the two parties. In some elections, as in most of
the 1972–1976 cycle, both parties experience a withdrawal of support,
and the senior member experiences a substantially greater withdrawal of
support than its junior partner. In others cycles, as in the first and middle
parts of the 1994–1998 cycle, the senior member actually gains voter
support, and the junior member loses. Yet in other cases, such as early on
in the 1976–1980 cycle, both parties lose support, but the loss by the
junior member is greater than that of the senior member. In sum, there is
no obvious pattern of loss of voter support by small parties compared
with that of large coalition parties.

One might still wonder whether difference in vote share is the
appropriate way to measure changes in party support. After all,
the loss of 3 percentage points for a party that enjoys 35 percent of the
voters may be different from the same drop in support for a party
enjoying 6 percent. Figure 5.4 examines the change in support for the
senior and junior coalition members (in black and gray, respectively)

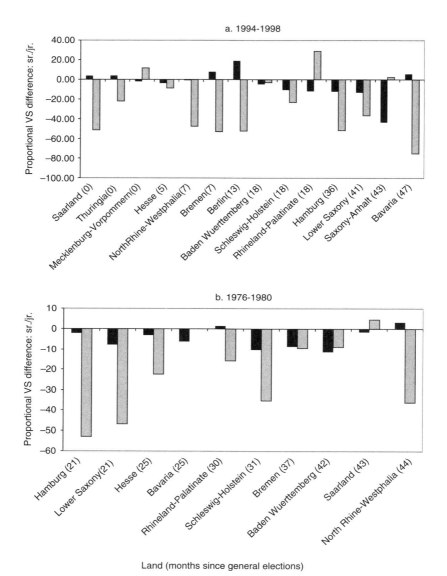

FIGURE 5.4. Vote-share differential proportions: senior and junior coalition partners
Note: The black bars represent the fraction of votes lost (gained) by the senior coalition partner between federal and regional elections. The gray bars represent the same quantity for the junior coalition partner.

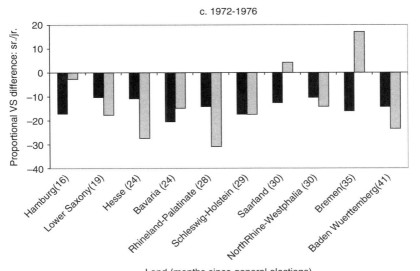

FIGURE 5.4. (continued)

as a *fraction* of their vote shares in the last federal elections.[5] The figure reveals that the volatility between federal and regional elections is greater for the junior member than for the senior member when measured in relative terms. It is not uncommon for the junior member to lose as much as 30 percent of its share. The volatility of support for the senior member is substantially smaller, hovering around 10 percent. Moreover, the gap between the two differences changes considerably from one election to another. In some elections, the relative loss of support is similar for the senior and junior members, while in others it is quite different. Overall, then, we do not observe that the senior incumbent incurs a greater loss of support than its junior partner.

Turnout. What part does turnout play in land elections? Turnout in federal elections is higher than in land elections: the average (non-weighted) turnout in federal elections across states is 84.9 percent in the relevant period, while the (non-weighted) average turnout in land elections is 73.9 percent. Does turnout differential account for the gap in vote share? Recall

---

[5] For each party, I calculate $\%difference_j^{t,l} = \frac{-100 \times \left(VS.Fed_j^{t-1,l} - VS.Land_j^{t,l}\right)}{VS.Fed_j^{t-1,l}}$, where $VS.Land_j^{t,l}$ is the vote share of party j in the elections for land l, and $VS.Fed_j^{t-1,l}$ is the vote share of party j in land l in the federal elections immediately preceding the land elections.

that the turnout hypothesis predicts a negative relationship: if a different cadre of voters turns out in regional elections compared with federal elections, then the greater the turnout differential from federal to state elections, the bigger the loss for the parties in power at the federal level.

Figure 5.5 displays the turnout differential between regional and federal elections against vote-share differential for each regional election in the relevant time frame (n = 107). For each election I calculate the difference between turnout in the land in federal elections and turnout in the same land in the regional elections that immediately follow. Thus, a higher score on the horizontal axis indicates a greater gap between (higher) turnout in general elections and (lower) turnout in regional elections. The figure reveals a weak negative, albeit not a striking, relationship between the two. Consistently, the correlation between the change of vote share between the two types of elections in a given state and the turnout differential between the two in the state is –0.17 (p-value = 0.09), suggesting a weak relationship: a greater drop of turnout is associated with moderately larger drop in voter support for the incumbent parties.

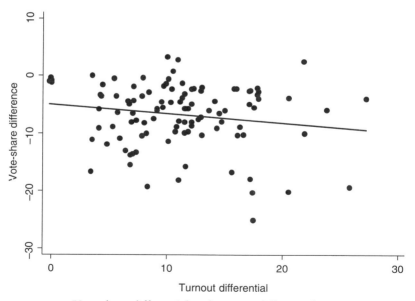

FIGURE 5.5. Vote-share differential and turnout differential

Note: For each land election, the figure presents difference in turnout between that election and the previous federal election on the horizontal axis, against difference in voter support on the vertical axis.

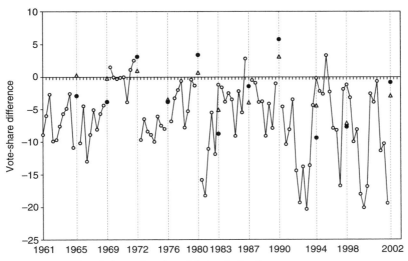

FIGURE 5.6. Trends in regional and federal elections

Note: Empty circles represent change in vote share for the coalition parties between federal and land elections. Vertical lines mark federal elections. Large black circles represent change in seat share for the parties in power federally, and the triangles represent the same quantity for the senior coalition partner alone.

Trend. Earlier I raised the possibility that each regional election is simply a time slice measuring voter sentiments. Land elections, according to this explanation, are not inherently different from federal elections. Rather, they are an opportunity to look at vote intentions leading up to the next federal elections. Figure 5.6 provides some insight into this possibility. The figure presents all federal and regional elections between 1961 and 2002, with vertical bars marking each federal election. Change of voter support for the federal incumbent between the last federal and regional elections is marked with an empty circle, and multiple elections are connected with a line. All measures are based on the second vote. The placement of elections on the horizontal axis reflects their chronological order. When more than one regional election took place at a given point, the graph presents the average change in vote share. The large black circles represent the change in seat share of the parties in power from one federal election to another, and the triangles the change in seat share for the senior partner in the coalition only.[6] For example, in the 1965 federal elections, the Christian

---

[6] The high degree of proportionality in the German system makes seat share and vote share based on the second vote highly compatible measures.

Democrats and Free Democrats – the coalition in power since the 1961 elections – lost 3 percent of their seats in the Bundestag. However, this loss was incurred by the Free Democrats; the Christian Democrats maintained their support level, as the relevant triangle indicates.

The figure allows us to evaluate whether the results of regional elections are consistent with subsequent federal elections. As the figure demonstrates, the results of the two types of elections are unrelated to one another in most cycles. Only in 1969, 1972, and to some degree in 1983 are the results of the federal arena consistent with those of the regional arena. In all other cycles, the figure reveals an appreciable difference between electoral results in the two arenas. This is true both when the change in the federal arena is measured for the two coalition partners and when it is measured for the senior member alone. Lastly, it is important to note that in eight out of the eleven federal cycles between 1965 and 2002, the parties in power were reelected to office. It seems, then, that regional elections are not simply a preview for federal elections, nor do they establish a trend that is then picked up at the federal arena.

Divided agenda. Do Germans think of the regional and federal arenas as two separate ones? Is the vertical electoral divergence simply a byproduct of federalism? What are voters concerned with when casting their ballot in regional elections? Do they think about politics in their own land or are they concerned with what is happening in Berlin? In a series of public opinion surveys conducted before surveys seven regional elections in 1982–1983, voters were asked about the role federal politics played in their vote decision in the land. In particular, they were asked: "Recently, it has been frequently said that federal politics plays an increasingly larger role during state elections. How about you: Is it more important for your decision what happens in (state) or in Bonn?" The weight a voter gives to federal politics in her regional vote choice is relevant for the framework we may use to analyze that choice. If few voters report such a connection, we can infer that regional elections are indeed about regional issues, and the political agenda is divided (Johnston and Cutler 2003). In other words, if the agenda is divided, neither the second-order framework nor the compensatory framework is relevant for understanding electoral divergence. However, if many declare that such a connection exists, either of the two frameworks (or yet another explanation) might apply.

Table 5.1 presents a summary of respondent reactions. As the table shows, the proportion of voters indicating that the federal arena

TABLE 5.1. *Perceived Importance of Political Arenas*

	State	Bonn	Both	Total
Bavaria	47.7	50.4	1.9	1073
Bremen	65.9	33.4	0.7	1015
Hamburg (6/82)	64.9	33.4	1.7	940
Hamburg (12/82)	63.0	35.4	1.7	1058
Hesse	58.1	36.6	5.3	995
Lower Saxony	51.4	48.6	0.0	1017
Rhineland-Palatinate	46.9	51.5	1.6	945
Schleswig-Holstein	54.0	42.0	4.1	1012
Average (unweighted)	56.5	41.4	2.1	

Note: Surveys were conducted in seven different states in 1982–1983. Respondents were asked: "Recently, it has been frequently said that federal politics plays an increasingly larger role during state elections. How about you: Is what happens in (state) or in Bonn more important for your decision?"

affects their choice varies, but is generally quite appreciable. It is as low as 33 percent in Bremen and Hamburg and as high as 50 percent and more in Bavaria and Rhineland-Palatinate. Altogether, on average, 41 percent report that federal politics affects their vote choice in the land, and 2 percent report that both federal and regional affairs make a difference. A substantial portion of the public, then, reports that the two arenas are linked in their view.

An examination of aggregate patterns of federal and regional governments across länder and time (Table 5.2) complements the picture. For each federal cycle between 1961 and 1998, I note the senior party in office at the federal level as well as the one in each of the regions. In gray are regional governments whose senior party is in agreement with the senior coalition party in the Bundestag. In stripes are regional unity governments. The table reveals several things. First, the degree of divergence between regional and national governments varies over time. Some cycles, such as the 1994–1998 cycle, are characterized by a great divergence between Berlin and the regional capitals, while others, as the 1969–1972 or the 1983–1987 cycles, are characterized by agreement. Second, different regions tends to go in different directions (see also Lohman et al. 1997). Some, like Bavaria, systematically turn to the right, while others, like Bremen or Hamburg, turn left. These strongly partisan länder, which have a clear political

TABLE 5.2. *Regional and Federal Governments: Convergence and Divergence*

	1961	1965	1969	1972	1976	1980	1983	1987	1990	1994	1998
Bundestag	CDU*	CDU**	SDP	SDP	SDP	SDP	CDU	CDU	CDU	CDU	SDP
Bavaria	CSU	CSU	CSU	CSU	CSU	CSU	CSU	CSU	CSU	CSU	
Lower Saxony	SDP	CDU+SDP	SDP	SDP	CDU	CDU	CDU	SDP	SDP	SDP	
Baden-Wuerttemberg	CDU	CDU+SDP	CDU	CDU	CDU	CDU	CDU	CDU	CDU	CDU	CDU
Hesse	SDP	SDP	SDP	SDP	SDP	SDP	SDP	SDP	SDP	SDP	CDU
North Rhine-Westphalia	CDU	CDU	SDP	SDP	SDP	SDP	SDP	SDP	SDP	SDP	SDP
Saarland	CDU		CDU	CDU	CDU		SDP	SDP	SDP	SDP	CDU
Schleswig-Holstein	CDU	CDU	CDU	CDU	CDU		CDU	CDU	SDP	SDP	SDP
Rhineland-Palatinate	CDU	CDU	CDU	CDU	CDU		CDU	CDU	SDP	SDP	SDP
Bremen	SDP	SDP	SDP	SDP	SDP		SDP	SDP	SDP	CDU+SDP	CDU+SDP
Berlin	SDP	SDP	SDP	SDP	SDP	CDU	CDU	SDP	SDP+CDU	SDP+CDU	SDP+CDU
Hamburg	SDP	SDP	SDP	SDP	SDP	SDP***	SDP****	SDP	SDP	SDP	SDP
Brandenburg									SDP	SDP	SDP+CDU
Saxony									CDU	CDU	CDU
Thuringia									CDU	SDP+CDU	CDU
Saxony-Anhalt									CDU	SDP	SDP
Mecklenburg–Western Pomerania									CDU	SDP+CDU	SDP

* At the federal level 'CDU' stands for CDU/CSU.

** In 1966, a national unity government was formed.

*** The CDU was unable to form a coalition.

Note: Each cell denotes the senior party in office, with the federal government in gray. Regional governments in agreement (by senior party in office) with the federal government in gray. Regional unity governments are in stripes.

direction, complement each other in the years in which they diverge from Berlin (e.g., Bavaria and Hamburg). Additionally, some länder are more often at odds with the government in Berlin (e.g., Saarland), while others are more often in agreement with it (e.g. Baden Wuerttemberg). Lastly, as the table shows, voters turn against both left-leaning federal governments and right-leaning governments, mitigating the suspicion that Germans have a taste for some specific vertical division of labor between left and right across political arenas.

The economy. How does a region's economy affect electoral outcomes? To test for the effect of the economy, I examined the effect of (quarterly) growth in the region on the same quantity of interest as used earlier – change in voter support for the incumbent from federal elections. I conducted the analysis in various ways, all yielding similar results, and here I report the results of the most elaborate analysis. I first examined the correlation between economic growth and vote differential over time, land by land. I then examined the correlation across regions, cycle be cycle. Neither analysis produced a systematic pattern – I did not detect a relationship between the economy in a region and support for the incumbent federal government. I also pooled all elections across regions and cycles. Still the data showed no systematic pattern.

One might wonder whether voters perceive economic performance in a region in comparison with other regions or with the country at large, rather than on its own. I repeated the analysis employing the difference between regional and national economic growth,[7] turning economic prosperity into a relative quantity of performance. Here, too, both state-by-state and cycle-by-cycle analyses showed no effect. Finally, I conducted one additional analysis utilizing the relative measure and pooling all elections and regions. Figure 5.7 presents this analysis, with growth differential on the horizontal axis and change in vote share on the vertical axis. As in the previous analysis, the data show no systematic relationship between the two.

On their own, then, each of the usual candidate explanations does not seem to account for the withdrawal in vote share. I now turn to a more comprehensive analysis.

Table 5.3 presents a preliminary breakdown of the withdrawal of support presented in Figure 5.2. The average vote-share loss of

---

[7] For the latter, I use annual rate.

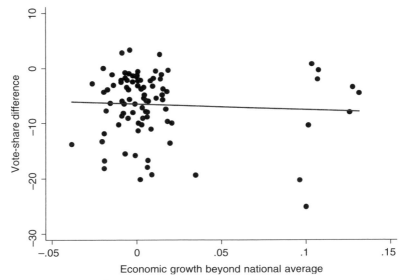

FIGURE 5.7. Vote-share differential and regional economy
Note: For each land election, the figure presents difference in economic growth between that land and the national average on the horizontal axis, against difference in voter support on the vertical axis. Regression line is superimposed.

TABLE 5.3. *Change of Vote Share – Some Comparisons*

	Mean	S.E.	(min, max)	N
Average change	−6.0	5.4	(−20.3, 3.3)	117
Average change w/o 1969	−6.6	5.2	(−20.3, 3.3)	107
Timing				
Staggered	−6.9	5.2	(−20.3, 3.3)	101
Concurrent	−0.7	0.7	(−1.2, 0.7)	6
Government ideology				
SPD in power (Fed)	−7.9	5.5	(−20.2, 2.5)	40
CDU in power (Fed)	−5.8	4.9	(−20.3, 3.3)	67
Post-unification				
West	−6.5	5.2	(−19.3, 2.5)	29
East	−9.2	8.7	(−20.3, 3.3)	15
Post-unification staggered				
West	−6.7	5.2	(−19.3, 2.5)	28
East	−12.4	8.0	(−20.3, 3.3)	11

members of the national coalition across all 117 länder is 6 percentage points. The distribution of these losses is left skewed, with a maximum loss of just over 20 percent and a maximum gain of 3 percentage points. While almost all federal cycles resemble the three cycles presented in Figure 5.1, the 1969 cycle (not presented separately) is an outlier to this pattern. After a center-right government was formed following the 1965 elections, a grand coalition was formed in January 1966, and remained in office until 1969. The 1969 cycle took place right after this first changing of the guard at the federal level since World War II, and the Christian Democrats were voted out of office. It is possible that voters considered this transition as a shift toward a unified center-left government, and therefore supported the SDP in land elections as well.[8] Furthermore, this early period of Ostpolitik in which West Germany attempted to establish a more harmonious relationship with East Germany is characterized by particularly high levels of optimism and momentum in German politics, and thus might break standard patterns. The following comparisons therefore include 107 elections, excluding the 1969 federal cycle.

Consistent with the compensatory prediction, a preliminary comparison of concurrent and staggered elections suggests that the loss is greater when voters know with certainty who has secured a majority in the Bundestag (an average of 6.9 percentage points in non-concurrent elections compared with 0.7 percentage points in concurrent ones). A comparison of loss of support during periods in which the left had control of the federal government versus periods in which the right was in power shows no systematic differences: the average loss when the SDP is the senior partner of the coalition is 7.9 percentage points, compared with 5.8 when the CDU/CSU is in office. Similarly, comparison of the regions of the former West Germany with those of the former East Germany shows no systematic pattern, with the average loss in the East somewhat larger, yet not statistically different (9.2 compared with 6.5 in the West). However, when examining staggered elections only, the vote-share loss in the former East is greater than in the West, with more than a 12 percentage point loss in the East compared with more than 6 in the West.

Table 5.4 presents the results of a multivariate analysis of 103 land elections, focusing on the same quantity as before – the change in vote

---

[8] I thank Daniela Stockmann for her investigation of the 1969 cycle and the possible reasons for this exception.

TABLE 5.4. *Change of Vote Share, Multivariate Analysis*

	Model 1	Model 2	Model 3
Non-concurrent	−9.75 (<.01)	−10.83 (<.01)	−10.49 (<.01)
Turnout differential		0.09 (.40)	0.07 (.53)
Growth in region			10.36 (.54)
Former East	−6.69 (<.01)	−6.98 (<.01)	−7.34 (<.01)
Post-unification	−0.21 (.88)	−0.42 (.77)	−0.30 (.84)
SPD in power	−1.32 (.33)	−1.50 (.26)	−1.30 (.35)
Constant	4.20 (.07)	4.46 (.06)	4.01 (.12)
R^2	.26	.26	.26
N	103	103	103

P-values in parentheses. Panel corrected standard errors.

share per land between federal and regional elections – as a dependent variable. I compare three different models. The first accounts for the timing of elections (concurrent or non-concurrent), the second adds turnout differential, and the third adds economic growth in the region. In addition, all three models control for general region (East vs. West), period (pre- vs. post-reunification), and government ideology (left-leaning vs. right-leaning). The results show a consistent pattern. Most importantly, non-concurrent regional elections result in about a 10 percent drop of support for the parties in power. Importantly, these results hold once turnout differential and economic growth are taken into account (Models 2 and 3, respectively). Neither of the latter two, however, has a systematic effect on the change of voter support. That fewer voters turned out in regional elections compared with the federal baseline turnout in the land does not result in a systematic change of support, nor does economic growth in the region. Of the control variables, while the post-reunification period does not systematically differ from pre-reunification,[9] and government ideology does not have a systematic impact, the incumbent parties experience a greater loss of voter support in länder in the former East than in those in the former West. This finding is curious. To the extent that voters use land elections to balance the federal government, one might expect that those

---

[9] I also examined a more subtle specification in which I allowed the effect to increase over time, consistent with the increasing authorities of the Bundesrat. This specification did not yield any systematic results.

voters who were introduced to democratic governance only recently would be less accustomed to separation-of-power mechanisms compared with their experienced counterparts in the West. My data do not allow me to investigate the reason for this regional discrepancy. A possible, yet admittedly post-hoc, potential explanation is that voters in the former East are weary about the concentration of power in unified hands, and thus shun the parties of the federal government with greater zeal than do their counterparts in the former West.

This is an opportunity to bring into the analysis an additional important issue: the timing of the regional elections in the federal cycle. In their study of elections for the European Parliament, Marsh and Franklin (1996) find that the timing of the elections in the national cycle has a quadratic effect on the success of the party ruling at the national level. In those countries in which EP elections take place shortly after the national elections, voters reinforce their support for parties of the national government. The loss peaks when the elections take place half-way into the national cycle (see also Marsh 1998).

As Figure 5.2 shows, loss of voter support in land elections occurs immediately after the national elections. Dividing the electoral cycle into twenty segments of 0.05 each is illustrative. The average vote-share withdrawal in elections taking place in the first five segments of 0.05 of the federal cycle each (cumulatively, roughly the first year of a four-year cycle) are −5 percent for the first 0.05 of the cycle (N = 3), −7.7 percent for the second 0.05 portion of the cycle (N = 3), −6.8 percent for the third portion (N = 5), −4.4 percent for the fourth portion of the cycle (N = 7), and −9.8 percent for the last portion of the first year (N = 7). This tracing of the raw data of electoral outcomes early in the cycle, then, suggests that the withdrawal of support reaches a substantial magnitude shortly after the federal elections.

Although the separate cycles of the regions in the German system offer possibilities for a nuanced analysis of regional–federal electoral politics, they also raise questions as to what voters have in mind when they vote in their region at various times in the federal cycle. As I explain in Chapter 2, the compensatory logic relies on the premise of prospective voting. Voters overshoot or pull in a certain direction in anticipation of post-electoral dilution. This might work differently depending on when in the federal cycle regional elections take place. It is easy to see this logic at work early on in the cycle: shortly after a federal government is elected, voters might vote with knowledge of the direction that compromise will likely take in the coming four years. The motivation is somewhat less clear, however, toward the end of a cycle. When regional elections take place only months prior to the next federal elections, voters may not have a clear expectation about future policy; the government currently in office may or may not be reelected. It is thus harder to know what to balance against. While I am unable to examine voter considerations per se, as I will show, the results of elections taking place toward the end of the cycle do not systematically differ from those of elections taking place in other periods.

To gain further understanding of the effect of timing of the elections, I reestimated the models presented earlier, but included in the analysis a linear and quadratic specifications of timing measured as the fraction of time since the federal elections (as calculated in Figure 5.2). The timing of regional elections is relevant for two reasons. First, although not an inherent part of the core theoretical prediction, second-order elections were found to produce the greatest loss for the parties in power at midterm (van der Eijk and Franklin 1996). The quadratic specification can capture this effect. Second, consistent with a hypothesized explanation in the presidential arena, it is possible that the federal government spends its political capital on policy decisions, some of which are unpopular, and consequently incurs electoral losses. If this is the case, the loss of support may become more severe with time, as the government spends more and more of its capital. The linear specification can capture this effect. If voters react to political capital spending by withdrawing their support from the federal government, then the later in the cycle regional elections take place, the greater the withdrawal of support (a negative coefficient of a linear relationship).

Table 5.5 presents the results of six models, including combinations of turnout differential and economic growth as before, as well as combinations of timing (linear and quadratic specifications). As before, the models also control for region, period, and government ideology. The table illuminates several things. First, in all three quadratic specifications, the quadratic element holds statistically. Additionally, the explanatory power of the quadratic model is greater than that of the linear model across all specifications (R^2 of 0.21, 0.22, and 0.23 in the quadratic specification compared with 0.15, 0.16, and 0.19 in the three linear specifications). An examination of the linear and quadratic

TABLE 5.5. *Change of Vote Share, Multivariate Analysis Incorporating Timing*

	Model 1	Model 2	Model 3	Model 4	Model 5	Model 6
Time	−3.88 (.04)	−23.36 (<.01)	−3.60 (.06)	−22.28 (<.01)	−3.82 (.03)	−20.46 (<.01)
Time squared		19.28 (<.01)		18.35 (<.01)		16.42 (.02)
Turnout differential			−0.11 (.21)	−0.05 (.56)	−0.15 (.10)	−0.09 (.36)
Growth in region					34.88 (.03)	24.24 (.17)
East	−4.24 (.05)	−5.51 (<.01)	−4.21 (.04)	−5.43 (.01)	−5.72 (<.01)	−6.36 (<.01)
Post unification	−0.28 (.86)	−0.76 (.60)	−0.02 (.99)	−0.61 (.69)	0.32 (.85)	−0.31 (.84)
SPD in power	−1.45 (.37)	−0.33 (.83)	−1.17 (.46)	−0.24 (.87)	−0.47 (.76)	0.15 (.92)
Constant	−3.43 (.01)	−0.34 (.84)	−2.56 (.10)	−0.06 (.97)	−3.11 (.05)	−0.71 (.72)
R^2	.15	.21	.16	.22	.19	.23
N	103	103	103	103	103	103

P-values in parentheses. Panel-corrected standard errors.

effects shows a non-monotonic effect peaking between 0.6 and 0.62 of the cycle, roughly two years and five months into the federal cycle. However, an examination of the magnitude of the effect suggests that it is quite limited. As an example, under all three quadratic models, the predicted difference in loss of support between 0.3 of the cycle and 0.6 of the cycle (or 0.6 and 0.9), slightly over a year, is less than 2 percentage points of support. This is consistent with Figure 5.2, which does not present a striking quadratic pattern of the raw data. As for the additional variables, as before, the electoral cycle in the East is more dramatic in magnitude than in the West, but the left does not systematically differ from the right, and the pre-reunification period does not differ from post-reunification.

It might be helpful to take stock of the findings up to this point. The analysis reveals two sets of results. First, it establishes that national incumbents lose support in staggered regional elections. Second, it tests and rejects a set of candidate explanations found in the literature. Specifically, I demonstrate that the senior coalition member does not suffer a systematically greater loss than the junior member. I also show that the parties gaining from that loss are those ideologically opposed to the incumbent. Furthermore, a greater gap in turnout between federal and land elections within a land does not result in a greater loss of support for the national incumbent. The combination of these findings mitigates the second-order elections explanation and the surge and decline explanation. However, I find a minor effect of timing: the loss of voter support peaks shortly after midterm. I also demonstrate that the results of regional elections in Germany are not simply part of a trend – they do not predict subsequent national elections. I then show that the electoral discrepancy varies across regions but does not vary with party ideology. This, in combination with evidence showing that voters consider both national and regional arenas when casting their ballot in their region, suggests that the electoral divergence is not about vertically divided agendas. Lastly, I show that a thriving economy does not decrease the loss for the national incumbent. And although the data utilized here do not allow me to test the compensatory thesis directly, the combination of the aggregate tests, the analysis of the available individual-level data, the elimination of competing explanations, and the indirect tests, along with the direct tests in the other arenas presented in the previous chapters, come together to support the compensatory thesis.

5.4 GERMAN FEDERALISM AS A CASE STUDY

Unlike my empirical analysis in the parliamentary and presidential arenas, my analysis of vertical balancing in federations focuses on a single country. This choice has its advantages and pitfalls. On the one hand, although German länder obviously do differ from one another, with the exception of timing, there is little institutional variation relevant to my argument, allowing me enough leverage to test the effect of institutional variation. On the other hand, focusing on a single country over time allows for a controlled comparison more easily than cross-polity analysis does. In addition, the focus on a single country (and the availability of data) enables me to complement my aggregate data analysis with individual-level analysis. Nonetheless, the theoretical argument applies beyond the German case. The results from Germany, I argue, can be generalized to other federations and multi-level governance systems. Here I discuss the generalizability and the limitations of such an inference.

The German party system is regionally integrated. Although länder are different in their support of various parties, with the exception of the CSU in Bavaria, the party system is similar across länder. This is not the case in all federal systems. Lack of integration of regional and national party systems can be a result of several factors. Jeffery and Hough (2003) propose that the relationship between national and regional electoral dynamics depends on diversity across regions. The authors make a distinction between heterogeneous multi-level systems, such as Spain and Canada, and systems with relative homogeneity across regions, such as Germany. In the former, the authors argue, regionalist parties – those parties competing in only some regions or representing regional interests – lead to divergence between the regional or the national party systems. Thus, in regions that have a strongly defined sense of regional identity the party system tends to diverge from the national one, but in those that lack such identity, the regional electoral landscape is usually similar to the national landscape.

Analyzing sources of nationalization of party systems, Chhibber and Kollman (2004) contend that when the national government takes authority from the regions, a nationalized party system is more likely to evolve. When authority is centralized, voters have a greater incentive to vote based on national issues, and regional parties, for their part, have an incentive to take positions corresponding with their national sister parties, making party aggregation more likely.

Whether a consequence of heterogeneous population, heterogeneity in identity across regions, or concentration of authority at the subnational government level, a nationally disintegrated party system produces a different version of compensatory vote. In particular, compensatory vote may not result in the cycles of support and withdrawal of support of governing parties. After all, in a disintegrated party system a vote intended to compensate for the strength of party A at the national level might imply endorsements of different parties in different regions. At the extreme, since party labels have different meanings in different regions under a disintegrated party system, a vote for A in a given region can even balance the national party A.

In addition to the effect of partisan politics, the structure of federalism may affect how voters compensate for diffusion of power. As I discuss in Chapter 2, compensatory vote applies differently to interlocking federations than to dual ones. The vertical division of responsibilities between the länder and the federal government in Germany creates a system of interlocking political institutions. Germany is a cooperative federation, one in which, for a majority of policy areas, the federal government sets the policy framework and the länder are responsible for its implementation. Polities of dual federalism – those in which the central and regional governments split responsibility across jurisdictional lines – imply a somewhat different form of compensation. Under such systems, compensatory voting takes place *across policy areas* rather than within them.

Another factor is the degree of centralization of the multi-level governance system under study. Vertical compensatory vote may depend not only on how power is shared, but also on the degree to which it is shared across levels. Here I wish to put the degree of centralization of Germany in a comparative context. Schneider (2003) offers conceptualization and measurement of decentralization. He offers three core dimensions: fiscal decentralization – the degree to which the "central government cedes fiscal impact to non-central government entities"; administrative decentralization – the degree of "autonomy non-central government possesses relative to central control"; and political decentralization – the degree to which non-central government entities are authorized "to undertake the political functions of governance, such as representation"

(33). In a sample of sixty-eight countries (based on data from 1996), Germany is ranked twelfth on fiscal decentralization, twenty-seventh on administrative decentralization, and thirteenth on political decentralization, suggesting a high, but not outstanding, degree of decentralization. For instance, more decentralized than Germany on two or three of these dimensions are countries such as Argentina, Canada, Panama, and Russia, and on one of the three dimensions are Australia, Chile, India, Switzerland, the UK, and the United States.

Rodden (2004) offers a distinction among and interpretation of several aspects of decentralization: fiscal, policy, and political. He offers a modification to a commonly used expenditure decentralization measure. In particular, Rodden examines the expenditure that is funded by mobilization of "own-source" revenue through independent taxes and other means as a share of total government revenue. Rodden then offers a set of measures that capture different aspects of subnational revenue autonomy, and in particular, draws attention to the role of political institutions in decentralization. Of thirty-nine countries, Germany is fourteenth in its degree of decentralization on this dimension, neighboring with Australia, India, Italy, Peru, and Spain. German federalism, then, is neither exceptionally centralized nor decentralized, making it a good middle-of-the-road test case.

5.5 VERTICAL DIVERGENCE IN OTHER MULTI-LEVEL ELECTIONS

Does electoral divergence between federal and regional levels travel beyond Germany to other federations and multi-level governance systems? Various authors have analyzed vertical discrepancy in voter support across levels of government. These studies vary in the polities they examine, levels of government, time periods, and the explanations they offer. While I do not analyze the sources of vertical discrepancy here, I review several contexts in which such a discrepancy exists – namely, national and regional elections in Austria, Canada, and Spain, and national and local elections in Denmark. In reviewing these cases, I point to vertical divergence as a common regularity. Importantly, I do not argue that, contrary to explanations invoked by the respective authors, compensatory vote is the engine behind it. Indeed, I am unable to establish such a conclusion. Rather, I suggest that vertical electoral divergence in different polities and contexts *may* have a common source – vertical compensatory vote – perhaps in addition to other factors, some of which are systematic, and others idiosyncratic to specific contexts. Such a common source can be a topic of future comparative research. Finally, I also discuss a case in which compensatory vote is an unlikely explanation for vertical electoral divergence – namely, elections for the European parliament.

Examining vote switching between local, regional, and national levels of government in Denmark, Elklit and Kjaer (2006) find that a considerable portion of Danish voters switch (or split) their vote across different government levels. In 2001, 37 percent of voters diverged in their local and national votes, 27 percent diverged in their national and regional votes, and 32 percent in their regional and local votes. That said, amalgamation of municipalities resulted in decline of vote switching in the 2005 elections. Once local party systems were united, and thus became more similar to the national party system, voters had less of a necessity to switch their votes. Nonetheless, a substantial amount of votes switching remained (32 percent, 26, and 26, for the three comparisons here, respectively). Moreover, the proportion of "unnecessary" splitting – voters who could have voted straight ticket across levels but chose not to do so – increased over time.

Divergence between federal and land elections has also been observed in Austria (Abedi and Siaroff 1999). This divergence varies both over time and across the nine Austrian länder. More than fifty years after World War II, the average dissimilarity between the national vote and the nine regional votes has increased considerably. Abedi and Siaroff show that the increase varies by party. In particular, the Austrian People's Party experienced the greatest divergence between land and national vote in the 1983–1995 period, followed by the Socialist Party. The authors identify substantial variation across länder in which some regions experience counter-cyclical patterns, while others are in harmony with federal trends.

Canada is a particularly interesting (and complicated) case of provincial–national electoral divergence. Among the many federations in the democratic world, Canada presents perhaps the clearest case of cross-regional heterogeneity. Johnston and Cutler demonstrate that federal–provincial divergence "has been ubiquitous since at least the turn of the twentieth century" (2003, 1). Two-thirds of Canadian provincial elections between 1909 and the 1990s resulted in regional governments that differed in their partisan composition from the government in Ottawa. Here, too, there is variation across provinces. Results in Ontario are most often at odds with federal results, followed by Quebec, and results in the more peripheral provinces are on average similar to those in Ottawa. The authors also observe change over time – depending on the measure of dissimilarity, the 1930s to 1940s and the 1960s were periods of relatively little divergence between the provincial and the federal vote.

Although not constitutionally a federation, Spain presents an interesting case of multi-level governance. In particular, the high heterogeneity of the population across regions, the difference in the degree of autonomy across regions, and the decentralization of the state accompanied by increase of authorities to the regions over time create a fascinating puzzle of vertical power sharing in which voters are embedded. de Miguel Moyer (2007) analyzes vertical patterns of elections across regions and parties in Spain between 1982–2003. She finds that, unlike in Germany, the party in power at the national level does not always lose support at the regional level. That said, she finds variation across parties, with the Spanish Socialist Workers Party (PSOE) suffering greater losses when holding national office compared with the People's Party (PP). de Miguel Moyer draws a distinction between national and regional parties, the latter being parties that contest elections (regional or general) only in a limited part of the territory (4), and demonstrates that in almost all cases during the period investigated, national parties did poorly in regional elections compared to their performance in the previous national elections. This pattern varies across regions in a fashion consistent with the normal vote (along the lines found in Lohmann et al. 1997). Furthermore, the relative strength of national vs. regional parties within the national government has an effect on the magnitude of the loss, implying a compensatory logic of some sort by voters.

While the compensatory logic may be a relevant factor in some cases, it is less relevant in others. And it is important to examine not only cases in which it may account for electoral divergence across levels, but also cases in which compensation does not belong.

It is well established that since the first direct elections for the European Parliament in 1979, national governments suffer losses in elections for the European Parliament (van der Eijk and Franklin 1996). Are these losses a result of compensatory vote? The same reasons I note earlier that make second-order elections a candidate explanation for results of these elections make compensatory vote a less relevant explanation. If European voters do not perceive the European Parliament as one that provides input for national policy, then in their vote at the European level there is no special reason to suspect that they take into account post-electoral compromise between national and supra-national levels. This, of course, might change with time as the European project progresses and more and more Europeans consider Brussels to be a relevant point of reference. As things stand now, however, compensatory logic is probably not an appropriate framework for understanding these elections.

5.6 CONCLUSION

My contribution in the analysis presented in this chapter is twofold. First, I further our understanding of the relationship between regional and federal elections in Germany. Using aggregate data from 11 federal and 117 land elections and individual-level data from a subset of these elections, and taking into consideration various explanations, I demonstrate how voters use land elections to compensate for vertical power sharing between the central and regional governments. Second, I put previous analyses of German land elections in the context of a broader argument about compensatory vote and institutional power sharing. Unfortunately, my data do not allow me to test the compensatory vote thesis directly. My analysis implies, however, that this is a specific case in which voters work around the institutional mechanisms that convert their votes to policy. And while an over-time, within-case analysis provides a controlled comparison, it lacks variation in some aspects. Such additional sources of variation may be helpful for further research.

I have discussed concurrent and non-concurrent elections (legislative and presidential or regional and federal) as uncertain and certain, respectively. The effect of uncertainty, however, goes beyond the dichotomous difference between concurrent and staggered elections. Not all concurrent elections are equally uncertain. In some federal elections, the results can be easily predicted, while in others the margin is small, or coalition considerations can lead in different directions. In the German case, since there are so few cases of concurrent elections, the distinction between levels of uncertainty in concurrent elections does not carry much empirical weight. Nonetheless, in other polities or in a cross-sectional analysis of a large enough number of concurrent elections, such variation can play an important role in providing further insight into the issue of uncertainty.

Another aspect of the subtle effect of uncertainty is the degree to which the regional policy can change at any given time. Since policy in federations is determined by both the central government and every single region, the degree of uncertainty depends on the number and relative weight of regions whose assemblies are up for election at a given time. In federations in which each region is on its own electoral cycle, along with a change in regional assemblies and governments, the composition of the upper chamber changes time and again during the course of a federal cycle. When only a few, or relatively small, regions hold elections, the electoral pull needed to shift policy is greater. When numerous, or large, regions hold elections simultaneously, the level of uncertainty regarding policy is greater. Therefore, other things being equal, loss of support for the national incumbent party will be greater when elections in any given region are isolated from other regions compared with when they are clustered in groups. Similarly, in federations in which the number of representatives in the upper chamber varies by region, loss of support for the national incumbent party will be greater when small regions hold their elections compared with when larger ones hold them. With sixteen regions (or twelve before reunification) usually scheduled either separately from one another or in group of two to three, the German case does not provide us enough with variation to draw empirically on this factor. As with the previous implication, cross-country empirical variation can shed light on this question.

The degree of national integration of the party system is yet another factor that may affect compensatory vote. I have discussed here how Germany compares with other multi-level governance systems in this respect. I only add the study of compensatory vote in non-integrated party systems as a potential topic of future research. How voters balance across institutions when party labels stand for different things across levels and regions, and how they do so when some parties compete only in some regions of the country, are relevant questions for many federations.

These factors, not present in Germany, may play a role in other multi-level governance systems. Additional studies incorporating them in other countries may shed light on the mechanisms of compensatory vote and feed back into further theorizing on the rich texture of institutionally embedded voting.

PART III

THEORETICAL IMPLICATIONS

6

Conclusion

6.1 SUMMARY

This book analyzes voter considerations under various institutional regimes. The key principle driving it is simple: voters are concerned with policy, and their vote choice reflects the institutional path that shapes policy formation. This simple principle carries broad implications both for voter choice and aggregate election outcomes, and provides a unifying explanation for a variety of empirical regularities in electoral politics.

I focus on three electoral arenas: parliamentary, presidential, and federal democracies. In the parliamentary arena, the institutional path of post-electoral compromise passes among parties in parliament and between coalition and opposition. A variety of mechanisms and practices facilitate power-sharing and compromise among these actors. This path, I show, is reflected in voter choice. Knowing that their votes will be diluted down the line, voters often overshoot and support parties that diverge ideologically from their own views. How much do they overshoot? Importantly, the degree of compensatory vote depends on the degree of power sharing facilitated by institutional mechanisms. Drawing on cross-polity institutional variation, I demonstrate that the more such mechanisms are present, the more voters support parties whose positions differ from their own views. Where the process of policy formation is consensual, voters compensate. Where it incorporates policy inputs of fewer actors, voters stick with parties ideologically similar to them. Finally, polities characterized by a high degree of compensatory vote are also those in which a smaller proportion of voters support parties ideologically closest to them.

In both the presidential and federal arenas, multi-office elections are held either concurrently or non-concurrently. In presidential democracies, cross-institutional power sharing is horizontal, between the executive and the legislature. In federations, it is vertical, between the national and regional governments. The same principle – compensation for power sharing and compromise – has a different manifestation under these institutional regimes. In presidential systems, the party of the president often loses support in legislative elections held non-concurrently with presidential elections. In federal systems, the federal government often loses support in non-concurrent regional elections. The compromise is cross-institutional, and so is the overshooting. Voters in presidential democracies compensate for horizontal power sharing by balancing the president with their legislative votes. Similarly, voters in federations compensate for vertical dilution of their votes by balancing the federal government with their regional votes. In the presidential arena, I show that the magnitude of the loss is correlated with institutional power sharing. Drawing on variations in the constitutional authorities of presidents, I demonstrate that the loss of electoral support is related to the relative impact of policy inputs of the executive – the more authority the constitution grants to the executive, the greater the loss her party suffers in legislative elections.

This framework indeed assumes longer time horizons on the part of voters than current theories of issue voting – namely, directional or proximity voting – but, as I discuss earlier, the framework does not assume a great degree of sophistication. Dutch voters, for instance, have not seen a single party win a majority in decades; thus the notion of post-electoral negotiations is not foreign to them. In fact, multi-party government is probably the only form of government with which many Dutch voters are familiar, and is part of their everyday political life. Thus, although they probably know little about, say, procedures of agenda control in the Tweede Kamer, they are not surprised by parliamentary compromise. Similarly, although it is unlikely that many Norwegian voters are steeped in the details of the Board of Presidents meetings, they likely expect that, as has been the case time and again, no single party will secure a majority in the Storting. The same intuition holds for voters in presidential or federal democracies. It is unlikely that Argentinean voters know the scope of cabinet dismissal authority that their constitution grants to their president compared with that of the American president, but their votes indicate an intuitive sense that some bargaining will take place after the elections. Similarly, German voters are likely unaware of the subtleties of power sharing between the federal government and the länder, but their choices reflect an intuitive understanding that neither Berlin nor any of the regional capitals will shape policy on its own. An important related factor is that politicians often campaign with compensatory rhetoric, sometimes using explicit language of balance, coalition, and veto; the media, for its part, often report and present the political situation of compromise using intuitive metaphors. In sum, even the most general sense that voters might have about power sharing has traces in their choices.

6.2 COMPENSATORY VOTE ACROSS INSTITUTIONAL REGIMES: SOME REFLECTIONS

At the outset of this project, I highlighted four potential contributions of the study. It is time to revisit these statements. The first, I proposed, was focusing on voter choice as having longer time horizons than usually conceptualized, and as aimed at policy rather than only at party positions or individual representatives. Since elections are concerned with electing parties or representatives, not forming policy, voters vote for a party among the parties on the ballot, but look over the party's shoulder to the next stage, that of policy formation, and, importantly, allow that next stage to guide them in their party choice. They choose a party that will best serve them in that next stage. This insight allows us to examine in a new light why voter choice so commonly deviates from what our models about party choice predict: we typically focused solely on the stage in which votes are converted to seats, but it is also the stage in which seats are converted to policy that guides voters.

Second, and strongly related to the first, was the view of voter choice as institutionally embedded. Tremendous effort has been dedicated to the fascinating question of how voters vote. As far as issues are concerned, voters are said to support either parties whose positions are as similar as possible to their own (proximity voting) or those whose positions are in the same direction as, but somewhat more intense than, their own views (directional voting). Since both approaches focus on voter evaluation of parties or candidates, the institutional context is not, and indeed need not be, part of the picture of voter choice. If, however, as I have established, voters are concerned with policy, the institutions that shape how votes turn into policy are reflected in the vote itself.

Third is the ongoing debate between supporters of proximity theory and those of directional theory. Numerous studies mentioned here examine voter choice under either of these frameworks. Most studies find that mixed decision rules best represent voter behavior, and some conclude that the question cannot be resolved using the data at hand. Focusing on policy and incorporating institutions into the analysis allows me to reframe the debate. I identify voting of a directional nature as compensatory vote. Voters, I argue, often support parties whose positions differ from their own views when they expect those parties to be more effective in pulling policy in a desired direction. Given this understanding of voter considerations, institutional variation allows me to predict when proximity considerations and when compensatory considerations will dominate voter choice.

Finally, I proposed that the framework put forth in this study offers an underlying principle that allows us to unify explanations for electoral regularities across polities. The patterns of voter choice under the parliamentary, presidential, and federal environments that I identify are specific examples of a general underlying compensatory logic, a logic that voters employ in the face of power sharing. This underlying principle allows me to examine the specific forms of power sharing present in different systems (such as the three examined in this study) and use a wide lens to approach electoral regularities in a given polity.

The importance of policy for voters is not novel – it can be traced back to Downs's (1957) seminal work. The problem is that while policy and the position of the winning party are identical in Downs's two-party system, in (almost) all democratic polities they are not. Thus, equating policy with parties, political scientists have inadvertently dropped an important part of the picture.

Conceptualizing voter utility as defined over policy rather than simply over parties on the ballot gives us tools for understanding a wide array of electoral regularities at both the individual level and in aggregate outcomes. Of course, it does not imply that parties in and of themselves are a negligible consideration for voters. We cannot and should not ignore party positions, nor should we ignore partisanship. Voters may still have strong allegiances to parties, and parties may still be an important filter through which voters understand the world around them. Keeping in mind the difference between party positions and policy, however, widens our conceptual lens. The immediate question that follows is how voting geared to the former differs from voting geared to the latter, and what are the implications of such a distinction. The answer calls for institutionally embedded analysis of voter choice.

Proximity voting, this study shows, is but one specific decision rule on a continuum of decision rules ranging from purely proximity to purely compensatory. If we are willing to consider voters as concerned with policy, then we should also recognize that our understanding of voter choice as support for the party ideologically most proximate to the voter is appropriate *only* when voting for that party is identical to voting for policy. This is the case only under a democratic arrangement in which a single actor in power determines policy in its entirety. Let us sketch out, then, what such a regime would look like in each of the three arenas on which I focus in this study. The conclusion will soon become clear – there is no such democratic institutional arrangement.

In the parliamentary case, voting for party platform is equivalent to voting for policy if a single party controls the policy-formation process in its entirety. This implies a single-party government with a solid majority (rather than a plurality), and an opposition that has no impact on bills proposed, on a plenary agenda and parliamentary committees, and is otherwise completely disempowered. In other words, other than by chance, proximity voting as a principle promotes one's preferred policy in those cases in which it is entirely inconsequential as to whether the opposition is to the left or to the right of the governing party. Needless to say, such situations are unlikely to be found in a functioning democracy. When we let the data speak, even in the UK of the late 1980s, arguably one of the most majoritarian empirical cases, voter choice had a compensatory component.

In the presidential arena, dilution of one's vote takes place across institutions. The stronger the institution with which a policy compromise will be negotiated, the more one's vote for another institution is watered down. Thus, although power sharing is highest when the president is relatively weak, given that the presidency is the center of gravity, a strong executive branch encourages compensatory vote in legislative elections. Proximity voting fully promotes one's preferred policy, then, when the cross-institutional dilution factor is nil. This is the case when the legislature has full control over policy formation, and the presidency none, and the constitution grants essentially no significant authorities to the president. Of course, significant authority of the president is part and parcel of what makes a presidential regime a presidential regime (Shugart and Carey 1992, 26). Thus, it is only in a hypothetical and impossible-to-define(!) case where there is no significant authority in the executive, a case in tension with the mere definition of presidentialism, that proximity voting as a guiding principle promotes one's preferred policy. Empirically, even where the executive branch is constitutionally limited, such as in the United States and in Peru, the data demonstrate that voters shun the party of the executive in power.

In the federal arena, maximum power sharing takes place when authority is distributed as equally as possible between the federal and regional governments. And as in the presidential arena, the stronger the central government, the more one's regional vote is watered down. Therefore a centralized federation encourages more compensatory vote than does a decentralized federation. Proximity voting at the regional level captures policy-oriented motivation in its entirety, then, in the hypothetical case in which regional votes are not diluted by the policy inputs of the central government. In this hypothetical situation, the regions of the federation are so loosely tied to the center such that voters consider each region to be an independent political unit in which policy is determined. Again, this hypothetical situation is by definition impossible. Empirically, although I did not analyze a highly centralized federation, my analysis demonstrated that in a middle-of-the-road federation, voters shun the parties in power and the central government in regional elections.

This discussion demonstrates once more that the insight we have been importing from Hotelling's metaphor of shops along a street and Downs's abstraction of a two-party system winner take-all either does not apply to most forms of governance to which we have imported it, or it applies only with too much of a shoehorning. Compensatory vote, whether in the particular form I propose here or via some other formalization that incorporates policy as an object of voter choice, is a framework that takes seriously the form of governance of the polity in which voters cast their ballots. In fact, proximity voting applies only to a specific form of governance – one with no power sharing. In other words, under no power sharing, the logic of proximity vote and that of compensatory vote converge.

6.3 COMPENSATORY VOTE AND MULTIPLE FORMS OF POWER SHARING

Compensatory vote is a framework of analysis. As such, it may take different specific forms. This study develops the framework, first in a universal form, and then in three variations applied to three central electoral arenas. Given the different nature of the three types of arenas I examine, I measure compensatory vote in each arena in a fashion related to the particular type of power sharing in that system. But compensatory vote is institutionally universal. How does compensatory vote in parliamentary Sweden compare with that in presidential Chile, and how does the latter compare with that in federal Germany? One might be interested in converting the three institutional regimes to a common ground and conceptualizing a universal measure of the degree of compensatory vote, along with a common scale for evaluating power sharing. On the institutional end, the veto-points framework (Tsebelis 1995, 2002) can come to our help. The framework enables us to compare "combinations and hybrids [of institutional and partisan regimes], such as comparing a unicameral presidential multiparty system with a bicameral parliamentary two-party system" (1995, 292). It may be fruitful to develop a unifying measure of compensatory vote and examine its co-variation with the number of veto players in the system. A potential such measure is the proportion of voters employing a compensatory strategy, where the specific strategy differs across electoral regimes. Another alternative is the average compensation in a polity, perhaps in terms of ideological distance between voters and the parties of their choice. However calculated, a universal measure of compensatory vote ought to capture the degree to which voters overshoot in preemption of the appropriate form of post-electoral compromise taking place in their institutional environment.

Consistently, power sharing is, of course, multi-faceted. In this book, I offer a first step in a new framework, and thereby focus on a single dimension of power sharing in each polity I analyze. I treat Germany as a case of compensatory vote in a federation, the United States as a presidential system, Switzerland as a parliamentary system, and so on. But, of course, Germany is not only a federal system, but also a parliamentary system with horizontal mechanisms of power sharing. The United States is not only a presidential system, but also a federation with a vertical division of labor, as is Switzerland, and so on. Each polity can be analyzed along different dimensions of power sharing, and importantly, the same polity can be analyzed along multiple dimensions simultaneously. A vote for the Bundestag, for instance, may take into account horizontal compensatory considerations regarding post-electoral negotiations among parties in the Bundestag, *as well as* horizontal and/or vertical compensatory considerations regarding cross-chamber compromise, *as well as* vertical compensatory considerations regarding power sharing with the länder. Similarly, a vote for the land assembly may both vertically compensate for policy inputs of the federal government and horizontally compensate for compromise with other parties in the assembly. A comprehensive analysis of compensatory vote, modeling the various aspects of compensation that hang on every single vote and may often create cross pressures, as well as their potential interaction, can be illuminating.

6.4 THEORETICAL IMPLICATION I: WHY VOTER CHOICE IS MENU DEPENDENT

In numerous studies of voter choice, scholars have observed an unintuitive, surprising pattern: voter utility for some parties is often affected by the presence or characteristics of other parties (see Alvarez and Nagler 1995, 1998 for original conceptualization and estimation, and Lacy and Burden 1999 and Quinn, Martin, and Whitford 1999 for further development of the idea).[1] Why, under the assumption of rationality, does voter utility for party A depend on the presence or characteristics of party B? Using Maximum Likelihood or Markov

---

[1] This property of utility, the Independence of Irrelevant Alternatives, has been modeled as a statistical matter in the econometric literature. See Ben Akiva and Lerman (1985).

Chain Monte Carlo models, these studies empirically analyze the dependence of voter utility for one party on another via the stochastic term of a statistical model: the unobserved component of the utility is correlated across alternatives. The results of the estimation indicate when cross-alternative dependence is present. While this literature reveals an interesting property of individuals' assessments of parties, political scientists are left with a curious, counterintuitive property of micro-level behavior begging for explanation.

Menu dependence (also referred to as choice-set effects) has also been theorized and experimented with extensively in the psychological literature (Huber, Payne, and Puto 1982; Simonson 1989; Tversky and Simonson 1993). Wedell (1991) examines several mechanisms that can account for menu dependence such as multidimensional weighting (whereby the saliences of different choice characteristics change once an additional choice is added to the choice set), value shifting (Parducci 1965) (whereby the values that subjects attach to characteristics change as a result of the presence of additional choices), and dominance valuing (whereby the global attractiveness of a choice changes once it dominates others).

The bulk of the literature on voter choice defines voter utility for parties in parallel with the way the psychological literature defines subject evaluation of alternatives: the utility is defined over party characteristics, and in particular party positions or the ideological distance between the voter and the party. The compensatory framework approaches menu dependence from a different angle. While voter utility for each party includes party characteristics, it is also defined over policy. And since policy in most cases is formed by multiple parties, voter utility for each party directly incorporates characteristics of other parties on the ballot. In particular, voter choice is menu dependent because the impact of each party on policy depeneds on the configuration of other parties and on their relative weight. When our imaginary voter described in Chapter 2 evaluates parties, asking what would policy look like in the presence or absence of party X, her answer depends on other actors in the political field and what impact each of these actors has. Depending on the location of the status quo and the positions (and weights) of other parties participating in policy formation in relation to the position of party X, X will pull policy toward or away from the voter and thereby increase or decrease voter utility.

Specifically, under the compensatory logic, voter assessment of each party in parliamentary systems depends on other parties in parliament or on the ballot (see Equation 2.12). In presidential and federal systems, the menu is cross-institutional, and includes not only parties on the ballot but also the party (parties) from the other governmental branch already in power. Thus, voter assessment of each party in the legislative race depends on factors that potentially dilute policy inputs of the legislature (see Equation 2.17) – namely, which party holds the presidency and how much impact the president has. In federations, voter assessment of each party in regional elections depends on the parties in power at the national level and, again, on the relative impact of each level and each region (Equation 2.18).

Recall the seesaw analogy. If a voter wishes to balance forces (parties or institutions more broadly) to her right with forces (parties or institutions) to her left, perfect balancing will yield policy identical to the voter's position. Such a policy-oriented voter will prefer a party to her right if the left is too powerful, and a party to her left if the seesaw tilts to the right. A party situated exactly at the voter's position will be less effective in balancing out any counterforce than a party at the opposite side of the counterforce with respect to the voter. Menu dependence is hard-wired into the voter's consideration: which party she supports depends on the placement of other parties and their relative strengths.

As an example, imagine a unidimensional policy space with a voter placed at $v_i = 0$ and three parties A, B, and C placed at $p_A = -1$, $p_B = p_C = 1$. The proximity model does not discriminate between the three parties: since A, B, and C are equally distanced from the voter, the model is consistent with any randomization across the three that the voter may employ. As a shorthand, we usually assume that each of the three parties equally distant from the voter may be endorsed with a probability of 0.33. However, the prediction of the proximity model in this case is curious. Is the similarity, and in fact identity, between parties B and C really irrelevant? Will our prediction indeed stay unchanged if party B shifted its position from 1 to -1? If not, what explains the difference between the three parties equally distant from the voter?

Reexamining the scenario with policy-oriented considerations in mind can reveal the difference among the three parties. If we accept the notion of policy being a compromise between the governing forces, assuming (an admittedly overly simplifying assumption) that the three parties have the same weight, it is easy to see that policy produced by the three is $P = 0.67$. Similarly, policy produced by a coalition of B and C ($P_{-A} = 1$) is farther away from the voter than policy produced by a coalition of A and B or A and C ($P_{-C} = P_{-B} = 0$). Thus the voter is worse off in the absence of A than she is in the absence of B or C. A's marginal impact on policy is greater, and it is greater because of the spatial characteristics of the parties *with respect to one another* – the complete substitutability of B and C. Employing the same analysis, one can see that under the second scenario in which $p_B = -1$, C's impact is greater, and therefore voter utility for C increases. Thus, if our voter is concerned with policy, she is likely to vote for party A in the first scenario and for C in the second, although the only difference between the two scenarios is B's placement.

In the illustration presented here A, B, and C are parties in parliament. Alternatively, we can think of the position of B as that of the president and of A and C as those of the legislative parties. Thus, when B is in power under the first scenario, the voter is more likely to endorse A over C. Under the second scenario, she will likely prefer C over A. Alternatively, B can be the position of the federal government and A and C those of regional governments, explaining why a voter might prefer A over C in some circumstances and C over A in others.

This example illustrates how a seemingly irrelevant party, and in fact any other potential party, may be relevant for voter calculation while evaluating each party alone – a statement counterintuitive at first glance under an assumption of rationality. The relevance of the "irrelevant" party is that it affects policy, and consequently the marginal impact of other parties on policy. A party placed ideologically near another one reduces the marginal effect of the party adjacent to it because of the substitutability of the two. The configuration of parties in the example is knife-edged: all three are equally distant from the voter. But the principle holds in the more general case as well. Realizing that policy is a product of political compromise, policy-oriented voters are likely to prefer parties ideologically farther away from their own positions to parties closer to them, depending on the configuration of the other parties in the political arena.

6.5 THEORETICAL IMPLICATION II: WHY PARTIES ARE SO EXTREME

Electoral processes take (at least) two to tango – voters and parties. And they take place in particular contexts. In this book, I analyze voters, and particularly, voter behavior under various contexts. Focusing on voter motivation under different institutional regimes, and offering a new framework for understanding voters, I take party behavior as given. But parties are obviously a key player, and there is no reason to think them a naive one. One of the questions asked in this study – why do voters often support parties whose positions differ from their own views – can be inverted: why do parties often place themselves away from their supporters?

Numerous studies analyzing party behavior have observed that parties are ideologically extreme relative to their supporters. Party positioning is generally attributed to two types of factors: institutional mechanisms and voter motivation. Here I review in brief a few examples from the voluminous literature. My purpose in doing so is to demonstrate that the findings of this literature are consistent with the compensatory logic, and to call for reexamination of theoretical accounts of party strategy, incorporating insights of this study.

Cox (1990) identifies institutional incentives for party and candidate positioning. He finds that when cumulation of votes (casting more than one vote to a given candidate) is prohibited, large district magnitude, small number of votes per voter, and partial abstention (not using all the votes that one may cast) all encourage ideological dispersion of parties. Correspondingly, ideological clustering of parties is promoted by smaller district magnitude, outlawing partial abstention, and increasing the number of votes per person. Additionally, having a small number of parties relative to the number of votes per person encourages centripetal tendencies of parties, but when the number of parties increases above a certain level, centrifugal forces prevail. Cumulation of votes, when allowed, promotes ideological dispersion in multi-member districts.

Dow (2001) compares party system dispersion in four polities: Israel (1992) and the Netherlands (1994) on the proportional side, and Canada (1993) and France (1998) on the majoritarian side. Borrowing Kollman et al.'s (1992) measure of centrality and dispersion, Dow calculates for each party system the ratio between the sum of squared distances between voters and the median voter, and the sum of squared distances between voters and each of the parties (averaged). He finds that the two proportional systems are characterized by a larger degree of party-system dispersion compared with that of the two majoritarian systems.[2] Relatedly, Warwick (2004) finds that parties tend to place themselves farther from a central tendency of their supporters. In a later study, analyzing the positions of parties in thirty-one countries, Warwick (2007) further explores this pattern, demonstrating that in multi-party coalition systems, parties placed away from the center indeed tend to diverge away from their supporters toward the poles of the ideological scale (of course, see also Sartori 1976 on this topic). However, Warwick also finds limited evidence for the convergence of moderate parties toward the center and toward each other, a convergence motivated by coalitional maneuvering. In summary, proportional representation, large district magnitude, and multi-party governments, all found in my analysis in Chapter 3 to predict compensatory voting, are also often associated with idelogical dispersion of parties.

Two recent works incorporate policy-oriented motivation on the part of voters as an incentive for party divergence. In a theoretical article, Merrill and Adams (2007) make a distinction between dominant party systems – systems in which policy is determined by a single party – and parliamentary mean systems – ones in which policy is determined by a weighted average of party positions. The authors show that while the policy formed is moderated in the latter compared with the former, positioning of parties in the presence of power-sharing mechanisms is either similar to or more extreme than positioning of parties under institutional settings characterized by dominant party systems. These results, however, depend on voter strategy. Under power sharing, if voters are instrumental, forward looking, and have policy considerations in mind, parties diverge from the center. If, however, voters are expressive, the party positions do not differ across systems. In a related study, Adams et al. (2005) explain party divergence away from the center. The authors incorporate policy, as well as non-policy incentives for voters, where for policy incentives they

<hr />

[2] However, see Ezrow (2008), who finds no systematic relationship between proportionality of an electoral system and party extremity.

employ a discounting model (inspired by Grofman 1985). Parties, they
assume, are vote maximizers. Three key principles – party loyalty,
voter discounting of party promises, and voter abstention – generate
centrifugal forces for party positioning. This combination of ratio-
nalistic and behavioral forces allows the authors to explain party
divergence as well as variation therein across polities.

These recent works are among the very first to incorporate policy-
oriented logic on the part of voters into our understanding of party
strategy. Examination of the party end of the picture depicted in
Figure 1.1 brings to the surface numerous puzzles about party behavior
in democratic systems beyond the question of dispersion. What explains
the variation in party placement across countries? In particular, why do
small non-centrist parties place themselves ideologically away from
their constituencies rather than next to their respective constituents?
And what explains changes over time in those cases in which the configuration of parties changes, but institutional environment is fixed?
Revisiting our theories of party strategy with the incorporation of
compensatory motivation by voters might shed light on these puzzles.

6.6 COMPENSATORY VOTE AND REPRESENTATION

The quality of representation is a key characteristic of democratic
polities. From Pitkin (1967) to Dahl (1989) to Manin (1997), different
aspects of representation and its history have occupied theorists of
democracy and political philosophers for generations. From an electoral point of view, representation is often examined as the congruence
between representatives and the electorate (Powell 2004), as well as
the responsiveness of the former to the latter. In an earlier work,
Powell (2000) analyzes the relationship between the median citizen
and government, demonstrating that government positions corres-
pond better with the positions of the median voter under proportional
representation than under majoritarian systems (see also Huber and
Powell 1994).

At the very beginning of this study, I contended that policy is the
real object of voter choice, and that parties are only a means. Voters
associate themselves with different parties under different political
constellations, they often shun those parties similar to them, and their
evaluation of parties is a reflection of instrumental considerations.

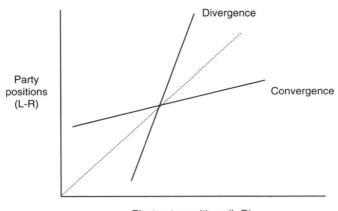

Party
positions
(L-R)

Divergence

Convergence

Electorate positions (L-R)

FIGURE 6.1. Voter and party ideological spectra

Nonetheless, the importance of the relationship between the positions of voters and those of parties should not be overlooked. Achen (1978) demonstrates that correlations between voters and representatives are not enough for evaluation of the quality of representation. He points out how easy it is to overlook the similarities and differences between preferences of voters and positions of parties. The framework of compensatory vote is not in tension with Achen's insight, but it does contend that when a discrepancy between voters and parties exists, it is not always an indication of a representation failure. We ought to examine the sources of discrepancy, and analyze whether voters choose parties different from them when they have an ideologically closer choice available on the ballot, or whether voters simply do not have their voices heard.

Figure 6.1 illustrates this point. On the horizontal axis are voter positions and on the vertical axis are party positions. The dotted line at a forty-five degree angle represents perfect correspondence between the two. The steep line represents a divergent party system: voter positions are projected onto a party system more dispersed than the electorate. The flatter line represents a convergent party system: parties are squeezed together, not reflecting the range of voters' positions. In the range of possible projections from voters to parties depicted here by only these two projections, each one has its representational qualities, along with some deficiencies. Of course, combinations of the two are possible as well. Parties can be dispersed on the edges of the political spectrum but tightly packed around the center.

Among the two systems presented here, over-dispersion of the party system does not endanger having voters' voice heard, but under-dispersion might. Although the center of gravity of the two systems may be identical, voters whose positions differ from the consensus are left unrepresented in the latter; the party system does not provide them with a meaningful choice. Of course, history provides ample of evidence for the perils of extremity. Yet it is easy to underestimate the perils of the lack of electoral options for voters who find themselves away from the consensus. This is particularly the case in societies in which democratic norms are not deeply instilled and the unrepresented may find other avenues to express their convictions, as well as in societies in which the variation among voter positions is substantial but is not reflected in the party system, and voters are pressed to find a party they perceive as "close enough," a choice that results in frustration. Institutional design is undoubtedly a crucial factor shaping the political landscape, but it is the interaction of institutions with society that takes polities on the path of history.

References

Aardal, Brent, and Henry Valen. Norwegian Election Study 1989 [computer file]. Norwegian Gallup Institute [producer]. Norwegian Social Science Data Services (NSD) [distributor].

Abedi, Amir, and Alan Siaroff. 1999. "The Mirror Has Broken: Increasing Divergence between National and Land Elections in Austria." *German Politics*, Vol. 8(1): 207–227.

Achen, Christopher H. 1978. "Measuring Representation." *American Journal of Political Science*, Vol. 22(3): 475–510.

2005. "Two-Step Hierarchical Estimation: Beyond Regression Analysis." *Political Analysis*, Vol. 13(4): 447–456.

Adams, James, Benjamin Bishin, and Jay Dow. 2004. "Representation in Congressional Campaigns: Evidence for Directional/Discounting Effects in U.S. Senate Elections." *Journal of Politics*, Vol. 66(2): 348–373.

Adams, James, and Samuel Merrill, III. 1999a. "Party Policy Equilibrium for Alternative Spatial Voting Models: An Application to the Norwegian Storting." *European Journal of Political Research*, Vol. 36: 235–255.

Adams, James, and Samuel Merrill, III. 1999b. "Modeling Party Strategies and Policy Representation in Mutliparty Elections: Why Are Strategies So Extreme?" *American Journal of Political Science*, Vol. 43(3): 765–791.

Adams, James F., Samuel Merrill III, and Bernard Grofman. 2005. *A Unified Theory of Party Competition: A Cross-National Analysis Integrating Spatial and Behavioral Factors*. New York: Cambridge University Press.

Aldrich, John H., and Richard D. McKelvey. 1977. "A Method of Scaling with Applications to the 1968 and 1972 Presidential Elections." *American Political Science Review*, Vol. 71(1): 111–130.

Alesina, Alberto, and Howard Rosenthal. 1995. *Partisan Politics, Divided Government, and the Economy*. Cambridge: Cambridge University Press.

Alesina, Alberto, N. Rubini, and G. Cohen. 1997. *Political Cycles and the Macroeconomy.* Cambridge, MA: MIT Press.

Alt, James E., and Alberto Alesina. 1998. "Political Economy: An Overview." In Robert E. Goodin and Hans-Dieter Klingeman, eds. *A New Handbook of Political Science.* New York: Oxford University Press.

Alvarez, R. Michael, and Jonathan Nagler. 1995. "Economics, Issues, and the Perot Candidacy: Voter Choice in the 1992 Presidential Election." *American Journal of Political Science*, Vol. **39**(3): 714–744.

 1998. "When Politics and Models Collide: Estimating Models of Multiparty Elections." *American Journal of Political Science*, Vol. **42**(January): 55–96.

 2000. "A New Approach for Modelling Strategic Voting in Multiparty Elections." *British Journal of Political Science*, Vol. **30**(1): 57–75.

Austen-Smith, David, and Jeffrey Banks. 1988. "Elections, Coalitions, and Legislative Outcomes." *American Political Science Review*, Vol. **82**(2): 405–422.

Avakumovic, Ivan. 1978. *Socialism in Canada: A Study of the CCF-NDP in Federal and Provincial Politics.* Toronto: McClelland and Stewart.

Bailey, Michael. 2001. "An Institutional Reconciliation of Proximity and Directional Voting." Georgetown University. Mimeo.

Barnes, Samuel H. 1997. "Electoral Behavior and Comparative Politics." In Mark I. Lichbach and Alan S. Zuckerman, eds. *Comparative Politics: Rationality, Culture, and Structure.* Cambridge: Cambridge University Press, 115–141.

Baron, David P., and Daniel Diermeier. 2001. "Elections, Governments, and Parliaments in Proportional Representation System." *Quarterly Journal of Economics*, Vol. **116**(3): 933–967.

Ben Akiva, Moshe, and Steven R. Lerman. 1985. *Discrete Choice Analysis: Theory and Applications to Travel Demand.* Cambridge, MA: MIT Press.

Blais et al. 2001. "Measuring Strategic Voting in Multiparty Plurality Elections." *Electoral Studies*, Vol. **20**(3): 343–352.

Brody, Richard A., and Benjamin J. Page. 1972. "Comment: The Assessment of Policy Voting." *American Political Science Review* **66**(2):450–458.

Burden, Barry C., and David C. Kimball. 1998. "A New Approach to the Study of Ticket Splitting." *American Political Science Review*, Vol. **92**(3): 533–544.

Cain, Bruce E. 1978. "Strategic Voting in Britain." *American Journal of Political Science*, Vol. **22**(3): 639–655.

Campbell, Angus. 1966. "Surge and Decline: A Study of Electoral Change." *Public Opinion Quarterly*, Vol. **24**: 397–418.

Campbell, James E. 1987. "A Revised Theory of Surge and Decline." *American Journal of Political Science*, Vol. **31**(4): 965–979.

 1991. "The Presidential Surge and Its Midterm Decline in Congressional Elections, 1868–1988." *Journal of Politics*, Vol. **53**(2): 477–987.

Chhibber, Pradeep, and Ken Kollman. 2004. *The Formation of National Party Systems Federalism and Party Competition in Canada, Great Britain, India, and the United States.* Princeton: Princeton University Press.

Cho, Sungdai, and James W. Endersby. 2003. "Issues, the Spatial Theory of Voting, and British General Elections: A Comparison of Proximity and Directional Models." *Public Choice*, Vol. **114**: 275–293.

Clark, William Roberts, and Matt Golder. 2006. "Rehabilitating Duverger's Theory: Testing the Mechanical and Strategic Modifying Effects of Electoral Laws." *Comparative Political Studies*, Vol. **39**(6): 679–708.

The Comparative Study of Electoral Systems (www.cses.org). CSES MODULE 1, 1996–2001. Ann Arbor, MI: University of Michigan, Center for Political Studies [producer and distributor].

The Comparative Study of Electoral Systems (www.cses.org). CSES MODULE 2, 2001–2005. Ann Arbor, MI: University of Michigan, Center for Political Studies [producer and distributor].

Cox, Gary W. 1990. "Centripetal and Centrifugal Incentives in Electoral Systems." *American Journal of Political Science*, Vol. **34**(4): 903–935.

1997. *Making Votes Count.* Cambridge: Cambridge University Press.

Dahl, Robert A. 1989. *Democracy and Its Critics.* New Haven: Yale University.

Dalton, Russell J. 1985. " Political Parties and Political Representation: Party Support and Party Elites in Nine Nations." *Comparative Political Studies*, Vol. **18**: 267–299.

Davis, Otto A., and Melvin J. Hinich. 1966. "A Mathmatical Model of Policy Formation in a Democratic Society." In J. L. Bernd, ed. *Mathematical Applications in Political Science II*, pp. 175–205. Dallas: Southern Methodist University Press.

Davis, Otto A., Melvin Hinich, and Peter C. Ordeshook. 1970. "An Expository Development if a Mathematical Model of the Electoral Process." *American Political Science Review*, Vol. **64**(2): 426–48.

de Miguel Moyer, Carolina G., 2007. "Electoral Patterns in Spain: Testing the Moderating Elections Hypothesis." Paper prepared for delivery at the European Consortium for Political Research, Joint Sessions. Helsinki, May 2007.

Dinkel, Rainer. 1977. "Der Zusammenhang zwischen Bundes und Landtagswahlergebnissen" *Politische Vierteljahresschrift*, Vol. **18**(3): 348–360.

Döring, Herbert. 1995. "Time as a Scarce Resource: Government Control of the Agenda." In Herbert Döring, ed. *Parliaments and Majority Rule in Western Europe.* New York: St. Martin's Press.

Dow, Jay K. 2001. "A Comparative Spatial Analysis of Majoritarian and Proportional Elections." *Electoral Studies*, Vol. **20**: 109–125.

Downs, Anthony. 1957. *An Economic Theory of Democracy.* New York: Harper & Row.

Druckman, James N. 2001. "Using Credible Advice to Overcome Framing Effects." *The Journal of Law, Economics, and Organization*, Vol. 17(1): 62–82.

Duch, Raymond. 2001. "A Developmental Model of Heterogeneous Economic Voting in New Democracies." *American Political Science Review*, Vol. 95(4): 895–910.

Duch, Raymond M., and Randolph T. Stevenson. 2008. *The Economic Vote: How Political and Economic Institutions Condition Election Results*. New York: Cambridge University Press.

Duverger, Maurice. 1954. *Political Parties*. New York: Wiley.

Edelman, Murray. 1964. *The Symbolic Uses of Politics*. Urbana: University of Illinois Press.

Elklit, Jørgen, and Ulrik Kjaer. 2006. "Split-Ticket Voting in Times of Sub-National Government Reorganization: Evidence from Denmark." Paper prepared for delivery at the symposium: Democracy, Divided Government and Split-Ticket Voting. Harvard University, May 26–27, 2006.

Elster, Jon. 1987. *The Multiple Self*. Cambridge: Cambridge University Press.

Enelow, James M., and Melvin J. Hinich. 1984. *The Spatial Theory of Voting: An Introduction*. New York: Cambridge University Press.

Erikson, Robert E., Michael B. MacKuen, and James A. Stimson. 2002. *The Macro Polity*. Cambridge: Cambridge University Press.

Ezrow, Lawrwnce. 2008. "Parties' Policy Programmes and the Dog That Didn't Bark: No Evidence That Proportional Systems Promote Extreme Party Positioning." *British Journal of Political Science*, Vol. 38(3): 479–497.

Financial Times Information. September 15, 2002.

Fiorina, Morris. 1996. *Divided Government*. Boston, MA: Allyn and Bacon.

Frymer, Paul, Thomas P. Kim, and Terri L. Bimes. 1997. "Party Elites, Ideological Voters, and Divided Party Governments." *Legislative Studies Quarterly*, Vol. 22(2): 195–216.

Gabel, Matthew J., and John D. Huber. 2000. "Putting Parties in Their Place: Inferring Party Left-Right Ideological Positions from Party Manifestos Data." *American Journal of Political Science*, Vol. 44(1): 94–103.

Gaines, Brian J., and Christophe Crombez. 2004. "Another Look at Connections Across German Elections." *Journal of Theoretical Politics*, Vol. 16(3): 289–319.

Gamson, William. 1961. "A Theory of Coalition Formation." *American Sociological Review*, Vol. 26(3): 373–382.

Globe and Mail. "The New Democrats." January 23, 2006.

Golder, Matt. 2005. "Democratic Electoral Systems around the World, 1946–2000." *Electoral Studies*, Vol. 24(1): 103–121.

Golder, Sona N. 2006. *The Logic of Pre-electoral Coalition Formation*. Columbus: Ohio State University Press.

Grofman, Bernard. 1985. "The Neglected Role of the Status Quo in Models of Issue Voting." *Journal of Politics*, Vol. 45: 230–237.

Haaretz, February 8, 2006. "The New Campaign Slogan of Meretz: Meretz in the Left – The Person in the Center" (my translation), by Yuli Khromchenko.

Heath, A. et al., British General Election Study, 1987 [computer file]. 2nd ed. Colchester, Essex: UK Data Archive [distributor], SN: 3887.

Hellman, Joel, and Joshua Tucker. 1998. "Post-Communist Elections Project Coding of Presidential Powers." [Database online] Available from http://www.wws.princeton.edu/~jtucker/pcelections.html.

Heston, Alan, Robert Summers, and Bettina Aten, Penn World Table Version 6.1, Center for International Comparisons at the University of Pennsylvania (CICUP), October 2002.

Hix, Simon. 1998. "Election, Parties, and Institutional Design: A Comparative Perspective on European Union Democracy." *West European Politics*, Vol. 21(3): 19–52.

Holmberg, Søren. 1989. "Political Representation in Sweden." *Scandinavian Political Studies*, Vol. 12: 1–36.

Hotelling, H. 1929. "Stability and Competition." *Economic Journal*, Vol. 39: 41–59.

Huber, Joel, John W. Payne, and Christopher Puto. 1982. "Adding Asymmetrically Dominated Alternatives: Violations of Regularity and the Similarity Hypothesis." *Journal of Consumer Research*, 9: 90–98.

Huber, John D., Georgia Kernell, and Eduardo L. Leoni. 2005. "Institutional Context, Cognitive Resources and Partisan Attachments across Democracies." *Political Analysis*, Vol. 13(4): 365–386.

Huber, John D., and G. Bingham Powell, Jr. 1994. "Congruence between Citizens and Policymakers in Two Visions of Liberal Democracy." *World Politics*, Vol. 46: 291–326.

Huber, John D., and Charles R. Shipan. 2002. *Deliberative Discretion? The Institutional Foundations of Bureaucratic Autonomy*. New York: Cambridge University Press.

Hug, Simon, and Pascal Sciarini. 2000. "Referendums on European Integration: Do Institutions Matter in the Voter's Decision?" *Comparative Political Studies*, Vol. 33(1): 3–36.

International Herald Tribune. September 13, 2002. "Schröder and Fischer Present United Front." By Judy Dempsey.

Iversen, Torben. 1994a. "Political Leadership and Representation in West European Democracies: A Test of Three Models of Voting." *American Journal of Political Science*, Vol. 38(1): 45–74.

Iversen, Torben. 1994b. "The Logics of Electoral Politics." *Comparative Political Studies*, Vol. 27(2): 155–189.

Jacobson, Gary C. 1990. *The Electoral Origins of Divided Government*. Boulder, CO: Westview.

Jeffery, Charlie, and Dan Hough. 2003. "Regional Elections in Multi-Level Systems." *European Urban and Regional Studies*, Vol. 10(3): 199–212.

Johnston, Richard, and Fred Cutler. 2003. "Popular Foundations of Divided Government in Canada." Paper prepared for delivery at the Annual Meeting of the Canadian Political Science Association, Halifax, Nova Scotia.

Kedar, Orit. 2005. "When Moderate Voters Prefer Extreme Parties: Policy Balancing in Parliamentary Elections." *American Political Science Review*, Vol. **99**(2): 185–199.

2005. "How Diffusion of Power in Parliaments Affects Voter Choice." *Political Analysis*, Vol. **13**(4): 410–429.

2006. "How Voters Work around Institutions: Policy Balancing in Staggered Elections." *Electoral Studies*, Vol. **25**(3): 509–527.

Kern, Holger Lutz, and Jens Hainmueller. 2006. "Electoral Balancing, Divided Government, and 'Midterm' Loss in German Elections." *Journal of Legislative Studies*, Vol. **12**(2): 127–149.

King, Gary, Michael Tomz, and Jason Wittenberg. 2000. "Making the Most of Statistical Analyses: Improving Interpretation and Presentation." *American Journal of Political Science*, Vol. **44**(April): 347–361.

Kollman, Kenneth, J. H. Miller, and Scott E. Page. 1992. "Adaptive Parties in Spatial Elections." *American Political Science Review*, Vol. **86**: 929–937.

Krämer, Jorgen, and Hans Rattinger. 1997. "The Proximity and the Directional Theories of Issue Voting: Comparative Results for the U.S. and Germany." *European Journal of Political Science*, Vol. **32**: 1–29.

Kreppel, Amie. 2006. "Understanding the European Parliament from a Federalist Perspective: The Legislatures of the United States and the European Union Compared." In Anand Menon and Martin A. Schain, eds., *Comparative Federalism: the European Union and the United States in Comparative Perspective*. New York: Oxford University Press.

Krosnick, John A. 2002. "The Challenges of Political Psychology: Lessons to be Learned from Research on Attitude Perception." In James H. Kuklinski, ed. *Thinking About Political Psychology*. Cambridge: Cambridge University Press, pp. 115–152.

Lacy, Dean, and Barry C. Burden. 1999. "The Vote-Stealing and Turnout Effects of Ross Perot in the 1992 U.S. Presidential election." *American Journal of Political Science*, Vol. **43**(1): 233–255.

Lacy, Dean, and Philip Paolino. 1998. "Downsian Voting and the Separation of Powers." *American Journal of Political Science*, Vol. **42**(4): 1180–1199.

Laver, Michael, and Kenneth Benoit. 2005. "Estimating Party Positions: Japan in Comparative Context." *Japanese Journal of Political Science*, Vol. **6**(2): 187–209.

Laver, Michael, and William Ben Hunt. 1992. *Policy and Party Competition*. London: Routledge.

Laver, Michael, and Kenneth A. Shepsle. 1996. *Making and Breaking Governments: Parliaments and Legislatures in Parliamentary Democracies*. New York: Cambridge University Press.

Lehmbruch, Gerhard. 2000. "The Institutional Framework: Federalism and Decentralisation in Germany?" In Hellmut Wollmann and Eckhard Schröter, eds., *Comparing Public Sector Reform in Britain and Germany: Key Traditions and Trends in Modernisation*. Ashgate: Aldershot. pp. 85–106.

Lewis, Jeffrey B., and Gary King. 2000. "No Evidence on Directional vs. Proximity Voting." *Political Analysis*, Vol. 8(1): 21–33.

Lewis-Beck, Michael, 1990. *Economics and Elections: The Major Western Democracies*. Ann Arbor: University of Michigan Press.

Lewis-Beck, Michael, and Mary Stegmaier. 2000. "Economic Determinants of Electoral Outcomes." *Annual Review of Political Science*, Vol. 3: 183–219.

Lijphart, Arend 1999. *Patterns of Democracy: Government Forms and Performance in Thirty-Six Countries*. New Haven: Yale University Press.

Lohmann, Susanne, David W. Brady, and Douglas Rivers. 1997. "Party Identification, Retrospective Voting, and Moderating Elections in a Federal System." *Comparative Political Studies*, Vol. 30(4): 420–449.

Lupia, Arthur. 1994. "Shortcuts versus Encyclopedias: Information and Voting Behavior in California Insurance Reform Elections." *American Political Science Review*, Vol. 88(1): 63–76.

2002. "Deliberation Disconnected: What It Takes to Improve Civic Competence." *Law and Contemporary Problems*, Vol. 65(3): 133–150.

Lupia, Arthur, and Matthew D. McCubbins. 1998. *The Democratic Dilemma*. Cambridge: Cambridge University Press.

Macdonald, Stuart Elaine, Ola Listhaug, and George Rabinowitz. 1991. "Issues and Party Support in Multiparty Systems." *American Political Science Review*, Vol. 85(4): 1107–1131.

Macdonald, Stuart Elaine, and George Rabinowitz. 1993. "Direction and Uncertainty in a Model of Issue Voting." *Journal of Theoretical Politics*, Vol. 5(1): 61–87.

Macdonald, Stuart Elaine, George Rabinowitz, and Ola Listhaug. 1998. "On Attempting to Rehabilitate the Proximity Model: Sometimes the Patient Just Can't Be Helped." *Journal of Politics*, Vol. 60(3): 653–690.

2001. "Sophistry versus Science: On Further Efforts to Rehabilitate the Proximity Model." *Journal of Politics*, Vol. 63(2): 482–500.

MacKuen, Michael B., Robert S. Erikson, and James A. Stimson. 1992. "Peasants or Bankers? The American Electorate and the U.S. Economy." *American Political Science Review*, Vol. 86(3): 597–611.

Manin, Bernard. 1997. *The Principles of Representative Government*. Cambridge: Cambridge University Press.

Marsh, Michael. 1998. "Testing the Second-Order Election Model after Four European Elections." *British Journal of Political Science*, Vol. 28: 591–607.

Marsh, Michael, and Mark N. Franklin. 1996. "The Foundations: Unanswered Questions from the Study of European Elections, 1979–1994." In van der

Eijk, Cees, and Mark N. Franklin, eds., *Choosing Europe? The European Electorate and National Politics in the Face of Union*. Ann Arbor: University of Michigan Press, pp. 11–32.

McDonald, Michael D., and Ian Budge. 2005. *Elections, Parties, Democracy: Conferring the Median Mandate*. New York: Oxford University Press.

Mebane, Walter R., Jr. 2000. "Coordination, Moderation, and Institutional Balancing in American Presidential and House Elections." *American Political Science Review*, Vol. 94 (1): 37–58.

Meguid, Bonnie M. 2005. "Competition Between Unequals: The Role of Mainstream Party Strategy in Niche Party Success." *American Political Science Review*, Vol. 99(3): 347–359.

Merrill, Samuel III, and James Adams. 2007. "The Effects of Alternative Power-Sharing Arrangements: Do 'Moderating' Institutions Moderate Party Strategies and Government Policy Outputs?" *Public Choice*, Vol. 131: 413–434.

Merrill, Samuel III, Bernard Grofman, and James Adams. 2001. "Assimilation and Contrast Effects in Voter Projections of Party Locations: Evidence from Norway, France, and the USA." *European Journal of Political Research*, Vol. 40: 199–221.

Möller, Tommy. 1999. "The Swedish Election 1998: A Protest Vote and the Birth of a New Political Landscape?" *Scandinavian Political Studies*, Vol. 22(3): 261–276.

Niemi, Richard G., Guy Whitten, and Mark N. Franklin. 1992. "Constituency Characteristics, Individual Characteristics, and Tactical Voting in the 1987 British General Election." *British Journal of Political Science*, Vol. 22(2): 229–254.

Onizuka, Naoko. 2005. "Re-examining Issue Voting in Japan: Direction vs. Proximity." Paper presented at the Annual Meeting of the American Political Science Association, Boston, Massachusetts.

Parducci, A. 1965. "Category Judgment: A Range-Frequency Model." *Psychological Review*, Vol. 72(6): 407–418.

Page, Benjamin I. and Robert Y. Shapiro. 1992. *The Rational Public*. Chicago: the University of Chicago Press.

Pitkin, Hanna Fenichel. 1967. *The Concept of Representation*. Berkeley: University of California Press.

Powell, G. Bingham, Jr. 1986. "American Voter Turnout in Comparative Perspective." *American Political Science Review*, Vol. 80(1): 17–43.

2000. *Elections as Instruments of Democracy*. New Haven: Yale University Press.

2004. "Political Representation in Comparative Politics." *Annual Review of Political Science*, Vol. 7: 273–296.

Powell, G. Bingham, and Guy D. Whitten. 1993. "A Cross-National Analysis of Economic Voting: Taking Account of the Political Context." *American Journal of Political Science*, Vol. 37(2): 391–414.

Proksch, Sven-Oliver, and Jonathan B. Slapin. 2006. "Institutions and Coalition Formation: the German Elections of 2005." *West European Politics*, Vol. **29**(3): 540–559.

Quinn, Kevin M., Andrew D. Martin, and Andrew B. Whitford. 1999. "Voter Choice in Multi-Party Democracies: A Test of Competing Theories and Models." *American Journal of Political Science*, Vol. **43**(4): 1231–1247.

Rabinowitz, George. 1978. "On the Nature of Political Issues: Insights from a Spatial Analysis." *American Journal of Political Science*, Vol. **22**(4): 793–817.

Rabinowitz, George, and Stuart Elaine Macdonald. 1989. "A Directional Theory of Issue Voting." *American Political Science Review*, Vol. **83**(1): 93–121.

Reif, Karlheinz, and Hermann Schmitt. 1980. "Nine 2nd-order National Elections: A Conceptual Framework for the Analysis of European Elections Results." *European Journal of Political Research*, Vol. **8**(1): 3–44.

Rodden, Jonathan. 2004. "Comparative Federalism and Decentralization: On Meaning and Measurement." *Comparative Politics*, Vol. **36**(4): 481–500.

Rubin, Donald B. 1987. *Multiple Imputation for Nonresponse in Surveys.* New York: John Wiley & Sons.

Samuels, David J. and Matthew Soberg Shugart. 2003. "Presidentialism, Elections, and Representation." *Journal of Theoretical Politics*, Vol. **15**(1): 33–60.

Sartori, Giovanni. 1976. *Parties and Party Systems: A framework for Analysis.* Volume I. London: Cambridge University Press.

Scheve, Kenneth, and Michael Tomz. 1999. "Electoral Surprise and the Midterm Loss in US Congressional Elections." *British Journal of Political Science*, Vol. **29**: 507–521.

Schneider, Aaron. 2003. "Decentralization: Conceptualization and Measurement." *Studies in Comparative International Development*, Vol. **38**(3): 32–56.

Schuessler, Alexander A. 2000. *A Logic of Expressive Choice.* Princeton: Princeton University Press.

Shugart, Matthew S. 1995. "The Electoral Cycle and Institutional Sources of Divided Presidential Government." *American Political Science Review*, Vol. **89**(2): 327–343.

Shugart, Matthew S. and John M. Carey. 1992. *Presidents and Assemblies: Constitutional Design and Electoral Dynamics.* Cambridge: Cambridge University Press.

Simonson, Itamar. 1989. "Choice Based on Reasons: The Case of Attraction and Compromise Effects." *Journal of Consumer Research* **16**: 158–174.

Stokes, Susan C. 2001. *Mandates and Democracy: Neoliberalism by Surprise in Latin America.* Cambridge: Cambridge University Press.

Strøm, Kaare. 1990. *Minority Government and Majority Rule.* Cambridge: Cambridge University Press.

Tsebelis, George. 1995. "Decision Making in Political Systems: Veto Players in Presidentialism, Parliamentarism, Multicameralism, and Multi-partyism." *British Journal of Political Science*, Vol. **25**: 289–325.

　　2002. *Veto Players: How Political Institutions Work*. Princeton: Princeton University Press.

Tsebelis, George, and Euardo Elamán. 2005. "Presidential Conditional Agenda setting in Latin America." *World Politics*, Vol. **57**(3): 396–420.

Tsebelis, George, and Tatiana P. Rizova. 2007. "Presidential Conditional Agenda Setting in the Former Communist Countries." *Comparative Political Studies,* Vol. 40(10): 1155–1182.

Tversky, Amos, and Itamar Simonson. 1993. "Context-dependent Preferences." *Management Science* 39(10): 1179–1189.

van der Eijk, Cees, and Mark N. Franklin. 1996. *Choosing Europe? The European Electorate and National Politics in the Face of Union.* Ann Arbor: University of Michigan Press.

Warwick, Paul V. 2001. "Coalition Policy in Parliamentary Democracy: Who Gets How Much and When." *Comparative Political Studies*, Vol. **34** (10): 1212–1236.

　　2004. "Proximity, Directionality, and the Riddle of Relative Party Extremeness." *The Journal of Theoretical Politics*, Vol. **16**: 263–287.

　　2007. "Relative Extremism and Relative Moderation: Strategic Party Positioning in Democratic Systems." Paper prepared for delivery at the 2007 annual meeting of the American Political Science Association, Chicago, Illinois.

Wedell, Douglas H. 1991. "Distinguishing Among Models of Contextually Induced Preference Reversals." *Journal of Experimental Psychology* 17(4): 767–778.

Westholm, Anders. 1997. "Distance Versus direction: The Illusory Defeat of the Proximity Theory of Electoral Choice." *American Political Science Review*, Vol. **91**(4): 865–885.

　　2001. "On the Return of Epicycles: Some Crossroads in Spatial Modeling Revisited." *Journal of Politics*, Vol. **63** (May): 436–481.

Index

Abedi & Siaroff (1999) on vote-switching in Austria, 174

Achen (1978) on evaluating quality of representation, 194–95

Achen (2005) on interpreting results under uncertainty, 87–88

Adams & Merrill (1999)
comparing directional and proximity models, 20–21
on ideological distance between parties and supporters in Norway, 6–7

Adams, Bishin, and Dow (2004) on electoral cycles in presidential systems, 109

Adams, Merrill & Grofman (2005) on party divergence from center, 193–94

agenda-setting
compensatory vote and, 66, 88–89, 90, 91–93, 185
in parliamentary systems, 66, 75–76, 86–87, 185
presidential powers of, 136

Aldrich & McKelvey (1977) on possible distortion of party placements, 71–73

Alesina & Rosenthal (1995)

on presidential policy balancing in the U.S., 29, 29–30, 36, 108–09
on unexpected presidential race results and midterm loss, 113–14, 129

Alesina, Roubini & Cohen (1997) on political business cycles in U.S., 110–11

Alt & Alesina (1998) on economic voting, 151

alternative vote, 77–78, 84

Alvarez & Nagler (1995)
on choice-set effects and voter choice, 188–89
on economic voting, 124

Alvarez & Nagler (1998)
on choice-set effects and voter choice, 188–89

Alvarez & Nagler (2000)
on strategic voting under first-past-the-post, 56

Argentina
presidential powers in, 120–21

Austen-Smith & Banks (1988)
formal model of parliamentary voting, 21–22
seat-share and party impact, 74

parties
- assumptions in formal model about, 40
- dispersion and quality of representation of, 196
- extreme positions and compensatory vote, 192–94
- impact of under compensatory voting and ideological positioning of, 47–48
- instrumental view of, 3–4, 66
- measuring impact of, 73–76
- number of, 77–78, 86–88, 89, 91–93, 109–10, 111, 128, 133–34
- power and policy impact of, 55, 73–76
- strategy under compensatory vote of, 16, 192–94

party systems
- fragmentation of, 18, 21–22, 25, 33, 36–37, 56, 58, 62, 65, 68, 83–84
- ideological dispersion of, 6–7, 192–93, 195–96
- nationalization of, 83–84, 171–72, 174, 177

People's Party (Spain), vote-switching in regional elections and, 175

People's Party for Freedom and Democracy (VVD) (The Netherlands)
- demographics of voter support for, 79
- perception by voters of, 71–73
- purple coalition and, 27–28, 38–39

Peru
- presidential powers in, 120–21
- weakness of executive branch in, 185–86

Pitkin (1967) on representation and democracy, 194

policy balancing. *See* compensatory vote, in presidential systems

policy formation
- assumptions in formal model about, 41–42, 50
- in federal systems, 54
- in parliamentary systems, 43
- in presidential systems, 50

Powell & Whitten (1993) on economic voting, 11–12, 124

Powell (1986) on policy outcomes and turnout, 11–12

Powell (2000)
- on policy outcomes under proportional representation, 27
- on representation and democracy, 194

Powell (2004) on representation and democracy, 194

power-sharing
- compensatory vote and, *See* compensatory vote, power sharing and
- measurement of, 68, 85–87, 119–20
- policy formation and, 46, 102
- second-order elections and, 153

presidential systems
- aggregate data in analysis of, 116–17
- alternative explanations for vote-loss in, 110–15
- choice-set effects and voting in, 190
- compensatory vote in, *See* compensatory vote, in presidential systems
- concurrent elections and presidential party vote-share in, 8–9, 103, 104–06, 117, 118, 122–24, 131–33
- constitutional powers of president in, 118–21, 122, 139
- data used in analysis of, 14, 115–17, 138
- district magnitude and electoral cycles in, 125–27, 133–34

voter sophistication (*cont.*)
  directional vote and, 19–20, 40,
    182–84
  proximity vote and, 23–24, 32, 40,
    43, 95, 182–83, 183–84
  strategic vote and, 55–56
  variation in, 95
voters
  analysis under varying national
    contexts of, 66–67
  assumptions in formal model
    about, 40, 95
  choice-set effects and behavior of,
    188–91
  decision rule of, 7, 10–11, 12–13,
    15, 18, 81–83, 87–94, 137, 149,
    184, 185–87
  education and perceptions of party
    positions of, 71–73
  effects of institutions on, 10–12,
    13, 14, 15, 23–24, 25–26, 48,
    87–94, 181, 183–84
  expressive attachment of, 18–19,
    23–24, 25–26, 43, 45–46, 47,
    51–53, 66, 92, 95, 184–85,
    193–94
  modeling of, 14
  party dispersion and ideology of,
    196
  party preference and perceptions
    of party positions, 71–73
  policy orientation of, 3–4, 11–12,
    13, 22, 24, 25–26, 73, 94, 107,
    147, 181, 183, 184–87, 193–95

projection bias of. *See* projection
  bias
spatial model of, 18
support for extreme parties of,
  5, 6–7, 12, 24, 48, 65, 66,
  93–94
time horizon of, 3–4, 11–12, 40,
  73, 182–83
utility functions of. *See*
  compensatory vote;
  directional models; proximity
  models, voter utility function
  under

Warwick (2001) on coalition
  government bias toward
  parliamentary center of gravity,
  75–76
Warwick (2004) on difference
  between position of party and its
  supporters, 192–93
Warwick (2007) on difference
  between position of party and its
  supporters, 192–93
Wedell (1991) on choice-set effects,
  189
Westholm (1997, 2001)
  on debate between proximity and
    directional models, 12
  on measuring party positions,
    70–71

Zambia, presidential powers in,
  120–21

Frances Hagopian, *Traditional Politics and Regime Change in Brazil*

Henry E. Hale, *The Foundations of Ethnic Politics: Separatism of States and Nations in Eurasia and the World*

Gretchen Helmke, *Courts Under Constraints: Judges, Generals, and Presidents in Argentina*

Yoshiko Herrera, *Imagined Economies: The Sources of Russian Regionalism*

J. Rogers Hollingsworth and Robert Boyer, eds., *Contemporary Capitalism: The Embeddedness of Institutions*

John D. Huber and Charles R. Shipan, *Deliberate Discretion? The Institutional Foundations of Bureaucratic Autonomy*

Ellen Immergut, *Health Politics: Interests and Institutions in Western Europe*

Torben Iversen, *Capitalism, Democracy, and Welfare*

Torben Iversen, *Contested Economic Institutions*

Torben Iversen, Jonas Pontussen, and David Soskice, eds., *Unions, Employers, and Central Banks: Macroeconomic Coordination and Institutional Change in Social Market Economies*

Thomas Janoski and Alexander M. Hicks, eds., *The Comparative Political Economy of the Welfare State*

Joseph Jupille, *Procedural Politics: Issues, Influence, and Institutional Choice in the European Union*

Stathis Kalyvas, *The Logic of Violence in Civil War*

David C. Kang, *Crony Capitalism: Corruption and Capitalism in South Korea and the Philippines*

Junko Kato, *Regressive Taxation and the Welfare State*

Robert O. Keohane and Helen B. Milner, eds., *Internationalization and Domestic Politics*

Herbert Kitschelt, *The Transformation of European Social Democracy*

Herbert Kitschelt, Peter Lange, Gary Marks, and John D. Stephens, eds., *Continuity and Change in Contemporary Capitalism*

Herbert Kitschelt, Zdenka Mansfeldova, Radek Markowski, and Gabor Toka, *Post-Communist Party Systems*

David Knoke, Franz Urban Pappi, Jeffrey Broadbent, and Yutaka Tsujinaka, eds., *Comparing Policy Networks*

Allan Kornberg and Harold D. Clarke, *Citizens and Community: Political Support in a Representative Democracy*

Amie Kreppel, *The European Parliament and the Supranational Party System*

David D. Laitin, *Language Repertoires and State Construction in Africa*

Fabrice E. Lehoucq and Ivan Molina, *Stuffing the Ballot Box: Fraud, Electoral Reform, and Democratization in Costa Rica*

Mark Irving Lichbach and Alan S. Zuckerman, eds., *Comparative Politics: Rationality, Culture, and Structure, Second Edition*

Evan Lieberman, *Race and Regionalism in the Politics of Taxation in Brazil and South Africa*

Julia Lynch, *Age in the Welfare State: The Origins of Social Spending on Pensioners, Workers, and Children*

Pauline Jones Luong, *Institutional Change and Political Continuity in Post-Soviet Central Asia*

Doug McAdam, John McCarthy, and Mayer Zald, eds., *Comparative Perspectives on Social Movements*

Beatriz Magaloni, *Voting for Autocracy: Hegemonic Party Survival and Its Demise in Mexico*

James Mahoney and Dietrich Rueschemeyer, eds., *Historical Analysis and the Social Sciences*

Scott Mainwaring and Matthew Soberg Shugart, eds., *Presidentialism and Democracy in Latin America*

Isabela Mares, *The Politics of Social Risk: Business and Welfare State Development*

Isabela Mares, *Taxation, Wage Bargaining, and Unemployment*

Anthony W. Marx, *Making Race, Making Nations: A Comparison of South Africa, the United States, and Brazil*

Bonnie Meguid, *Competition between Unequals: The Role of Mainstream Parties in Late-Century Africa*

Joel S. Migdal, *State in Society: Studying How States and Societies Constitute One Another*

Joel S. Migdal, Atul Kohli, and Vivienne Shue, eds., *State Power and Social Forces: Domination and Transformation in the Third World*

Scott Morgenstern and Benito Nacif, eds., *Legislative Politics in Latin America*

Layna Mosley, *Global Capital and National Governments*

Wolfgang C. Müller and Kaare Strøm, *Policy, Office, or Votes?*

Maria Victoria Murillo, *Labor Unions, Partisan Coalitions, and Market Reforms in Latin America*

Ton Notermans, *Money, Markets, and the State: Social Democratic Economic Policies since 1918*

Aníbal Pérez-Liñán, *Presidential Impeachment and the New Political Instability in Latin America*

Roger Petersen, *Understanding Ethnic Violence: Fear, Hatred, and Resentment in Twentieth-Century Eastern Europe*

Simona Piattoni, ed., *Clientelism, Interests, and Democratic Representation*

Paul Pierson, *Dismantling the Welfare State? Reagan, Thatcher, and the Politics of Retrenchment*

Marino Regini, *Uncertain Boundaries: The Social and Political Construction of European Economies*

Marc Howard Ross, *Cultural Contestation in Ethnic Conflict*